IMAGES
of America

LUMBERTON

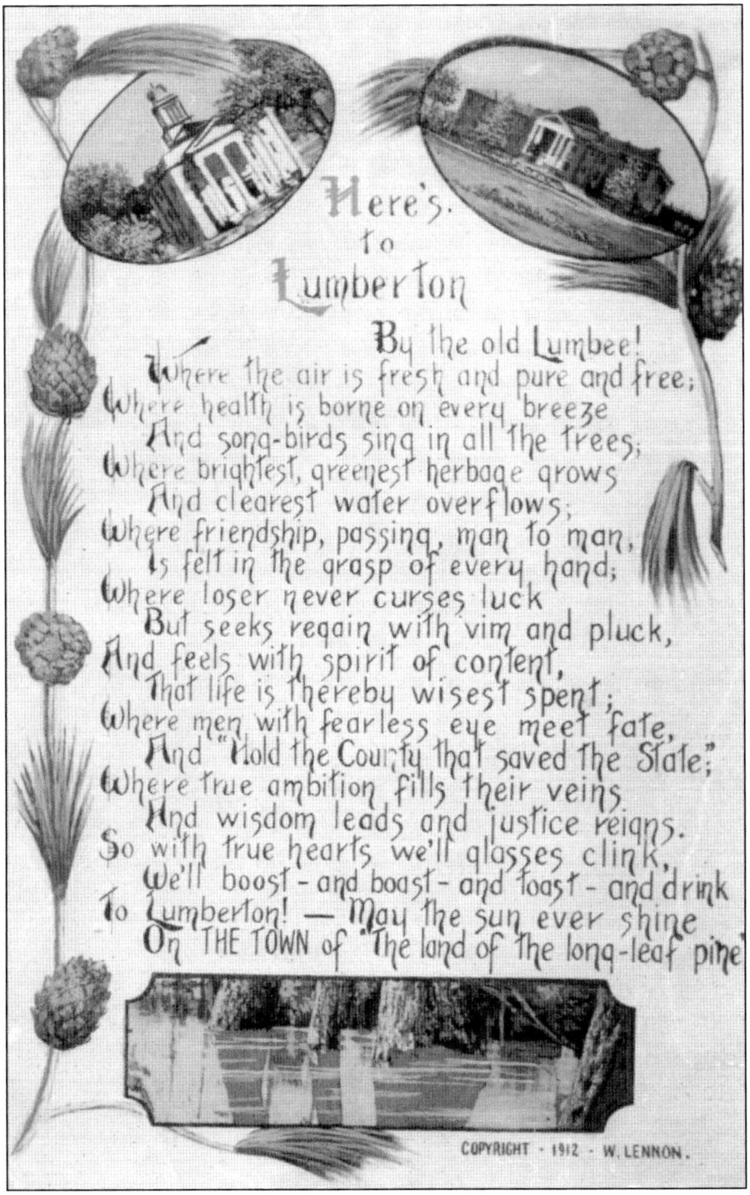

This 1912 poem by Woodberry Lennon tells of the positive aspects of Lumberton. Although he was an attorney, Lennon's talents and activities were also devoted to several other fields. He was an accomplished musician, able to play practically every wind or string instrument. He was also a mapmaker, and his 1922 map shows township lines, roads, swamps, millponds, roads, churches, schools, and other data, with an index to help one locate these items. (Courtesy of the Hubbard-Tyner Collection.)

On the Cover: The Lumberton High School band majorettes assembled here around 1948. (Courtesy of Gillespie Studio Collection, Robeson County History Museum.)

IMAGES
of America

LUMBERTON

K. Blake Tyner

ARCADIA
PUBLISHING

ISBN 978-1-4671-2025-8

Published by Arcadia Publishing
Charleston, South Carolina

Printed in the United States of America

Library of Congress Control Number: 2013933073

For all general information, please contact Arcadia Publishing:
Telephone 843-853-2070
Fax 843-853-0044
E-mail sales@arcadiapublishing.com
For customer service and orders:
Toll-Free 1-888-313-2665

Visit us on the Internet at www.arcadiapublishing.com

This book is dedicated to my late wife, Bess Tyner, and our son, McKay Tyner. Thank you for your love and support with this project.

Contents

Acknowledgments

Images of America: *Lumberton* has been a labor of love and a wonderful collaboration with current and former Lumberton citizens. I was able to find a large number of photographs and postcards in the collection that my late wife, Bess, and I have titled the Hubbard-Tyner Collection.

I want to thank all of individuals who opened their private collections and shared their cherished photographs with me. They include Lyl MacLean Clinard, Suzie McLeod Dedrick, Jane Carroll Lee, Rev. James Burt MacLeod, Ruth Ann Baker McLellan, Tom Parker, Frances Phillips, Alan Prevatte, Mitchell Prevatte, Marshall Shepherd, Merle and Ann Summers, Brad Thompson, Jackie Oliver Utz, Paul Valenti, Keith Vincent, and Catherine Currie Ward.

A project like this would have been impossible without numerous groups throughout Lumberton and the state. I would like to gratefully acknowledge the assistance from the Carolina Collection at the University of North Carolina (UNC) Chapel Hill, East Lumberton Baptist Church, First Baptist Church, Historical Robeson, Inc., Knuckles School, Library of Congress, Lumberton Police Department, Lumberton Rescue and EMS, Robeson County History Museum's Gillespie Studio Collection, and various Robeson Remembers collections, Robeson County Public Library (especially the Kate Biggs Collection), National Archives and Records Administration, North Carolina State (NC State) University Library, and the university communications and marketing department at the University of North Carolina at Pembroke (UNCP).

The entire staff of Arcadia Publishing has been wonderful to work with, especially my editor, Katie McAlpin; she has kept my feet to the fire throughout this process. At the University of North Carolina at Pembroke, I must thank my boss, art department chairman Dr. Richard Gay.

This book would not have been a possibility without my family—my late wife, Bess, and son, McKay, who have heard me say so many times over the past months, "Just five more minutes, let me finish this caption"—thank you!

INTRODUCTION

The historic city of Lumberton has served as the capital of "the State of Robeson," since it was created by the North Carolina General Assembly on November 3, 1788. Lumberton was officially incorporated in 1852, sixty-four years after its founding.

John Willis, referred to as the "father of Lumberton," was born in 1756 to Daniel Willis and Elizabeth Moore. In 1753, his parents settled on Saddletree Swamp in what was, at that time, the western part of Bladen County. John joined in the fight for independence from England and achieved the rank of colonel. After the Revolution, he achieved the rank of general while in the militia.

In the postwar period, he began acquiring large tracts near his family's holdings, becoming one the largest landowners in the area. In 1787, Robeson County was carved from North Carolina's mother county, Bladen. The area residents complained and petitioned that Bladen was too large and unwieldy to govern, and the new county was named for Col. Thomas Robeson, a proponent of its creation and a hero of the Revolutionary War Battle of Elizabethtown.

After the general assembly formed Robeson County from Bladen, John Willis and six others were tasked with establishing a county seat. The commission chose a parcel of land owned by Willis on the east bluffs of the Lumber River. In August 1787, Willis donated 170 acres of his Red Bluff Plantation to be used for the purpose. He named area Lumberton for the nearby Lumber River. The "father of Lumberton" went on to represent Robeson County as a state senator in 1787, 1788, 1789, 1791, and 1798. He served in the House in 1794 and 1795 and at the state convention of 1789 where North Carolina ratified the Constitution and became the 12th state. His business interests in the county included a planter as well as dealing in timber, tar, turpentine, and tanned hides. He also operated saw- and gristmills.

Surveyor Jacob Rhodes laid out the town and filed the plat on May 5, 1787, along with a plan to conduct a lottery to dispose of town lots. The lottery was held on August 14, 1787. Lots were laid off in half-acre size, with streets, a commons, and a public square. The lots not sold were rented out for the best prices obtainable.

The setting along the Lumber River made for a beautiful downtown. North Carolina's unofficial poet laureate, John Charles McNeill, in writing about the river said, "writing about the Lumber River, to a man who has spent his summers in dalliance with her, is like writing about his sweetheart. She is subject to change and as teasing as any girl that goes; and no human angel ever possessed more variable hues and tints and shadows in her misty eyes than this unconscious flirt."

In the late 18th and the 19th centuries, the lumbering and naval stores industries were very important to the region, and the river was a vital route for transporting their products. Logs that measured 100 feet were rafted downriver in the late 1800s to Georgetown, South Carolina. The Lumber River was designated as a National Wild and Scenic River and is part of the North Carolina Natural and Scenic River System.

The first county court session was held in February 1787 in a building on the plantation of General Willis. The justices were Abraham Barnes, John Willis, Elias Barnes, and Jacob Alford. The building, which was later purchased from John Willis and moved to Courthouse Square, was used until the second Robeson County Courthouse was built in 1848 to replace it as it had become expensive to maintain and repair. In 1851, the *Fayetteville Observer* reported, "The new courthouse is finished and is a handsome building and probably larger than any other in the circuit, but is not as convenient as some we have seen . . . we understand that it cost $7,500."

A wonderful account of the courthouse and Lumberton appears in George Alfred Townsend's 1872 book *The Swamp Outlaws, or, The North Carolina Bandits*, which tells the story of what is known locally as the Lowry War, which lasted from 1865 until 1872:

> We came to the weather-blackened, unpainted town of Lumberton, on the flowing Lumber River, a branch of the Pee Dee. This being Court week, the town of Lumberton was full. The Court House is built of brick, with a frame pediment above the eaves in the gable end, and the courtroom in the second story is covered with sawdust to keep the peace while Judge Clarke, one of the District Judges, goes through the comedy of justice. The courtroom is very crude, large and bare, and the Judge looks amazingly high up behind the long gallery where they expose him. He is a queer, affable old Judge, who has fought in the Mexican war, in the Confederate army, and commanded one of Holden's regiments against the Ku Klux Klan. Down before the Court House, where the people of the county are congregated, there is an old pole well in the public square, where they fill their gourds at the dripping bucket.

The third courthouse was built on the same site in 1908 and replaced in 1975 by the present building. The Robeson County Confederate Monument was unveiled in front of the courthouse on May 10, 1907, before a crowd of 7,000—including 500 Confederate veterans. The first to donate to the fundraising project was Lumberton attorney and future North Carolina governor Angus Wilton McLean. The monument has survived two courthouses and a major overhaul to the exterior of the current courthouse. Through time, the Confederate soldier has stood high above Elm Street, looking down on Lumberton as a silent reminder of the loss the county suffered during the Civil War.

The 1790s became a time of scandal for John Willis. First, he was involved with others—including John Grey Blount of Washington, North Carolina, and Jacob Rhodes, locally—in land speculation on a large scale. These speculations were in so-called "vacant lands" in North Carolina and Tennessee that had not previously been granted by Colonial government or the new states. Most of this land had been settled by others, so problems arose, and a grand jury was conducted in October 1794; Willis was indicted but not tried.

The 1797 North Carolina Senate election was a heated race between Gen. John Willis and John Gilchrist. After losing the race, Willis accused John Gilchrist of having been a Tory during the war with Great Britain and insisted on his removal from the Senate. Gilchrist was impeached and tried as a Tory. During the trial, many came forward to give character depositions concerning John Gilchrist, and the State Committee of Privileges and Elections found him entitled to a seat in the House.

It is possible that these scandals lead to Willis leaving Robeson County. By 1799, he had moved to Fayetteville and was practicing law. The September 5, 1799, issue of the *Wilmington Gazette* had an advertisement for the sale of his mill along with another 1,000-acre plantation adjoining the town of Lumberton, two townhouses, and 5,000 additional acres of land in the neighborhood. Willis offered to take lands in the district of Tennessee in partial exchange for these lands. In 1801, he and his family set out for the Natchez territory of Mississippi to begin a new life. Willis died in Natchez on April 22, 1802, and his wife followed in 1806. He is buried in Veterans Memorial Park near downtown Natchez.

When Lumberton incorporated in 1852, Dr. Edmund McQueen became the first mayor, and Col. John Rowland drew up the city ordinances and named the streets. The first town commissioners to serve were Edward Lewis, W.W. Gunn, J.M. Hartman, and R.S. French. One can only imagine what these first city fathers would think of Lumberton today. In 1852, there were no paved streets and no railroad tracks; now, not only are there miles of paved streets throughout town, there is also Interstate 95 running through town and bringing thousands of travelers every day.

An 1884 publication described the town—with its population of 1,200, twenty stores, five churches, sawmills, turpentine distilleries, and four hotels—as "one of the prettiest in the state." Land could be purchased for as little as $5 per acre. The Bank of Lumberton was organized in 1896; this was the first bank in Robeson County. Lumberton also became the first major industrial center with the opening of the first cotton mill in 1896, the cotton mill industry would provide jobs for several generations before dying out. Two years later, a group consisting of Caldwell & Carlyle, L.H. Caldwell and Q.T. Williams built the first tobacco warehouse. Later that same year, the Lumberton Tobacco Market was organized by a group of local businessmen, and by its 75th anniversary, Lumberton was home to 24 warehouses with more than 35 acres of space.

The Wilmington, Charlotte and Rutherfordton Railroad was the first to go through Lumberton and was finished soon before the beginning of the Civil War, providing rail service east and west of town. The Virginia and Carolina Southern Railroad was incorporated in 1907. Angus Wilton McLean was president and general counsel while J.F.L. Armfield was vice president and general manager. It had 65.8 miles of track and linked Lumberton with St. Pauls, Elizabethtown, and Hope Mills. It had four locomotives, seven freight and passenger cars and three gasoline motor cars.

Education has always been important to Lumberton's citizens. The Lumberton Academy was established by Gen. John Willis in 1791 with David Kerr as principal. Kerr was later the first presiding professor at the University of North Carolina. A 1794 law called for the governance of the town by five directors with power of taxation. Unobligated tax money was designed to support Lumberton Academy.

In 1891, Edward K. Proctor and A.C. Melke conceived the idea of a Baptist school in Lumberton. Proctor made the first contribution of $1,000, and Melke contributed $5,000. Berry Godwin donated the site, a valuable lot of 2.5 acres. This property was beside First Baptist Church. The Lumberton Post Office presently is located on part of the land. Baptist churches over the county made substantial contributions. The academy opened its doors in 1893. Prof. John Duckett, father of Mrs. K.M. Biggs, was the first principal. Gen. Thomas F. Toon was the principal of the intermediate department, and Mrs. Henry T. Pope was teacher of the primary department. In 1893, there were 166 pupils of whom 51 were boarders.

The price of board ranged from $3 to $4 monthly, but this did not include washing clothes. Washing cost 25¢ monthly. There was a charge of 10¢ to cover fuel and other incidental expenses. The school continued in operation until 1907 when the property was purchased by the Town of Lumberton and turned into the graded school.

In 1965, the community college movement in North Carolina expanded into Robeson County with the establishment of a technical institute. The unit was established at the Barker Ten-Mile Elementary School, seven miles north of Lumberton. Twenty full-time curriculum students enrolled during the first year of Robeson Technical Institute.

Today, Robeson Community College (RCC) is a comprehensive, open-door, two-year public institution of higher learning with a mission "to enhance the lifelong education opportunities for adults appropriate to their needs, interests, and abilities," according to its mission statement. RCC is located at the intersection of US 301 and Interstate 95 in Lumberton and consists of an 80-acre campus. Campus facilities occupy almost 200,000 square feet within classrooms, offices, and laboratories. RCC is one of the 58 colleges that comprise the North Carolina Community College System.

Robeson County was home to great number of Jewish families with a big concentration being in Lumberton. One of the most prominent was Aaron Weinstein. He immigrated from Lithuania to Baltimore and moved to Lumberton in the early 20th century. He chose Elm Street as the site for his general store, called "Weinstein's." He donated the land for the county's first synagogue on Water Street in 1908. The Weinstein store remained in the family until they closed it in 1987. This was an important year for the family because David Weinstein, Aaron Weinstein's grandson, took office as Lumberton's first Jewish mayor. He held the office until 1991 and was elected to the North Carolina State Senate in 1997. After serving 12 years in the state senate, Weinstein became the director of the state Highway Safety Program in 2009.

In the words of lawyer and historian Robert C. Lawrence, from his book *State of Robeson*, "Lumberton has indeed been fortunate in its citizens of foreign birth or descent, particularly those of German extraction, notably William Linkhauer, Christopher von Glahn, of Hanover, Germany, G. E. Rancke, Dr. Rudolph Vampill, and Arthur C. Melke."

Two or three years after the Civil War, Arthur C. Melke, a young German, arrived in Lumberton without friends or funds. He immediately showed a disposition to work, found one little job and then another, and soon had a position clerking. He saved his money, went into business for himself and was extremely successful.

His capital was small, but he was industrious, patient, and persevering. Thoroughly frank and honest in all his dealings with men, diligent in business transactions and prudent in his plans, he succeeded from the beginning and, while others in circumstances more favorable failed, his prosperity never waned. His career as a businessman is an example of the saying "honesty is the best policy." He was in the highest sense a self-made man, and young men starting in business can find no higher example than his life—a life of unceasing industry controlled by principle.

He was a brother-in-law of the late W.I. Linkhaw and of the late Frank Gough, and the business success achieved by them was largely due to the influence of Mr. Melke. C.B. Skipper, W. O. Thompson, and other prominent citizens of Lumberton were once employed by him.

He became a member of the Baptist church, being one of its strongest supporters financially and otherwise. He was another great friend to the needy. He hunted for the poor and told them in person and certainty what was needed. Besides his nets of charity, he would visit the sick, always carrying his Bible and reading the Scriptures and praying with the afflicted.

He acquired a large estate and was known for his charitable disposition and his willingness to assist and support any cause that he believed worthwhile. In his will, he gave generous benefactions to the Robeson Institute, and to the Baptist State Convention, Wake Forest College, Baptist Foreign Mission Board, and the institution now known as Meredith College. He left no descendants.

Jacob Wessell first immigrated to Wilmington around 1853 but moved back to Germany in 1855. In 1859, he immigrated to Lumberton and served as captain over a group of German volunteers during the Civil War. He was known in Lumberton for making brandy, which was a legitimate business and probably as well thought of as any, as evidenced by the following notices in the old paper, "Bring On Your Fruit I am now prepared to still fruit, such as apples, peaches and grapes at my distillery for one third of the brandy made from it J. Wessell, Lumberton, N.C., July 20th, 1878."

Lumberton is home to the Robeson County History Museum which was organized in 1986 as the Robeson County Heritage Showcase under the auspices of Robeson County Bicentennial to preserve and share the history of Robeson County.

The museum is housed in the reconstructed historic Southern Express Building along the banks of the Lumber River. The iron front building was constructed around 1910 across the street from the railroad depot by the late governor Angus W. McLean in the heart of Lumberton's business district.

The past decades have seen efforts to revitalize downtown Lumberton to its glory days. The historic Carolina Theatre was reopened as the Carolina Civic Center after major renovations. Recently, a group of concerned citizens formed the Rediscover Downtown Lumberton Committee to help facilitate a more active downtown.

One

Government and Health Care

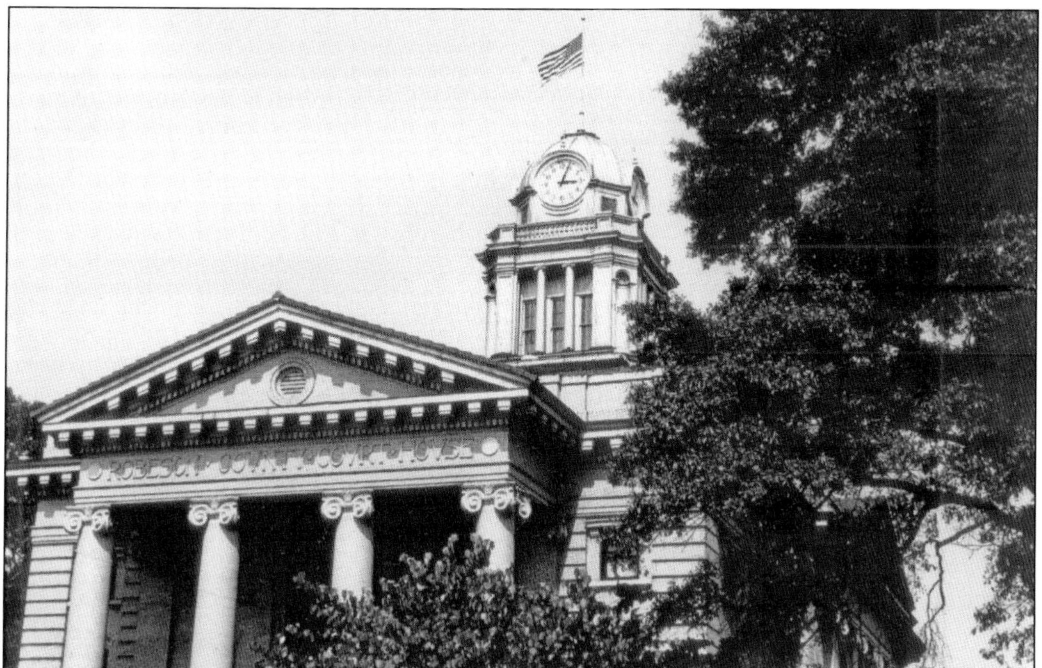

This great shot of the Robeson County Courthouse highlighting the tops of the columns and the clock tower was taken by Lumberton architect Hollis Ivey around 1973 and was rescued by Brad Thompson from a trash pile when Ivey's house was being cleaned out. The courthouse bell is preserved at the Robeson County History Museum, while the clock tower is abandoned in the woods at the Robeson County Fairgrounds. (Courtesy of Brad Thompson.)

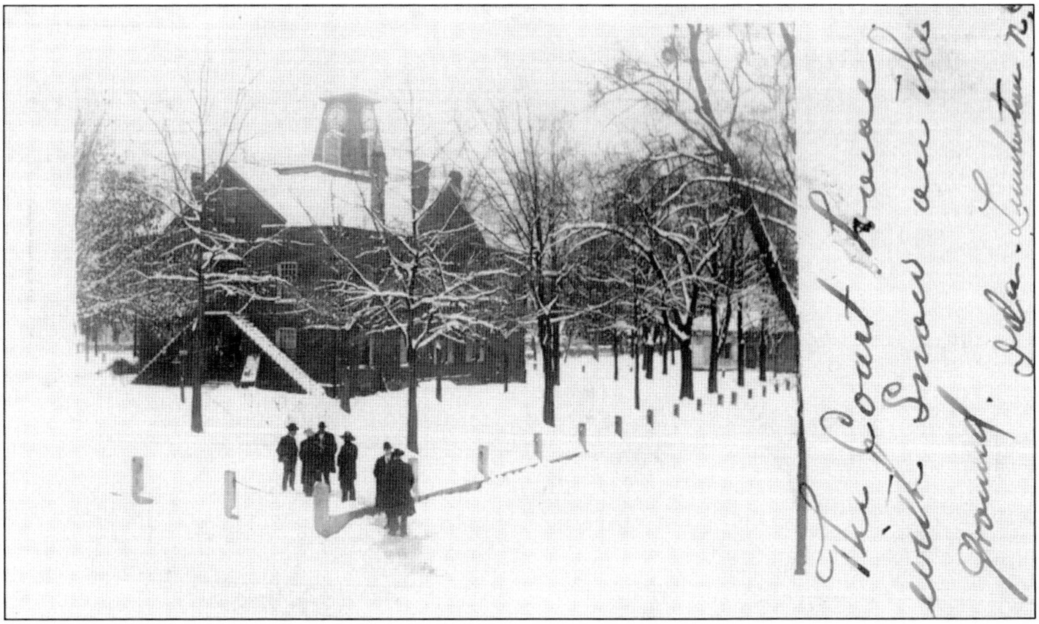

The second Robeson County Courthouse was built in 1848 to replace the original at a cost of $7,500. The 1872 book *The Swamp Outlaws, or, The North Carolina Bandits* states the "court room in the second story is covered with saw dust to keep the peace, it is very crude, large and bare, and the Judge looks amazingly high up behind the long gallery where they expose him." (Courtesy of Keith Vincent of courthousehistory.com.)

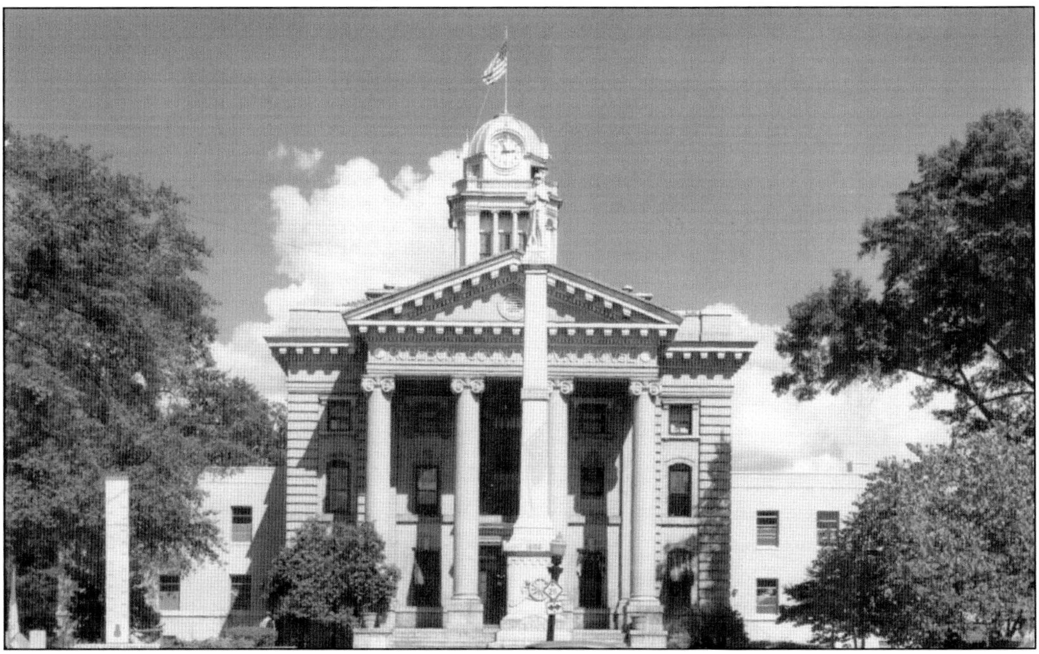

The third courthouse was constructed in 1908, and in 1950, additions were added to the back and both sides of the building. During the original construction, court was held in Dr. Rudolph Vampill's opera house at the corner of Elm and Sixth Streets. The building was razed in 1974 to make room for the fourth and current courthouse. (Courtesy of the Hubbard-Tyner Collection.)

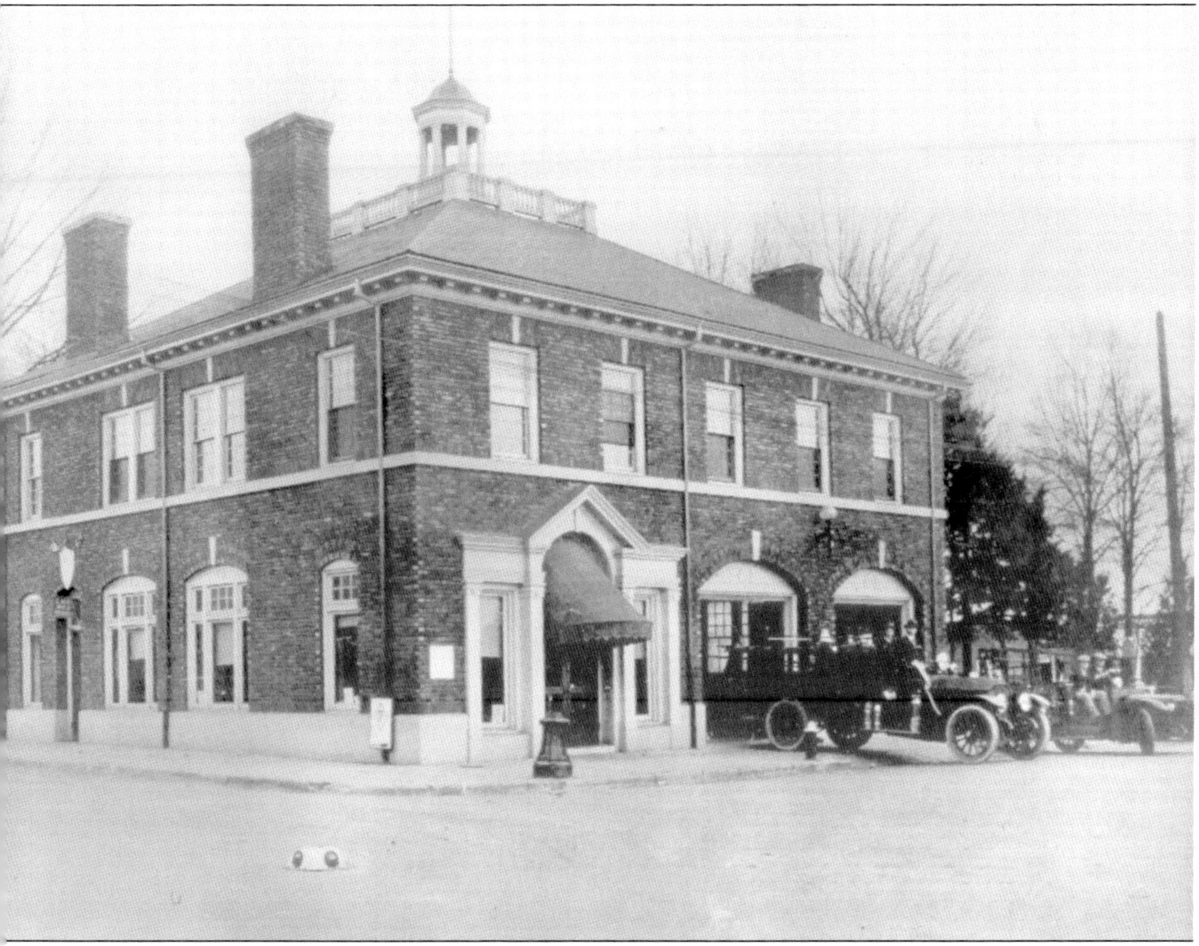

This building was constructed in 1917 by William Moody Burney to house the Lumberton City Hall and the police and fire departments. The city hall and police department moved out of the building in 1955, and the fire department relocated in 1978. The building also housed the library for a while. Fireman Rudolph Lewis remembered that the Carolina Theatre used to provide two movie tickets a week to the firemen. (Courtesy of the Hubbard-Tyner Collection.)

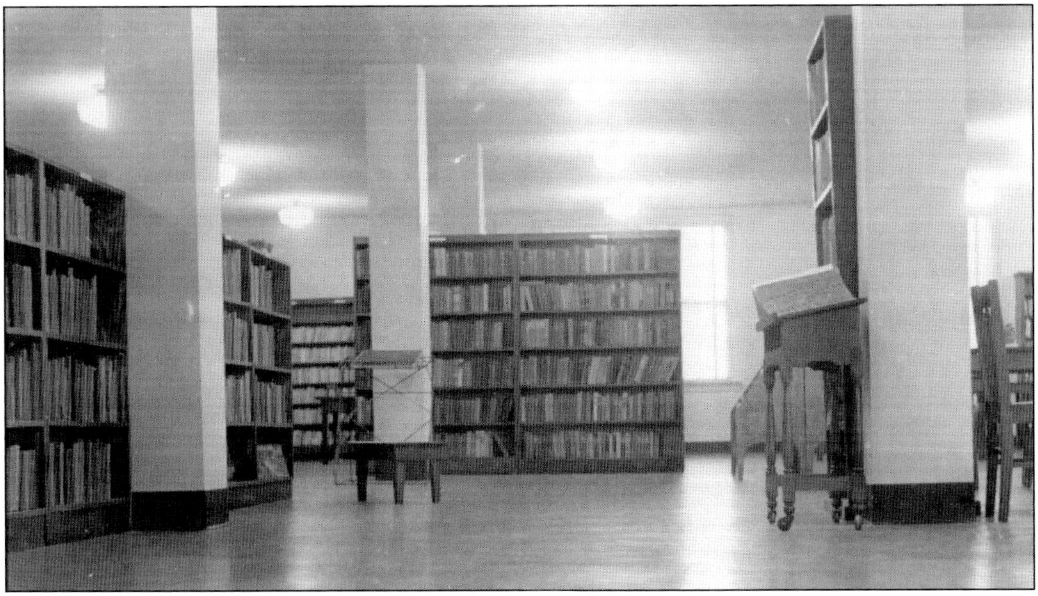

The Robeson County Public Library is seen here when it was housed in the old Thompson Memorial Hospital on the northeast corner of Cedar and Fifth Streets. Many share a common childhood memory of walking up the stairs and being overtaken by the smell of the books as they roamed the stacks with the floors creaking. (Courtesy of NC State University Library.)

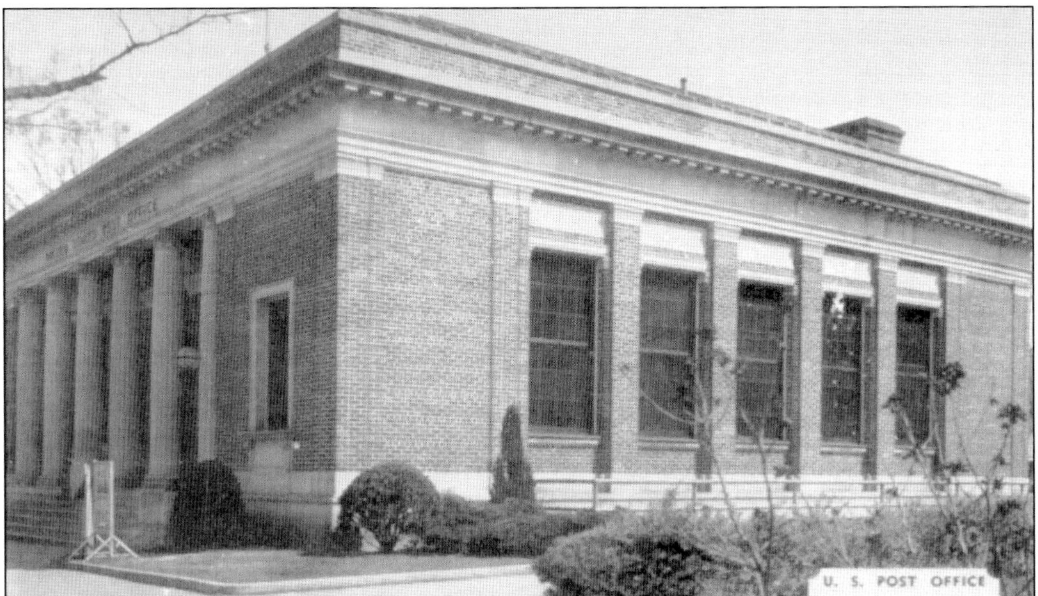

This Neoclassical Revival building was erected in 1931 as part of Pres. Franklin D. Roosevelt's Works Progress Administration at a cost of $75,000, with James A. Wetmore as the supervising architect. The redbrick building with granite detailing served for years as the main Lumberton Post Office. Located on Elm Street, it is now home to the law firm of Musselwhite & Branch. (Courtesy of the Hubbard-Tyner Collection.)

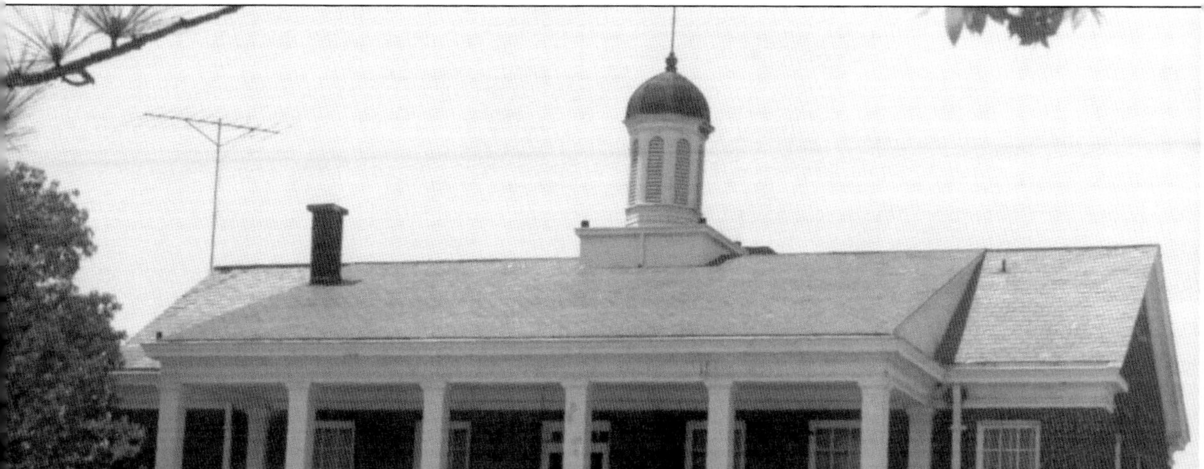

A new County Home was erected in 1924 at the fork of the Old Maxton and Red Springs Roads to replace the old one on East Fifth Street. Originally 37 acres, an additional 170 acres were later added. The building contained 131 rooms, and the number of inmates ranged through the years of its use from about 100 to 150. Its farm and dairy produced part of the food used by the home. The buildings later housed the county health department, the cancer clinic, and the department of social services. The Robeson County Health Department was organized in 1912 and was the first county health department in the United States. When Dr. B.W. Page was hired on February 19, 1912, he started an effort to improve the health problems of the county. This included addressing typhoid fever, hookworm disease, unsanitary conditions, smallpox, and high infant death. The main building above was named for Dr. Eugene Ramsey Hardin, the third county health director. (Courtesy of Historical Robeson, Inc.)

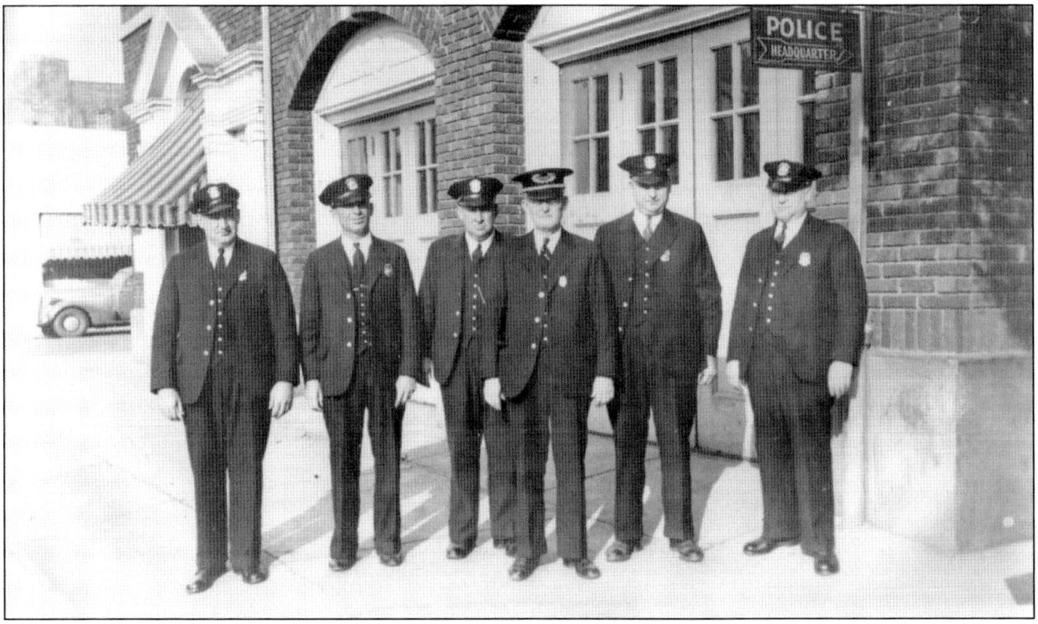

In 1937, Lumberton's efficient police department maintained a good law-enforcement record for the city under the direction of Chief J.T. McRainey. Pictured from left to right are J.S. Lassiter, A.R. Pittman, Randall Stephens, McRainey, F.L. Crump, and Hinton McLeod. Policeman Horace Wishart was absent when the above picture was made (Courtesy of the Lumberton Police Department.)

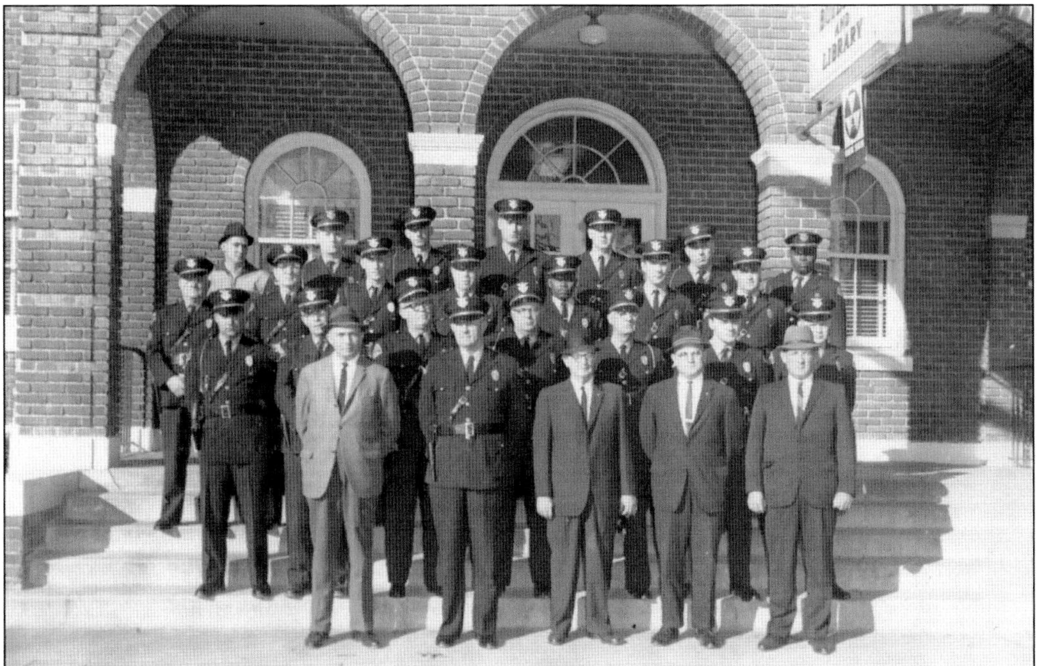

Lumberton's police department takes time to pose outside of city hall in the early 1960s. The current department is composed of 77 sworn and 13 non-sworn employees under the leadership of Chief Michael McNeill. (Courtesy of the Lumberton Police Department.)

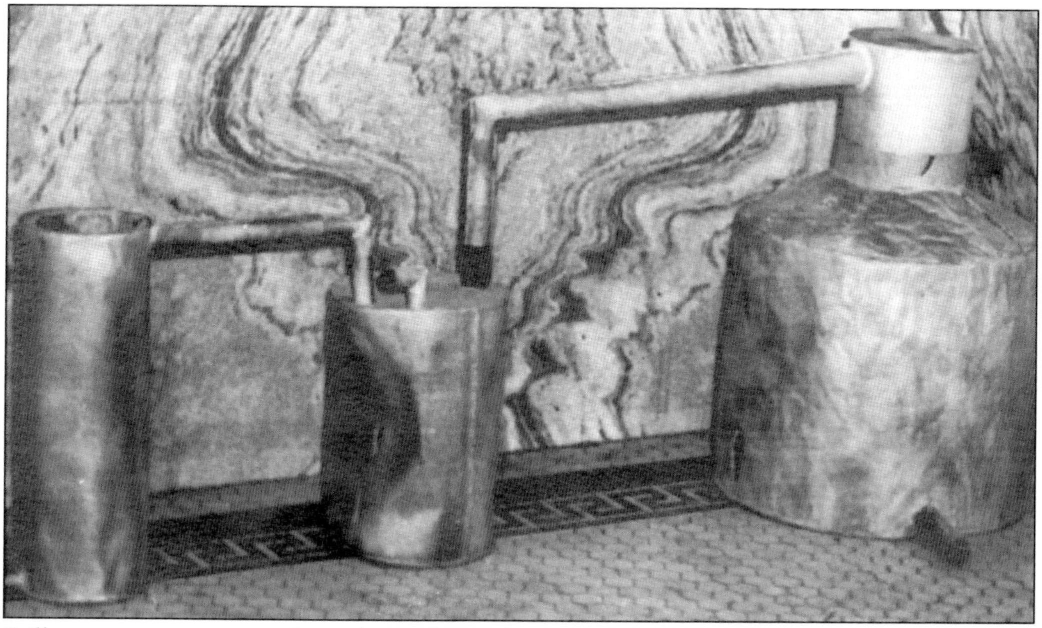

Stills were once commonplace; the making of moonshine was a family tradition, and the skill was passed on from father to son. In 1908, North Carolina was officially a dry state, which meant moonshining and bootlegging accounted for a large portion of the underground economy. This captured still was displayed in the Robeson County Courthouse in the 1950s. (Courtesy of Historic Robeson, Inc.)

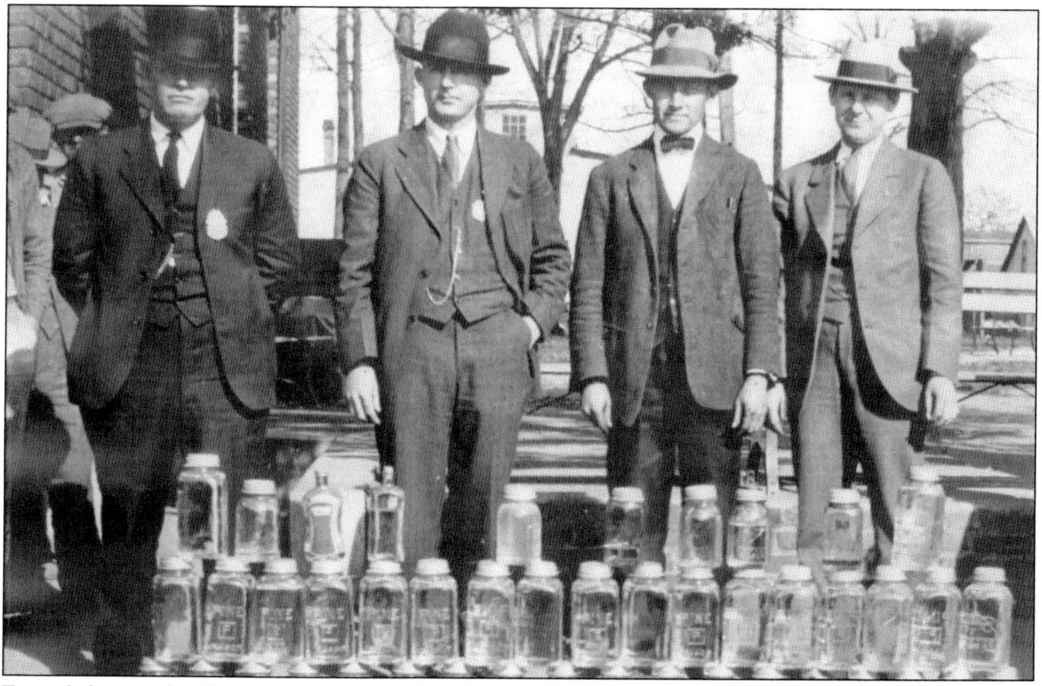

From left to right, Deputy Marvin Barker, Deputy Mel Ivey, Sherriff Pat Korneagy, and solicitor Frank Ertel Carlyle pose at the courthouse with the results of a still bust. Carlyle went on the serve in the US Congress from 1949 until 1957. (Courtesy of Historic Robeson, Inc.)

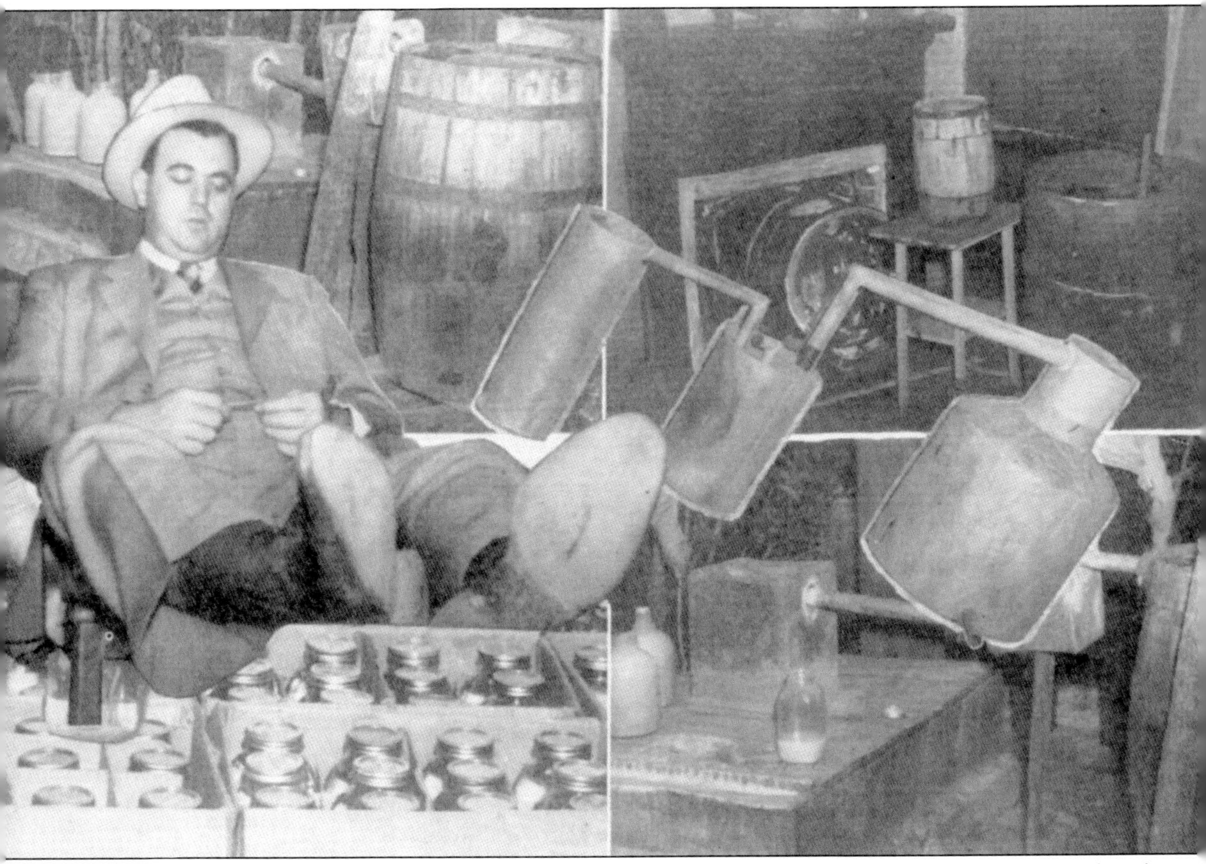

Sheriff Malcolm McLeod was the son of Lumberton Police Chief Alphus and Kate McLeod and was married to the former Mary Lois Allen. He was elected sheriff in November 1950 and held the position for 28 years. During his tenure, the department was enlarged from 13 deputies to 46, and he modernized it with new police vehicles and radios. He was known as the still buster; during his first four years in office he busted 2,967 stills, destroyed 6,831 gallons of liquor and 690,735 gallons of mash, and arrested 521 men in connection with the still operations. One major event during his tenure that received national attention was the KKK rally at Hayes Pond in Maxton, which was covered in *Life* magazine. When trying to disburse the crowd he told them "go home and watch 'Gunsmoke.'" (Courtesy Hubbard-Tyner Collection.)

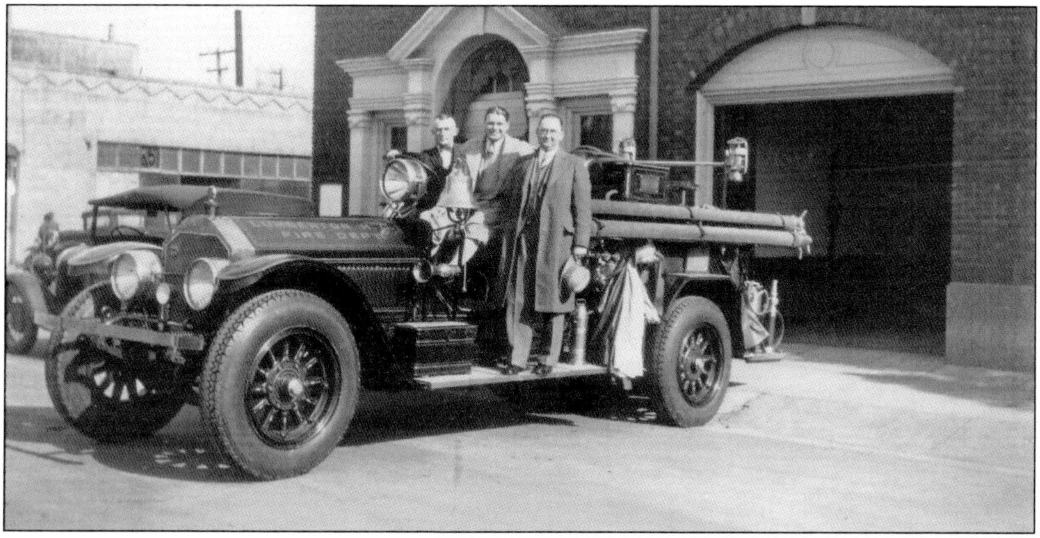

Ervin Mosby Johnson served as mayor of Lumberton from 1922 to 1943. He is shown standing on the running board of new fire truck with fire chief Ed Glover at the wheel and an unidentified man in between. (Courtesy of Johnson Collection, Robeson Remembers, Robeson County History Museum.)

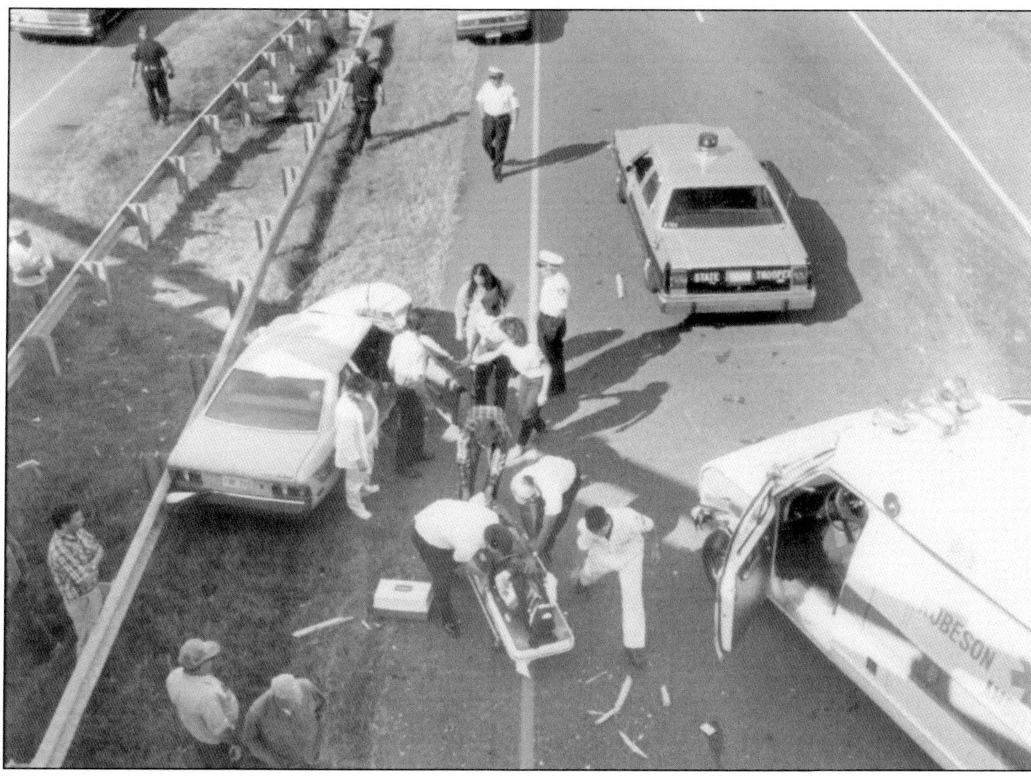

The Lumberton Rescue and EMS was founded as the Robeson County Rescue Squad after Hurricane Hazel hit the area in 1954. They originally covered all of Robeson County as well as Bladen and Columbus Counties, responding to hundreds of calls per month to help citizens and visitors to the city. (Courtesy of Lumberton Rescue and EMS.)

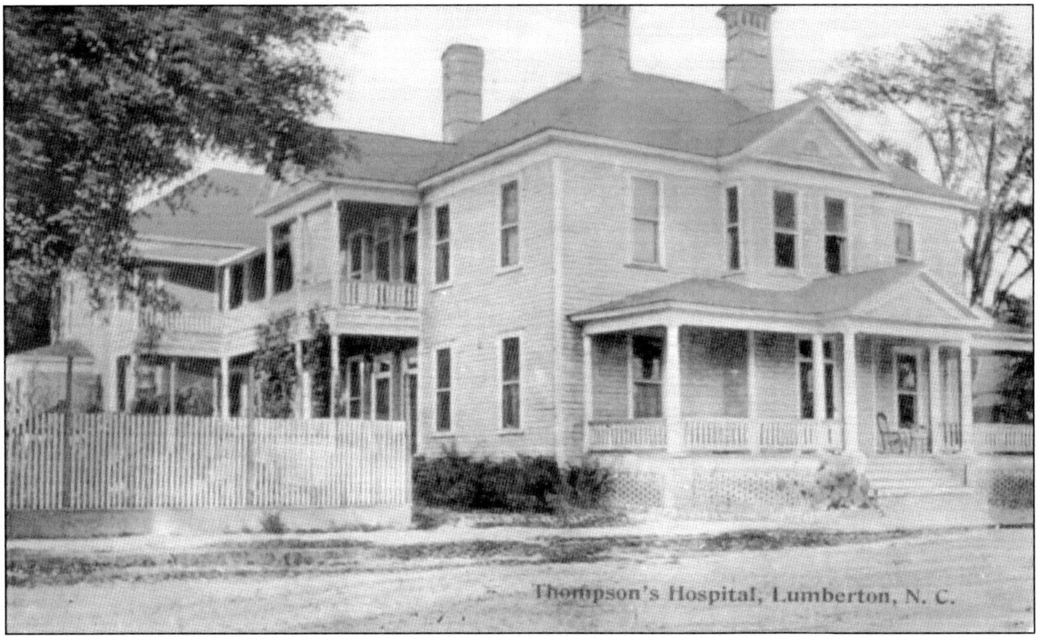

Thompson Hospital was organized in 1905 by Dr. Neill Archie Thompson Sr., Dr. Richard Gregory Rozier, and R.C. Lawrence. It was located in old Solomon Bennett home on the northwest corner of Pine and Fourth Streets. A 1910 advertisement in the *News and Observer* stated that the hospital cared for all classes of surgical, gynecological, and noncontagious medical patients, and the facility had superior operations rooms and two large wards. (Courtesy of the Hubbard-Tyner Collection.)

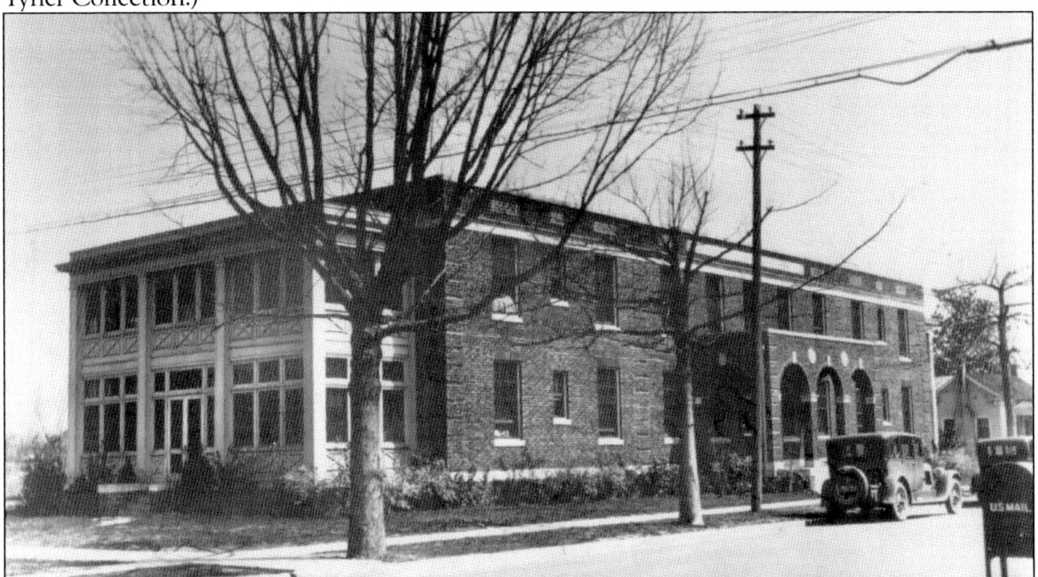

Dr. Neill Archie Thompson Sr. was killed in 1922 while crossing Fayetteville Street. Later, Under the leadership of Dr. Thomas C. Johnson, a new hospital was built on the northeast corner of Cedar and Fifth Streets in 1926. In 1955, the city offices, police department, and public library moved into the building. This structure was demolished in 2005 after the new city hall was built. (Courtesy of Robeson County History Museum.)

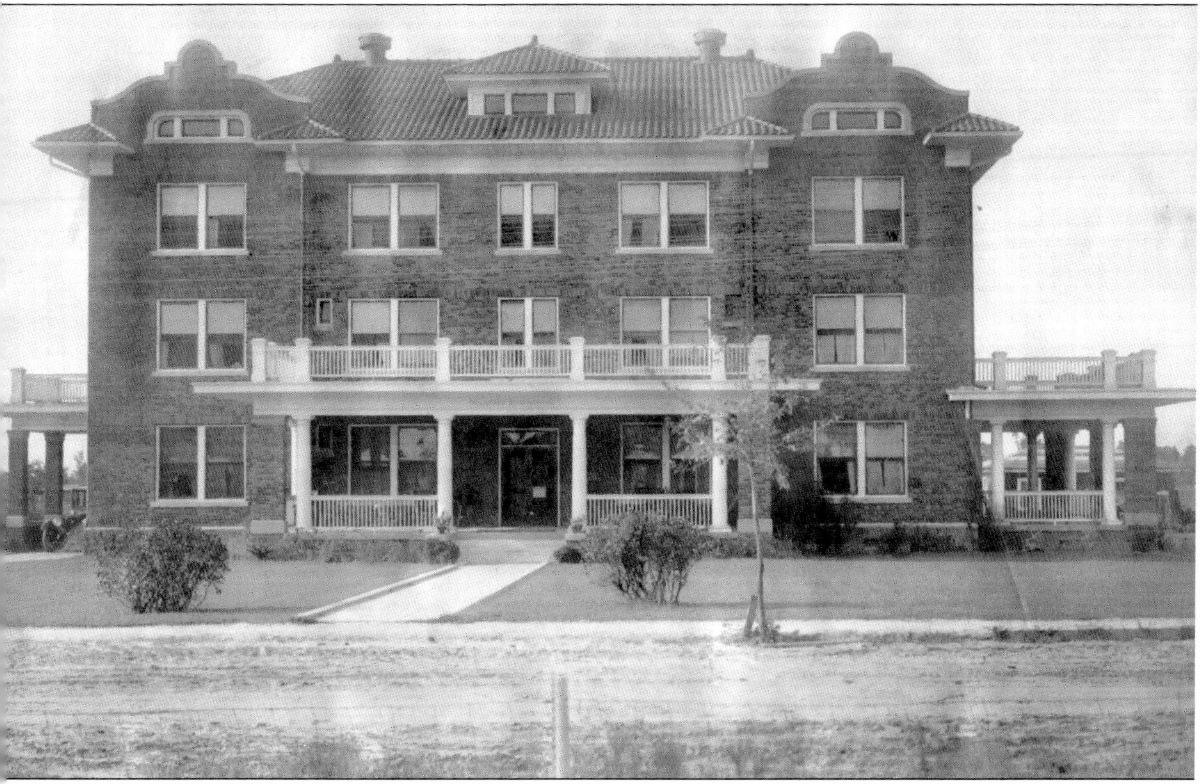

Dr. Horace Baker opened the Baker Sanatorium, a 75-bed facility located on North Chestnut Street, in January 1921. The dream began five years before on a Martha's Vineyard beach. On a summer day in 1917, Annie Ruth Caldwell and Horace, who had been introduced in Boston where they were in college, sat on the beach talking about her dreams of opening a new hospital that could treat her father, Robert David Caldwell. Annie and Horace were married on August 21, 1918, at the bedside of her father during one of his stays at Johns Hopkins Hospital. Robert had pernicious anemia, which required blood transfusions. At first, a doctor and volunteer would travel to Lumberton to do the procedure, but later he had to start making the trips to Johns Hopkins. Robert was instrumental in planning the hospital. The hospital took care of medical, surgical, and obstetric-gynecological cases. When Dr. Horace Baker died in 1945 the sanatorium merged with the Thompson Hospital, which was also under the Duke Endowment. In the 1950s, the structure became the Medical Arts Building. It is currently senior citizen apartments. (Courtesy of Ruth Ann Baker McLellan.)

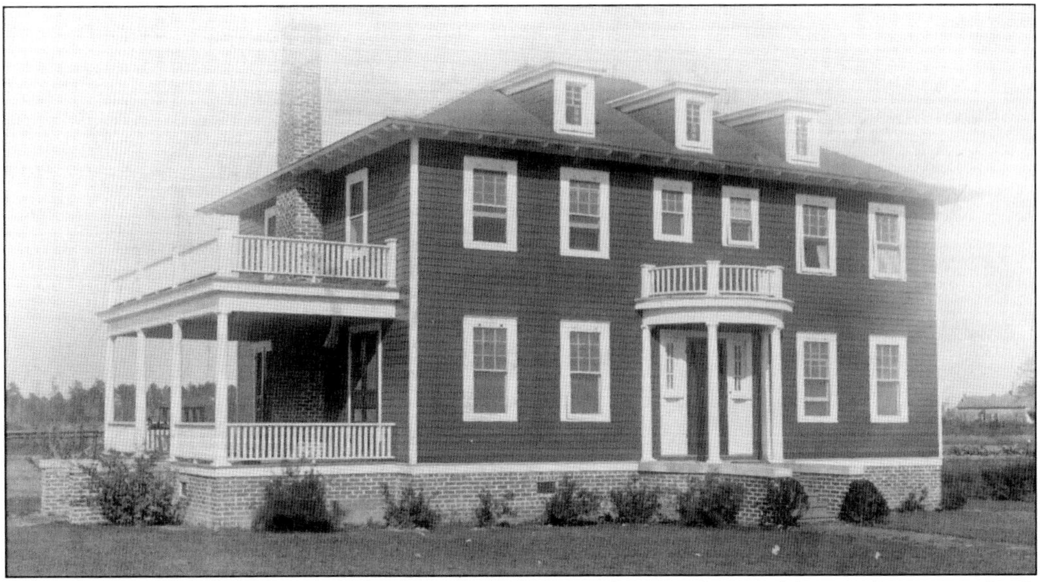

The Baker Sanatorium Nurses' Home and School was Lumberton's first prefabricated structure, built at a cost of $15,000. It was designed for the training of nurses to the highest point in efficiency. The home consisted of beautiful quarters for 20 nurses, with two baths, steam heat, electric lights, and all modern conveniences. The walls were painted, and the woodwork was white enameled. Study rooms, a library, and lecture rooms were provided. (Courtesy of Ruth Ann Baker McLellan.)

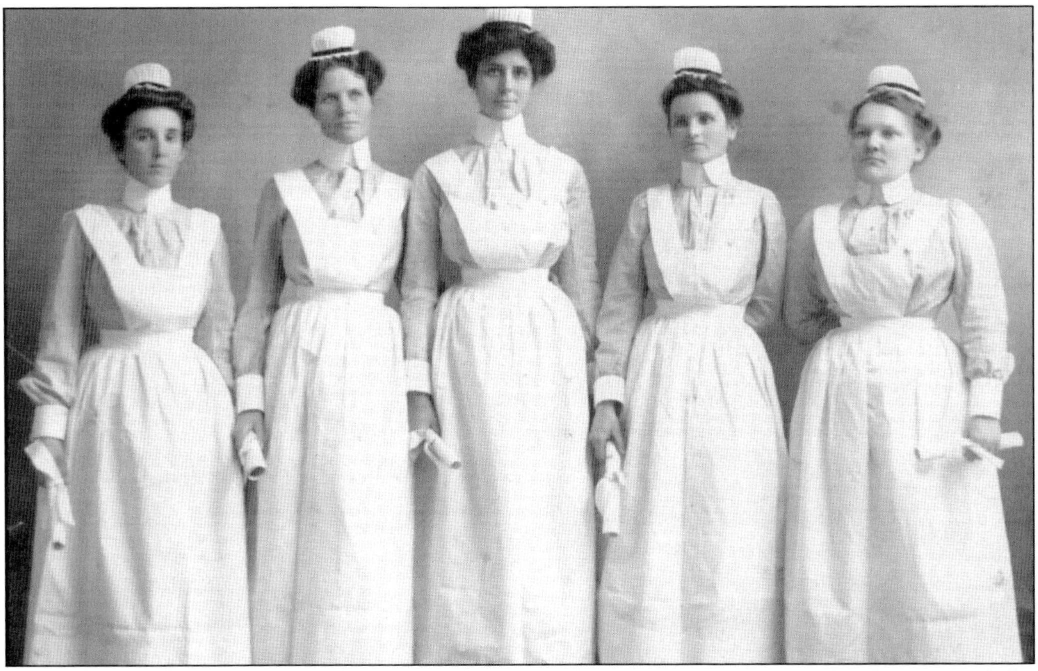

Shown here are early graduates of the Baker Sanatorium Nursing School. Dr. Baker opened the school after seeing a need for better-trained nurses, and he not only assumed medical teaching duties for the girls, he also was their Sunday school teacher each week. Baker's wife played her part by often filling the school and its celebrations with fresh flowers from her sunken garden. (Courtesy of Ruth Ann Baker McLellan.)

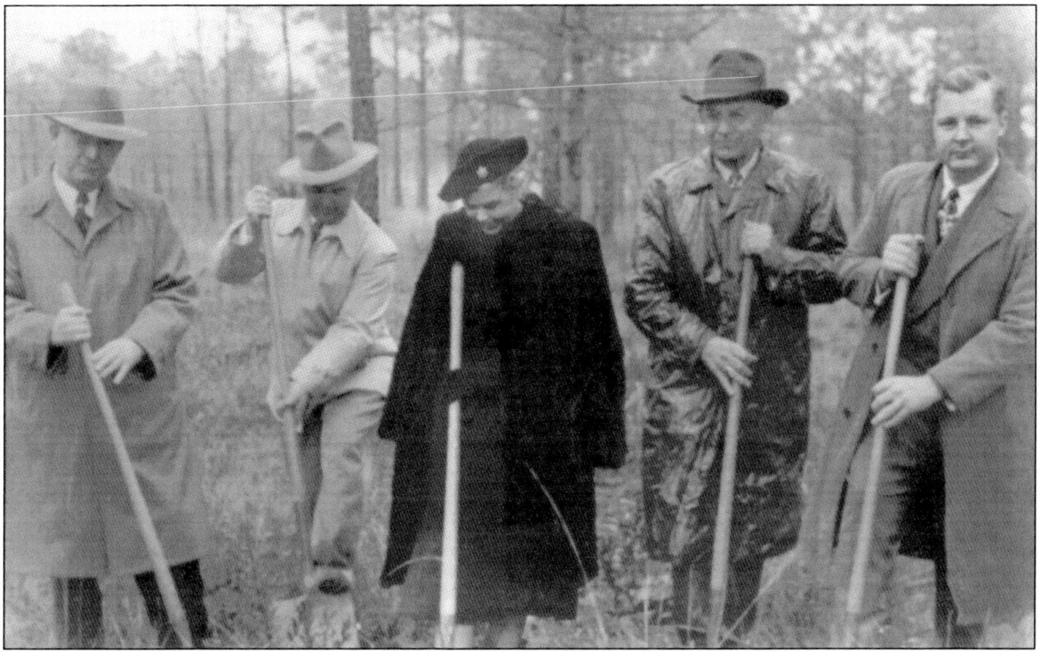

Turning the first shovels of dirt at the 1950 ground-breaking of the Robeson County Memorial Hospital are, from left to right, R.H. Livermore Sr., Wymon Scarborough, Annie Ruth Caldwell Baker, Lee Britt, and Hector MacLean. (Courtesy of the Livermores Collection, Robeson Remembers, Robeson County History Museum.)

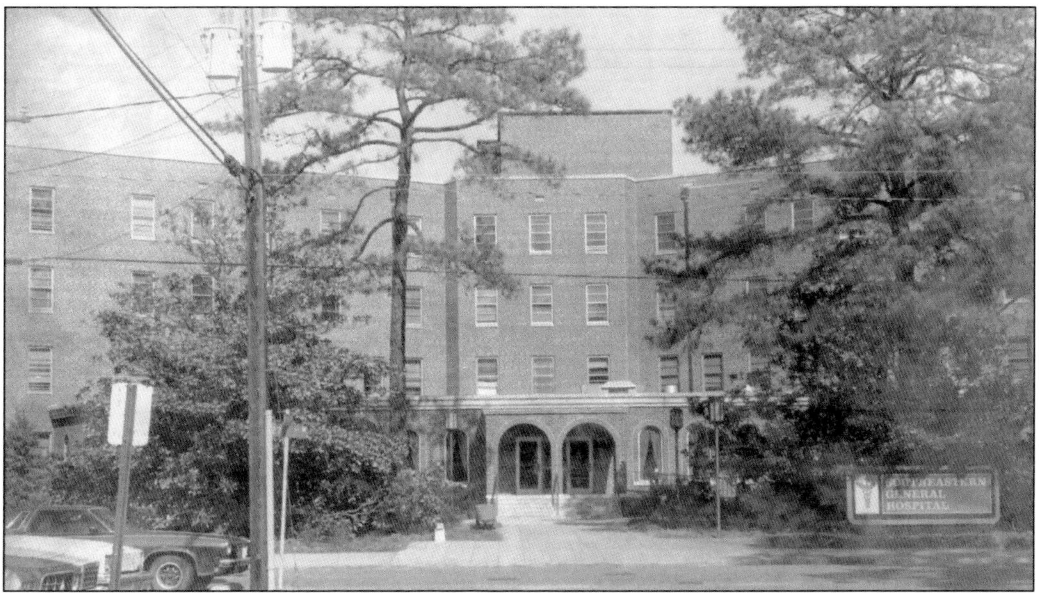

The Baker-Thompson Memorial Hospital performed surgical procedures at the Baker site while medical, pediatric, and obstetric cases went to the Thompson facility. The trustees decided that one new hospital could serve the needs of Robeson County better, and the result was the Robeson County Memorial Hospital, now Southeastern Health. The main building was completed in 1953 on a 10-acre site between Rowland and Elm Streets in North Lumberton. (Courtesy of the Andrews Collection, Robeson Remembers, Robeson County History Museum.)

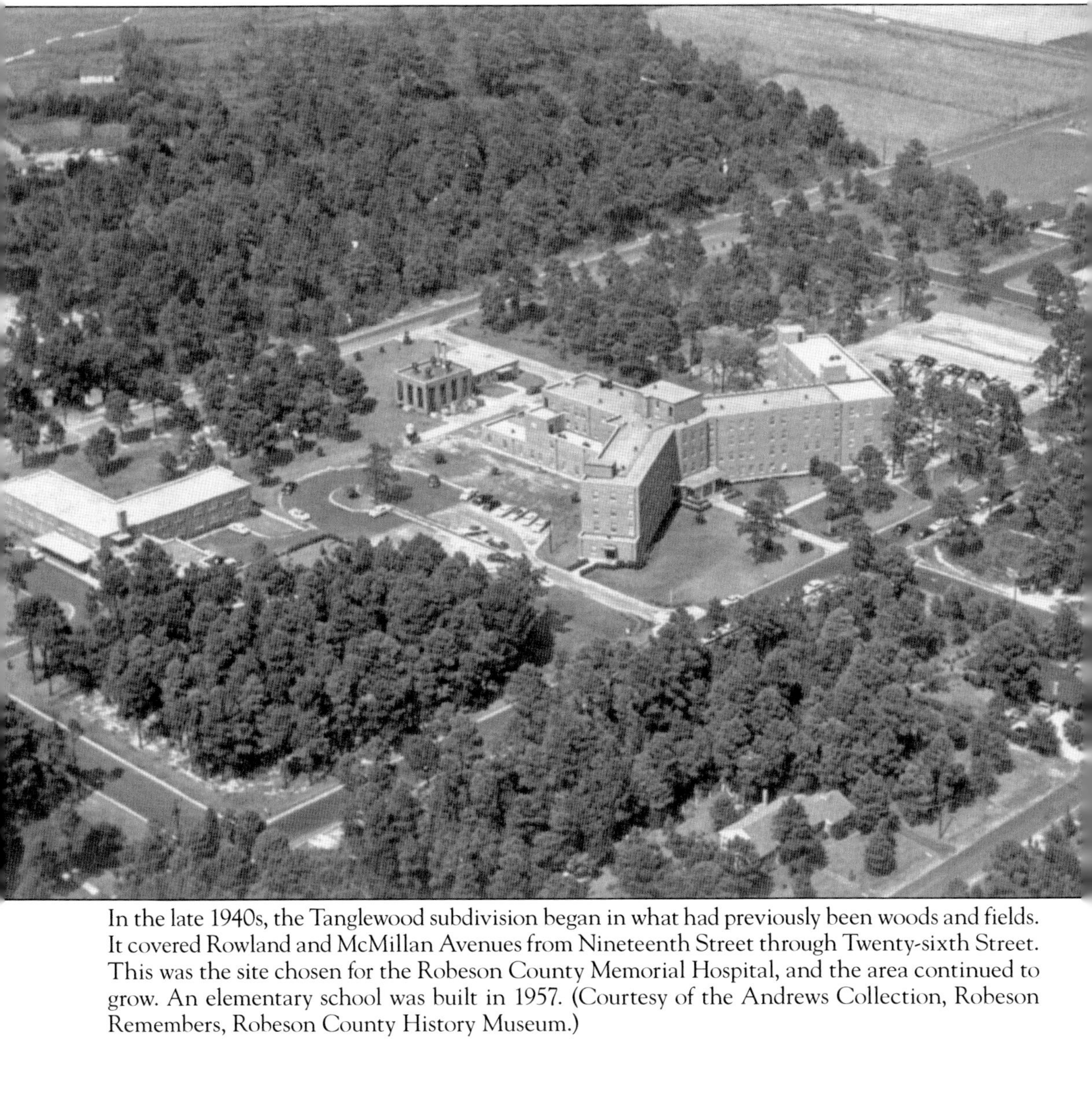

In the late 1940s, the Tanglewood subdivision began in what had previously been woods and fields. It covered Rowland and McMillan Avenues from Nineteenth Street through Twenty-sixth Street. This was the site chosen for the Robeson County Memorial Hospital, and the area continued to grow. An elementary school was built in 1957. (Courtesy of the Andrews Collection, Robeson Remembers, Robeson County History Museum.)

Two

Business and Industry

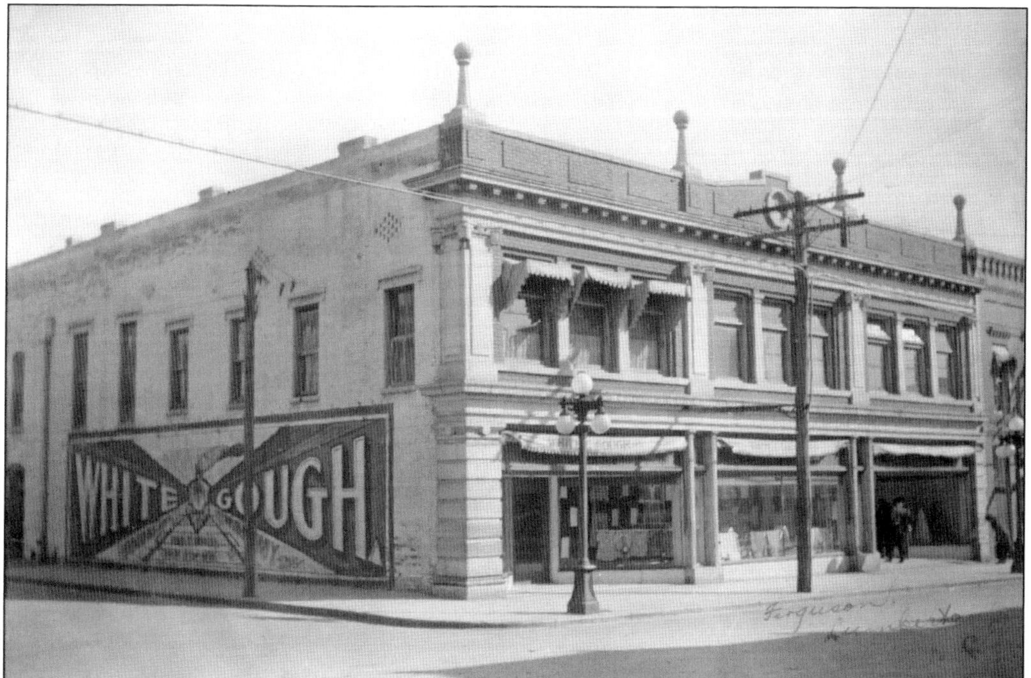

The Lumberton Telephone Company organized in 1896 and was housed on the second floor of the White and Gough Store. The company was purchased by Southern Bell in 1909. Russell Gordon Cashwell worked as a night operator in 1915, and 60 years later could still remember some of the most common numbers: J.H. Wishart Grocery, 1; Dr. H.T. Pope, 50, Hinds Market, 53; J.T. Biggs Company, 61; McMillan Drug Store, 75; K.M. Biggs Store, 80. (Courtesy Historic Robeson, Inc.)

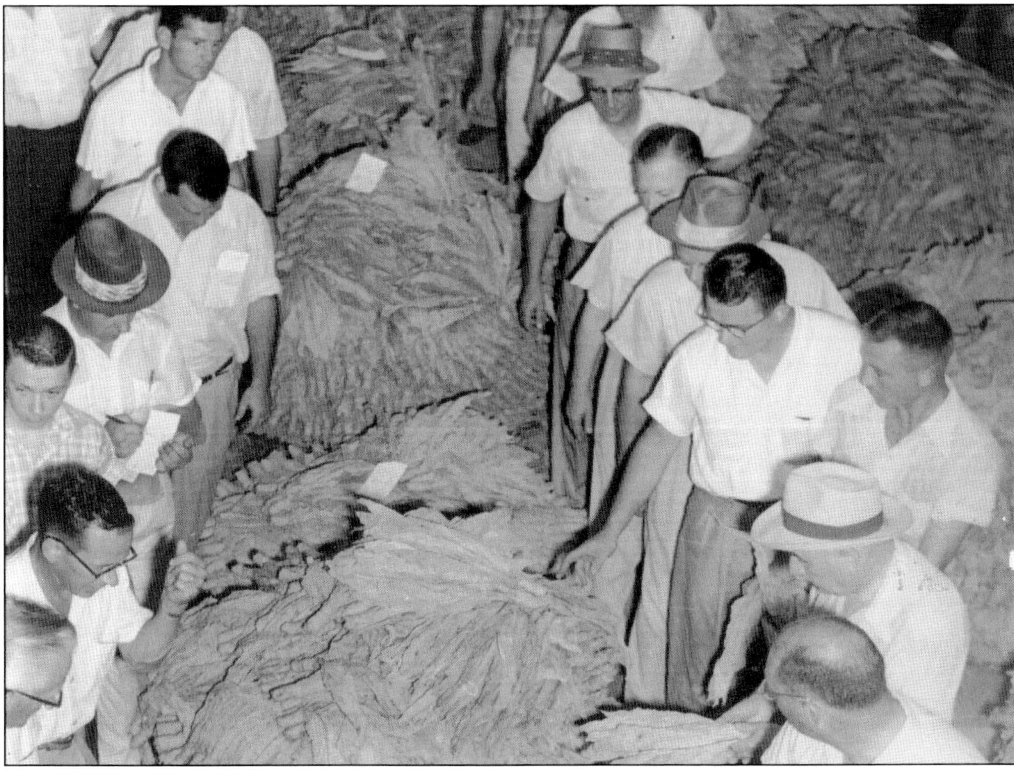

In 1898, Caldwell & Carlyle, L.H. Caldwell, and Q.T. Williams built the first tobacco warehouse at Lumberton. That same year, Kenneth M. Biggs and a small, civic-minded group organized the Lumberton Tobacco Market. By the 75th anniversary, there were 24 warehouses with more than 35 acres of space. (Courtesy of Historic Robeson, Inc.)

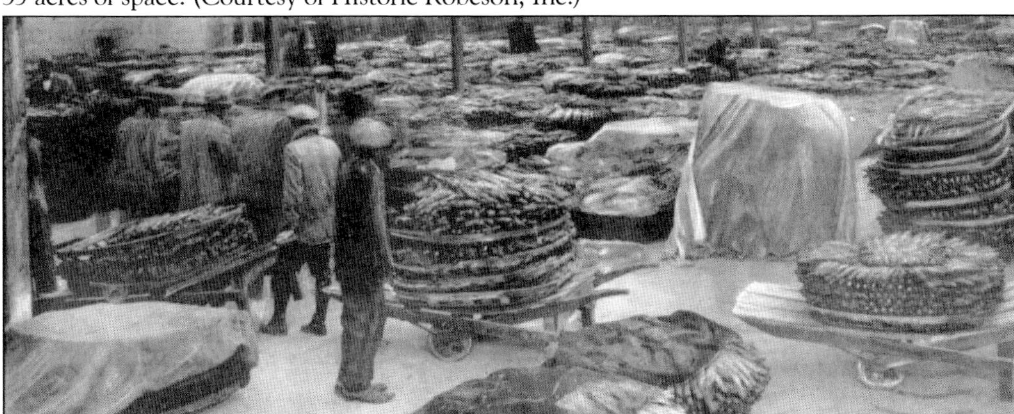

In 1973, the Lumberton Tobacco Market celebrated its 75th anniversary. The 24 warehouses were operated by six firms—Hedgepeth is operated by E.H. Collins and Albert Thornton Jr.; Star is operated by Hogan Teater, D.T. Stephenson, and Russell Teater; Smith is operated by Jack Pait; Cooperative is operated by L.D. West; Liberty is operated by R.H. Livermore Sr. and H.D. Goode; and Carolina is operated by J.L. Townsend Sr. and James Johnson. "Border Belt's Best" was the slogan of the Lumberton Tobacco Market. (Courtesy of the Carolina Collection, UNC-Chapel Hill.)

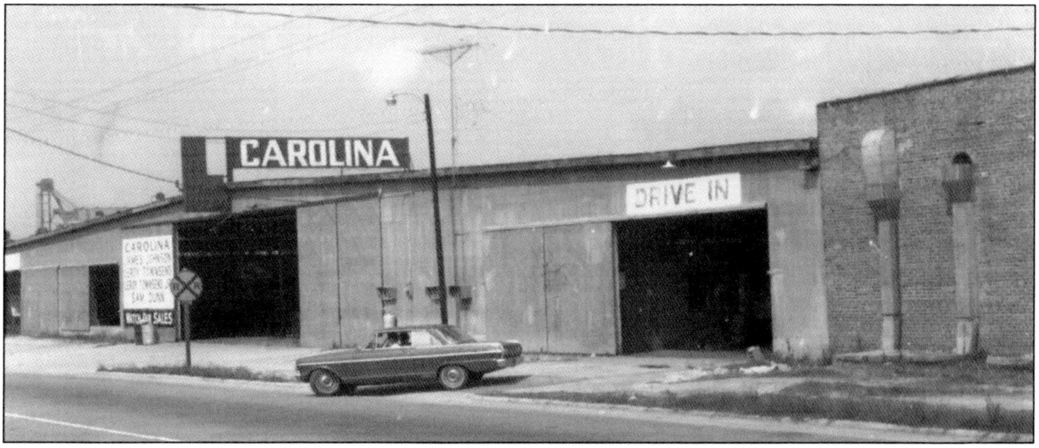

This photograph of the Carolina Tobacco Warehouse appeared in the July 27, 1970, issue of the *Robesonian*. It was owned by Leroy Townsend Sr., Leroy Townsend Jr., and James Johnson. By the mid-1990s, it was owned by David Stephenson, Gary Powers, and Bobby Britt, and in 1999, it merged with Rusty Livermore's Liberty Warehouse. (Courtesy of Historic Robeson, Inc.)

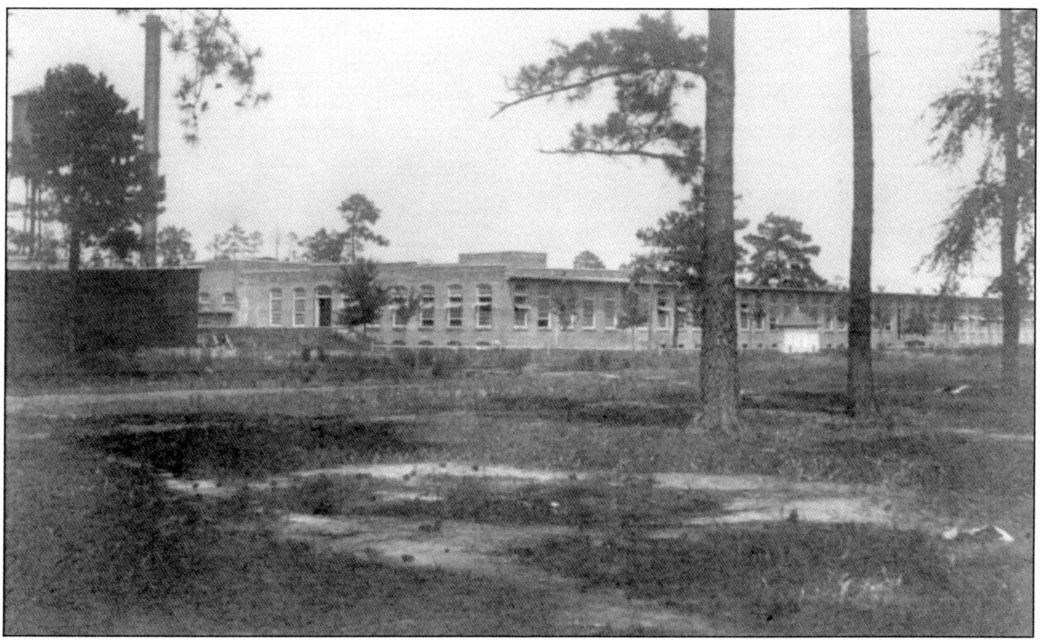

The National Cotton Mill was organized in 1906, a half-mile from the Lumber River on the Seaboard Airline Railroad, 1.5 miles west of Lumberton. The officers were George B. McLeod, president; R.C. Lawrence, vice president; and A.P. McAllister, secretary-treasurer. A school was operated most of the year on the property, and the children were encouraged to attend. Religious services were sponsored, as was entertainment for the young people. (Courtesy of the Hubbard-Tyner Collection.)

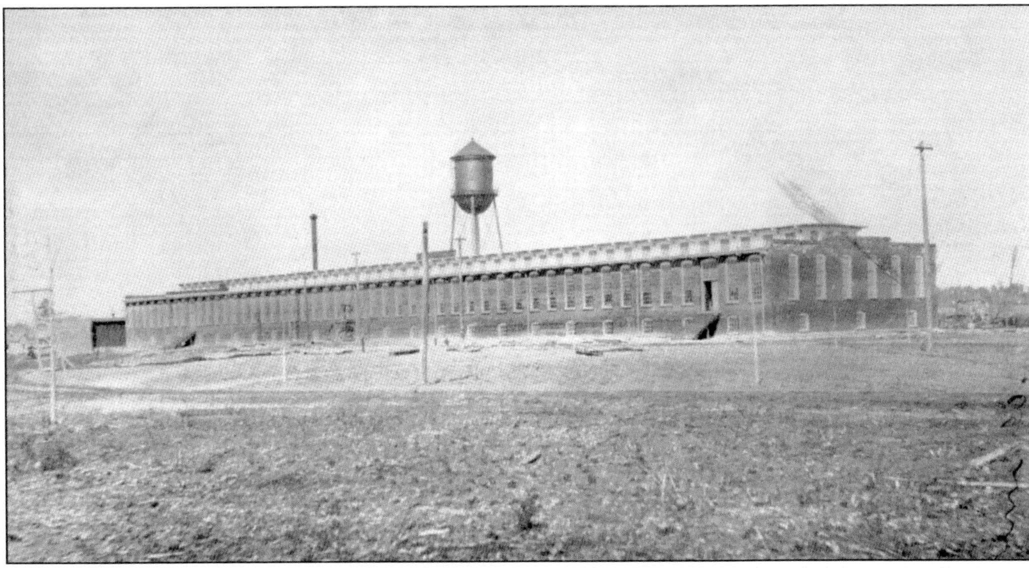

The first cotton mill, named the Dresden Cotton Mill, was organized in 1896 on the Seaboard Airline Railroad in East Lumberton. The company officers were R.D. Caldwell, president; A.W. McLean, vice president; H.B. Jennings, secretary-treasurer; and F.R. Gray, assistant treasurer. (Courtesy of the Hubbard-Tyner Collection.)

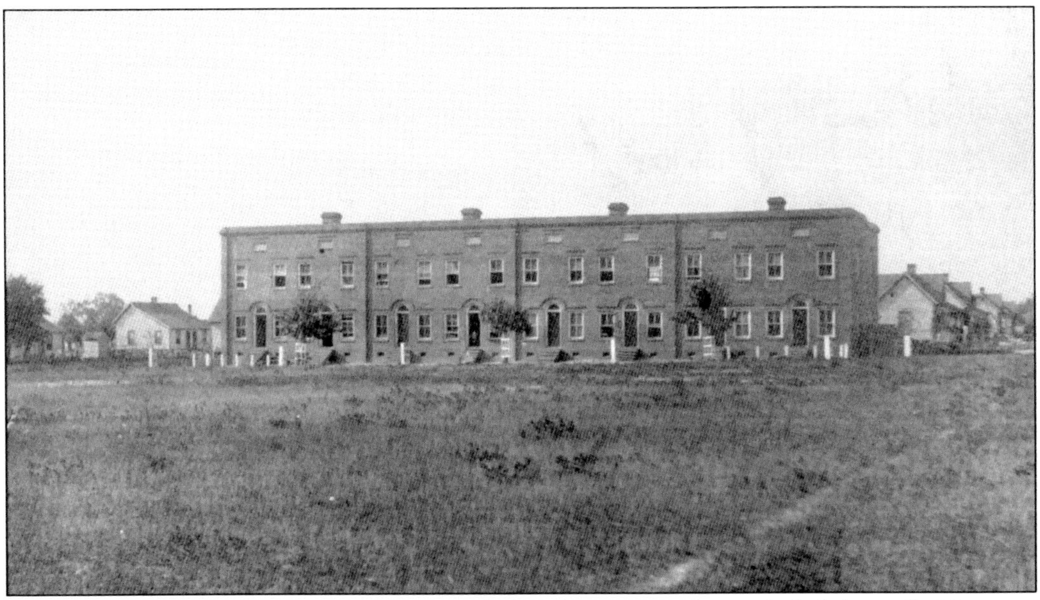

The Dresden Cotton Mill property consisted of a 75-acre tract that included the mill; 54 tenant houses; and this large two-story brick apartment for single male workers, containing eight apartments with four rooms each. Each dwelling had its own artesian well. The children attended the schoolhouse at the Lumberton Cotton Mill; the hall of the school also served the community as a place for religious services and entertainment. (Courtesy of the Hubbard-Tyner Collection.)

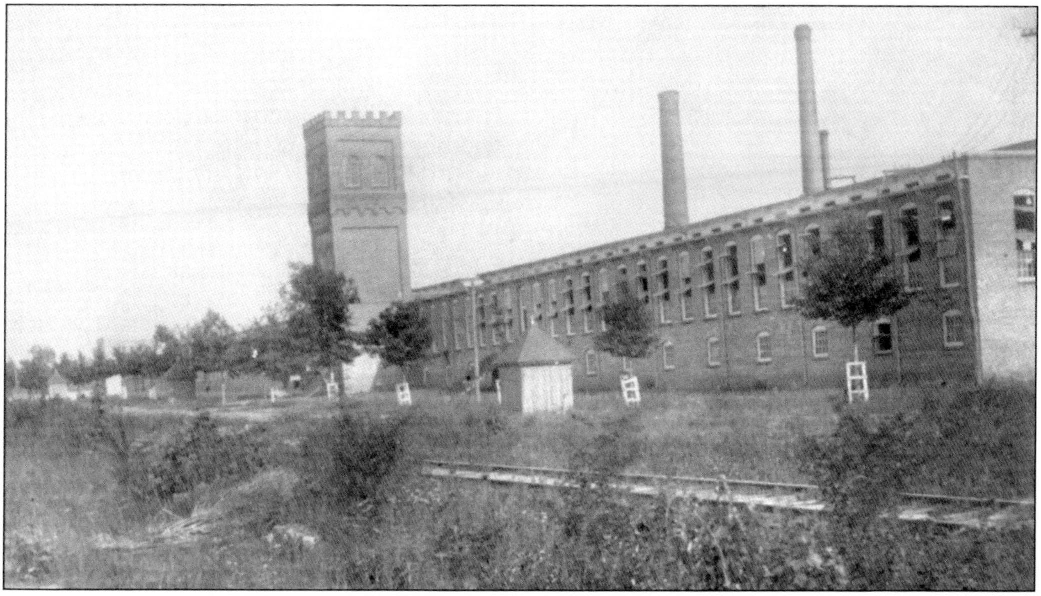

The Lumberton Cotton Mill was incorporated in 1900 with officers being R.D. Caldwell, president; A.W. McLean, vice president; H.B. Jennings, secretary-treasurer; and F.R. Gray, assistant treasurer. It was located in East Lumberton on the Seaboard Airline Railroad. The property covered 250 acres with the mill buildings, company store, public school, and 175 cottages. The main building was a one-story, 75-by-250-foot brick structure with 5,000 spindles. (Courtesy of the Hubbard-Tyner Collection.)

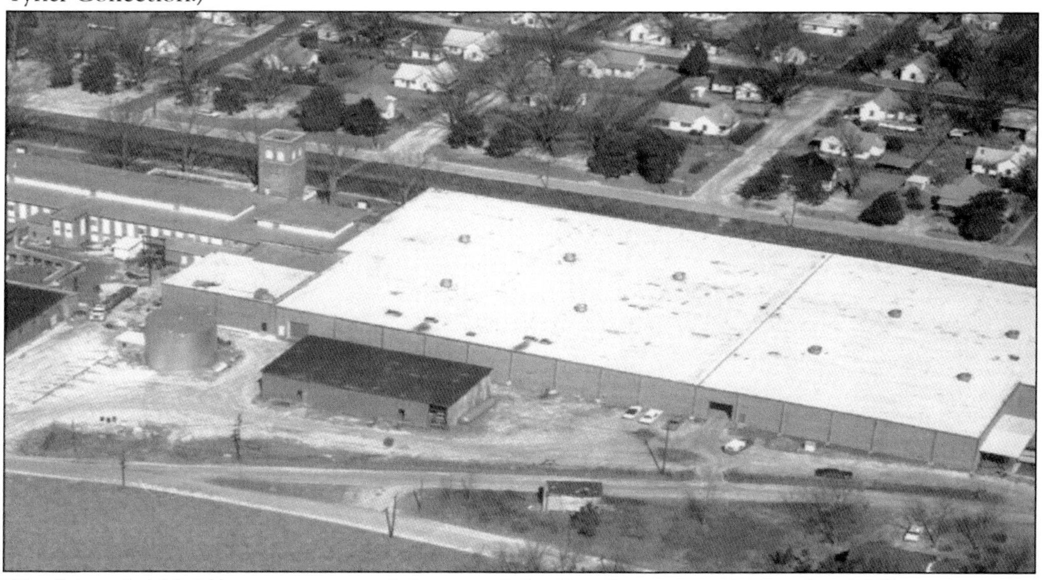

The Mansfield Mills were a consolidation of the Lumberton and Dresden Mills in 1922. In September 1934, there were calls for a national walkout of mill workers. The National Guard, under command of Capt. Eli Wishart, was on hand with local policeman. Of the 950 workers, only 8 belonged to the union; the others opposed the union and the walkout. Many of the nonunion workers brought squirrel guns and rifles, promising the out-of-towners a warm welcome. The out-of-towners were union men who traveled town to town to try and convince, sometimes by force, textile workers to join the union. (Courtesy of Frances Phillips.)

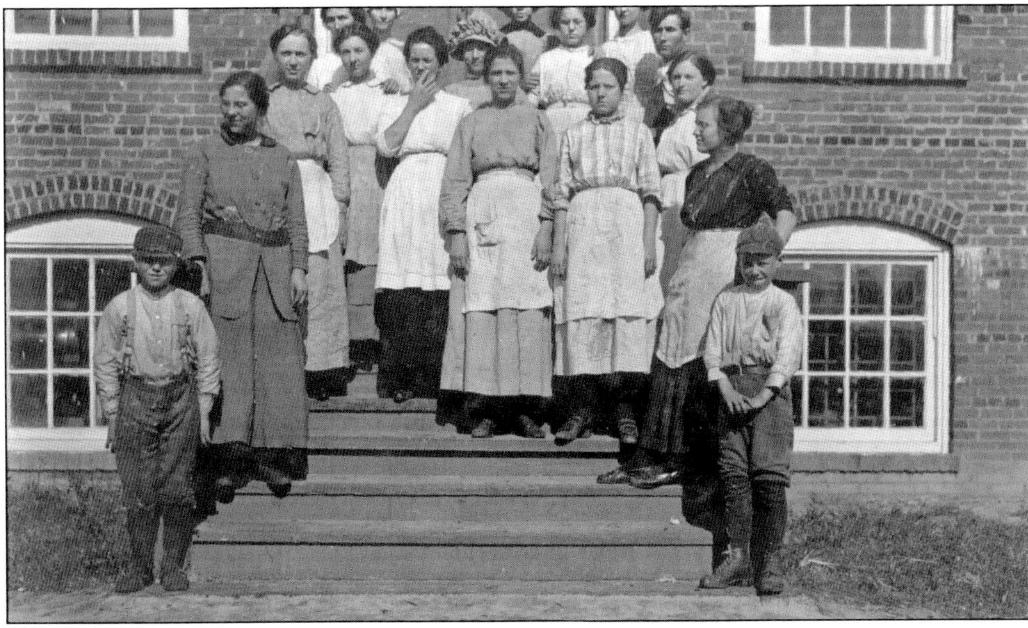

Lewis Hine is best known for his use of photography as a means to achieve social reform. In 1908, he became an investigator and photographer for the National Child Labor Committee. Between 1908 and 1916, he traveled extensively photographing child-labor abuses. Hine traveled to Lumberton in November 1914 and took this photograph at the Dresden Cotton Mills; he believed the two small boys were probably under the age of 12. (Courtesy of the Library of Congress.)

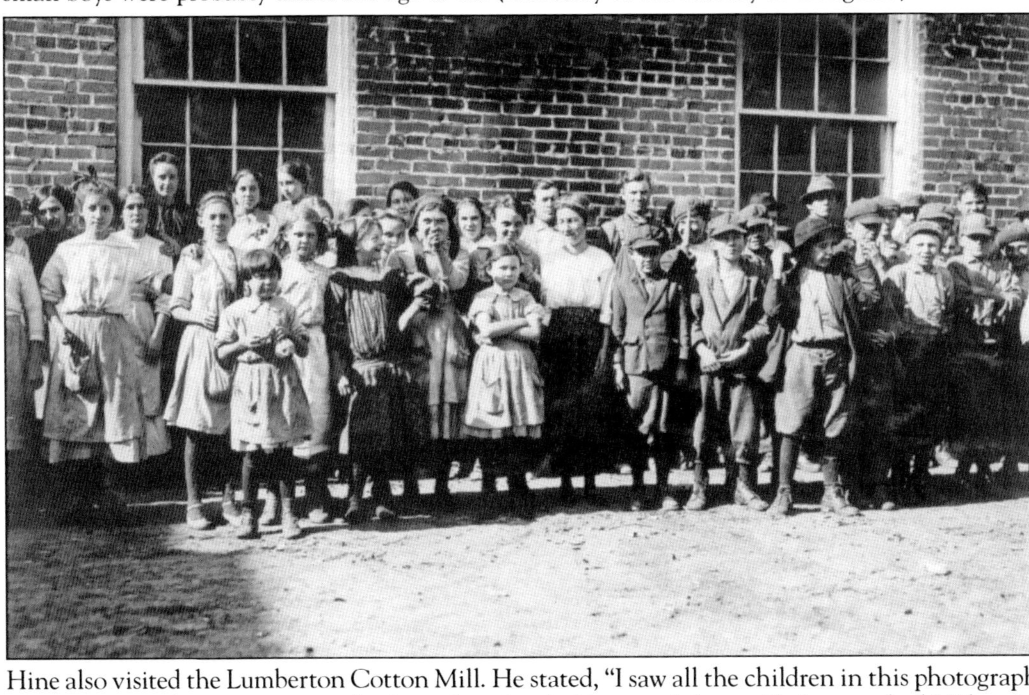

Hine also visited the Lumberton Cotton Mill. He stated, "I saw all the children in this photograph coming out and going in to work when the whistle blew, and they said they worked." The girl with crossed arms in the center is six-year-old Flossie Britt, who had been working several months steadily as a spinner for 30¢ a day. (Courtesy of the Library of Congress.)

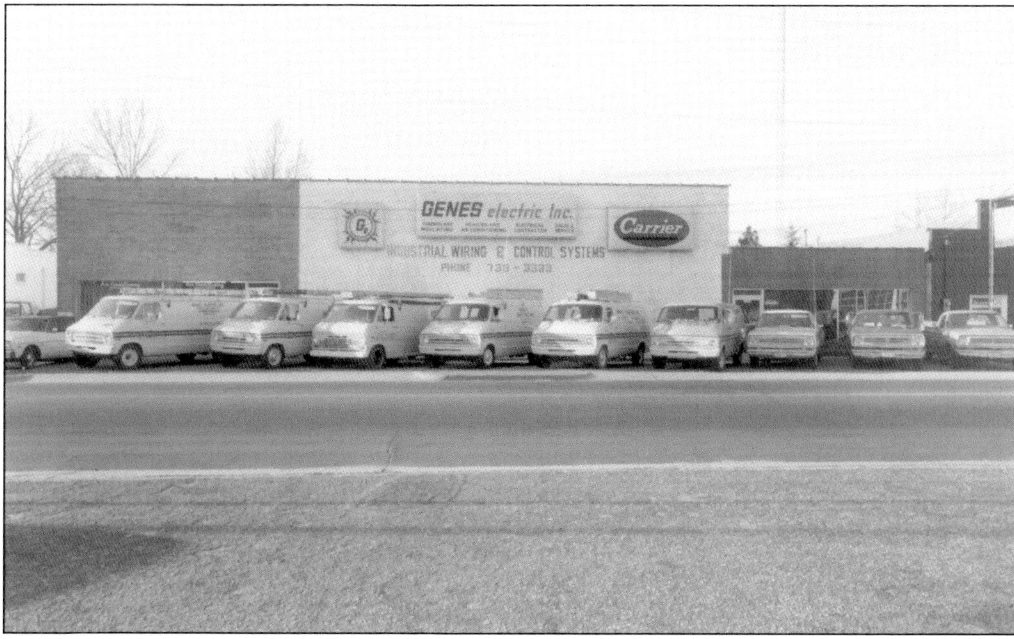

Gene's Electric was owned by Eugene "Gene" Knox Helgren. He cofounded Tri-Tex Knits, Inc., in 1974 and was one of the founders of Progressive State Bank, where he served on the board of directors. He was also involved in various other local business enterprises and was a longtime Mason at St. Alban's Lodge in Lumberton. (Courtesy of Mitchell Prevatte.)

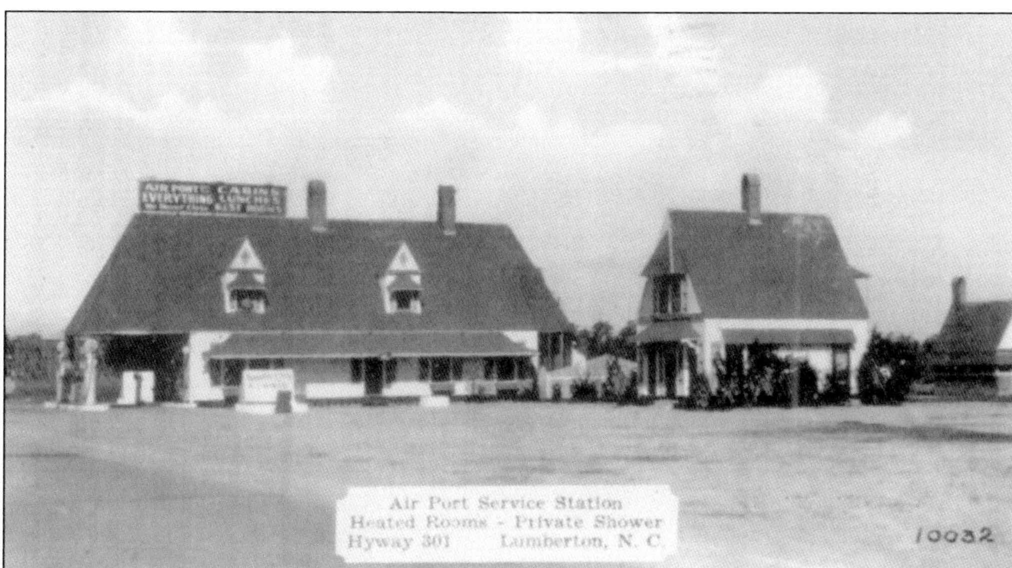

The airport café was located at the Lumberton Airport on the old Maxton Highway. According to the June 1947 issue of *Southern Wings*, Lumberton Airport was having an average of 20 planes a day, and the large part of them were from Latin America. There were so many Spanish-speaking patrons that the bathrooms and the menus at the airport restaurant were printed in Spanish and English. Horace Barnes is considered the father of Lumberton aviation. (Courtesy Hubbard-Tyner Collection)

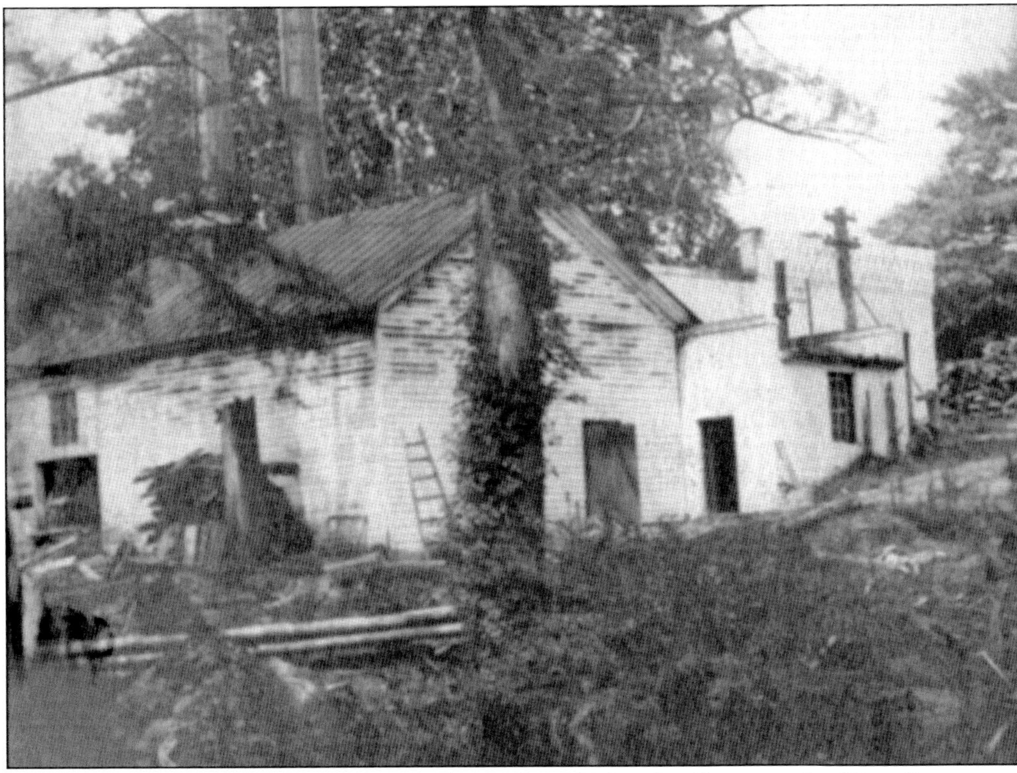

The original Lumberton Power Plant was located on the Lumber River south of First Street, near the area called "the Bottoms." The Bottoms was located in the area between the Lumber River and Elm Street below First Street. The area, which was made of up small wooden houses, was very prone to flooding. (Courtesy of the Carolina Collection, UNC-Chapel Hill.)

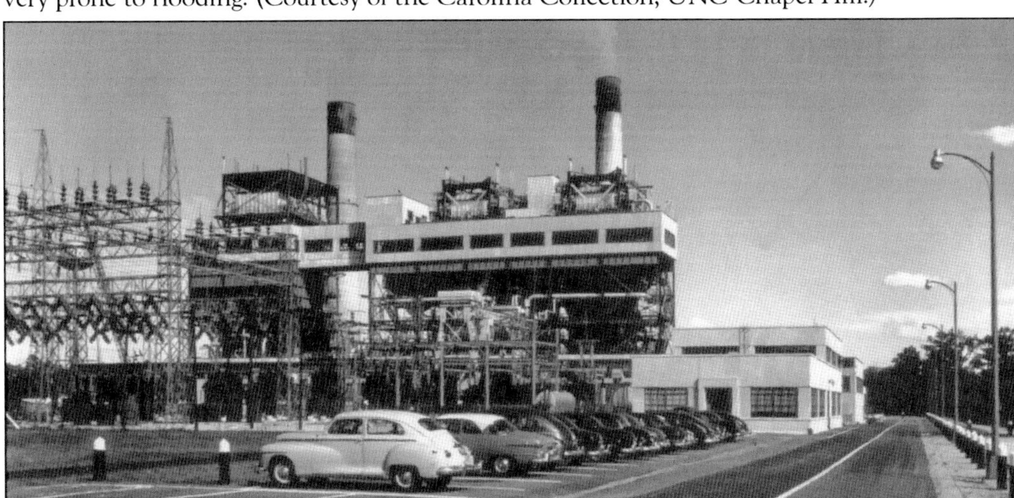

Progress Energy's W.H. Weatherspoon Power Plant opened in 1949 and is scheduled to be shut down by 2015. The site has always been a popular gathering spot. Many churches and families hosted cookouts and picnics on the grounds, and local teenagers gathered in the evenings, parking between the pine trees and listening to music while steaming up the car windows. (Courtesy of Frances Phillips.)

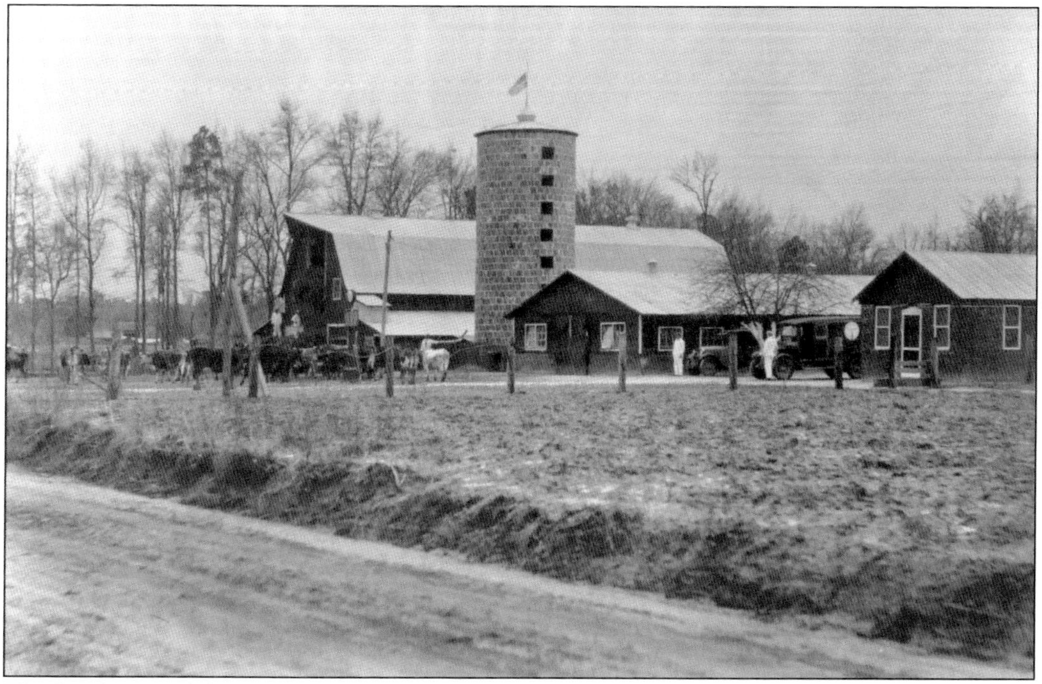

The family-owned dairies that provided milk to Lumberton's homes and schools were once common sites on the outskirts of town. Leighton D. Williamson's Maple Shade Dairy was located on Rural Route 3. (Courtesy of Historic Robeson, Inc.)

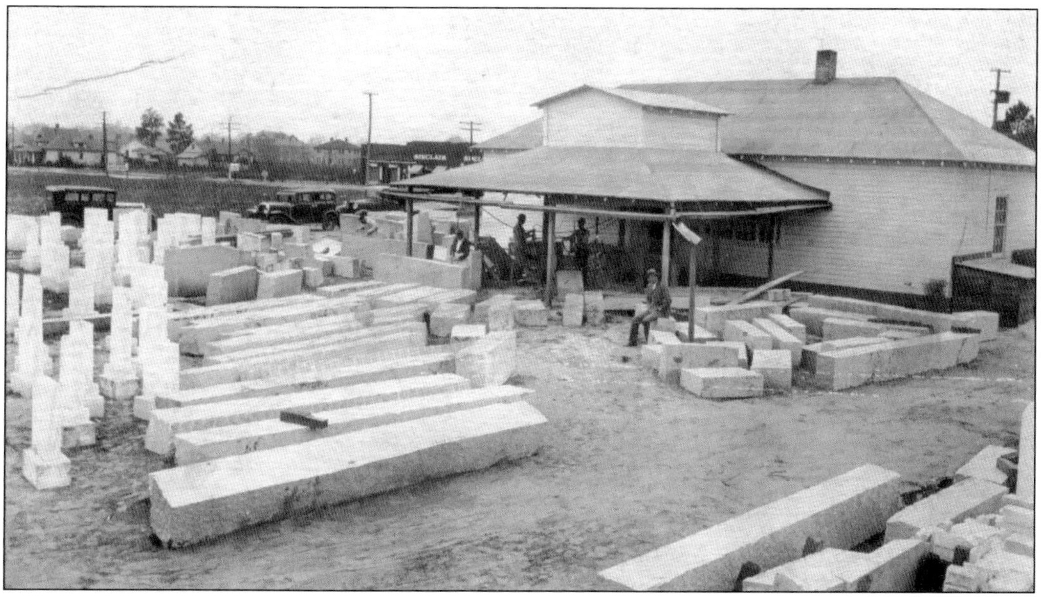

This is the work yard of the Southern Marble Works on Pine Street. The business was moved to Lumberton from Dunn in 1926 by Pres. Joseph Pearly Cooper. An advertisement stated that they made and installed 290 monuments that year. Copper's sons Howard and James joined him in the business. In 1959, the brothers started Gardens of Faith Cemetery, and in 1970, Lumbee Memorial Gardens. They were the first perpetual-care cemeteries in the area. (Courtesy of Cooper Collection, Robeson Remembers, Robeson County History Museum.)

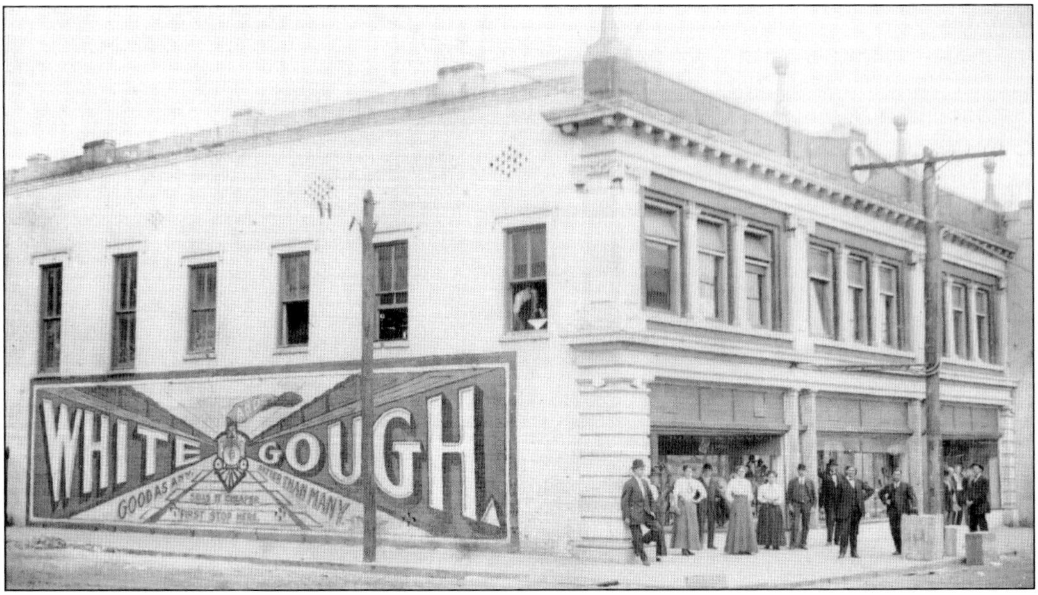

The third brick building in Lumberton was erected by A.C. Melke in 1866 to house the town's first department store. Melke's partners were Frank Gough and John Smith. Gough operated White & Gough at this location with Albert E. White. The store's motto was "Good as many better than many—Sells it cheaper first stop here." Later, the building was home to the Rayless Department Store. It was demolished in 1976 to make a parking lot for the courthouse. (Courtesy of Brad Thompson.)

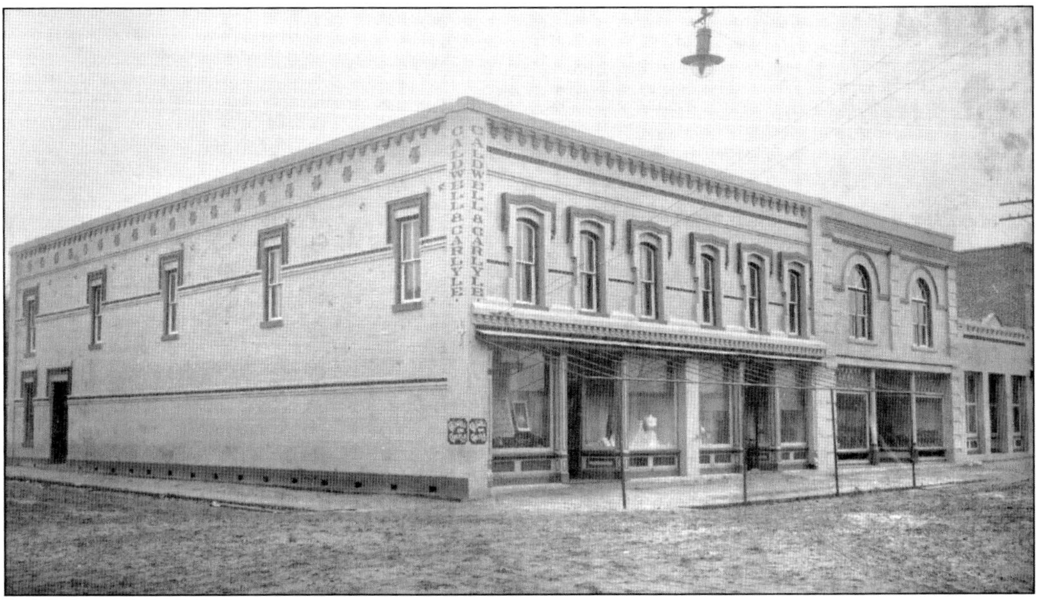

The store of Caldwell & Carlyle was located on the corner of Third and Elm Streets where the plaza is now located. It was a partnership between Robert David Caldwell and his brother-in-law William Watts Carlyle. Their store's slogan was "From the Cradle to the Grave" because it had everything one could need and even provided undertaking services. After Carlyle retired, the firm was renamed R.D. Caldwell & Sons. (Courtesy of Robeson County History Museum.)

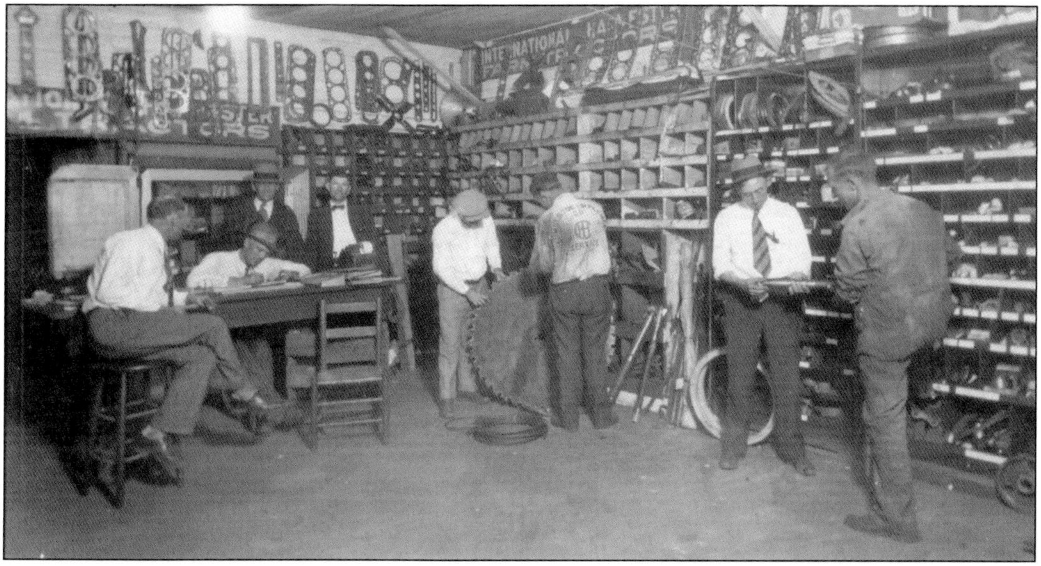

This photograph of Lumberton Implement Company appeared in the October 1, 1931, special issue of the *Robesonian*. The company, established in 1926 on the corner of Fourth and Pine Streets, carried a complete line of McCormick-Deering farm machinery. In 1938, John D. Stewart was listed as manager. The slogan was "Good Equipment Makes a Good Farmer Better." By 1956, Hector MacLean was listed as president, his brother-in-law W. Scott Shepherd was vice president, and J.B. Gleaton was secretary-treasurer and general manager. (Courtesy of Historic Robeson, Inc.)

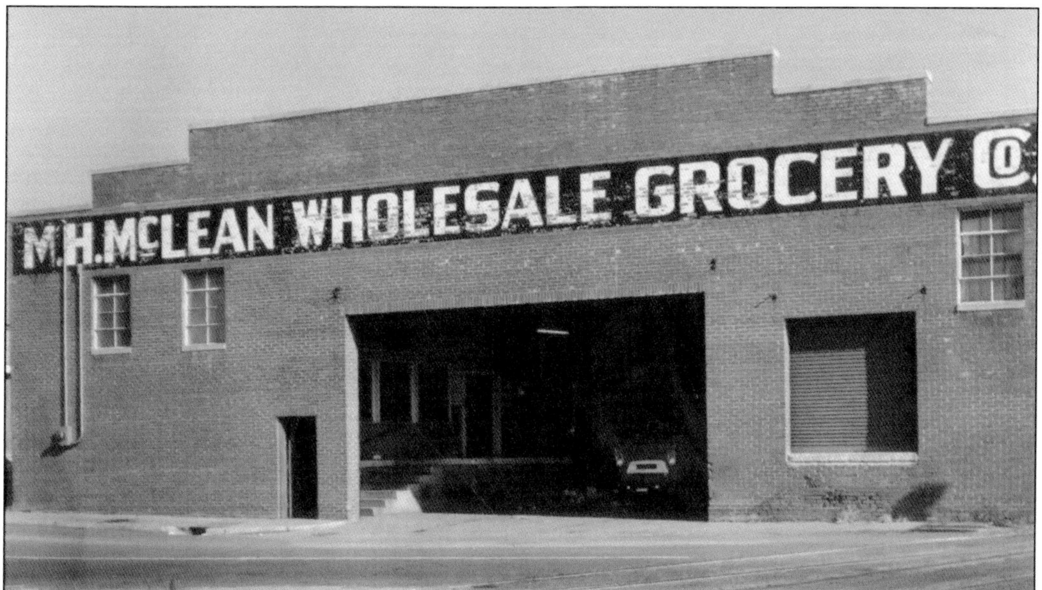

M.H. McLean Jr. followed the footsteps of his father into the wholesale grocery business; at the end of the Depression, he began his business in the family's garage. As the business grew, he relocated several times in the downtown area until 1946, when he built this structure on the site of the former train depot between Elm and Chestnut Streets. McLean Wholesale was sold in 1985 to Nash Finch Company. (Courtesy of the McLean Collection, Robeson Remembers, Robeson County History Museum.)

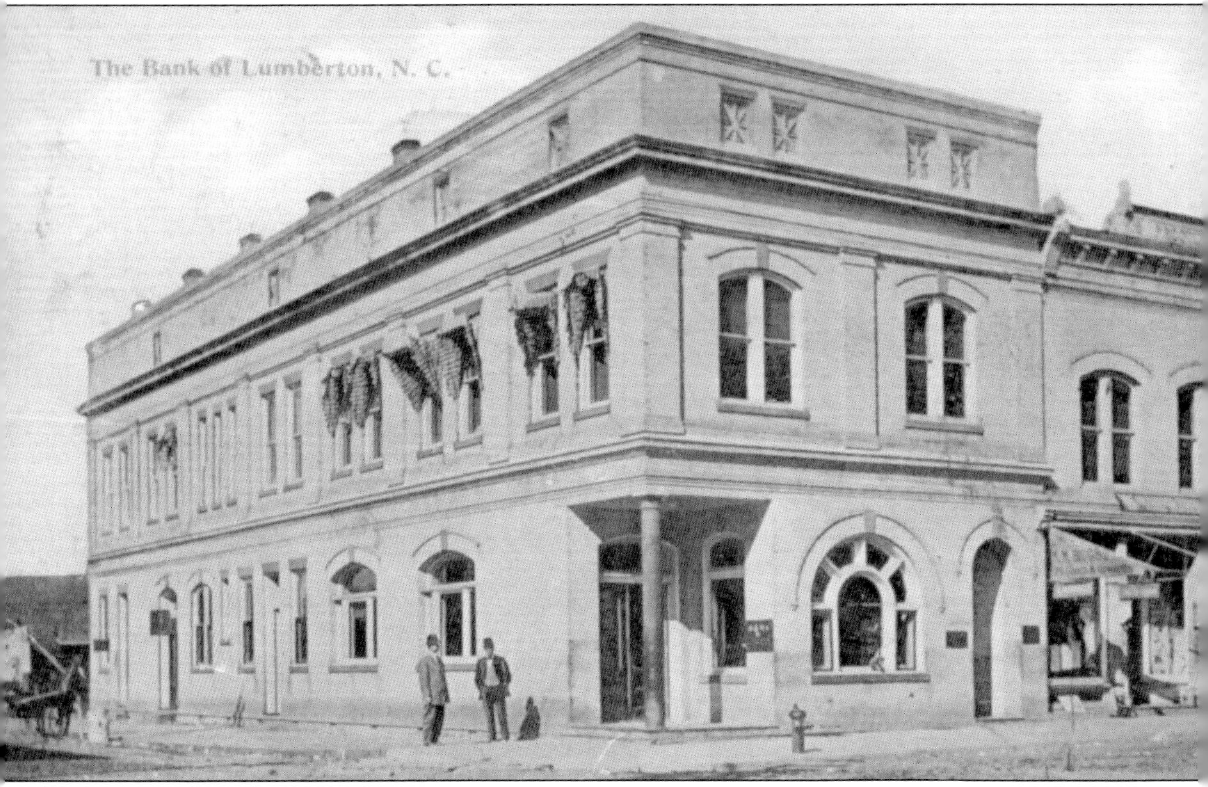

The Bank of Lumberton was organized in 1896; it was the first bank in Robeson County. The first president was T.A. McNeill, who resigned after six months, then Angus Wilton McLean became the bank's president and served until his death in 1935. McLean served as governor of North Carolina from 1925 to 1929. The next three presidents were Albert E. White, his son-in-law Dr. Russell Beam, and Morris Cobb. In 1952, McLean's son Hector MacLean joined the bank as counsel and in 1955 was elected president. During his 35 years of leadership, he oversaw the growth from one location and $11.1 million in assets to a $3.4-billion corporation with 149 banking offices throughout the Carolinas. The name was changed in 1959 to Southern National Bank and became the sixth-largest bank holding company in North Carolina and the fifth-largest in South Carolina. MacLean retired in 1990, and on August 1, 1994, the bank merged with Branch Banking & Trust. (Courtesy of the Hubbard-Tyner Collection.)

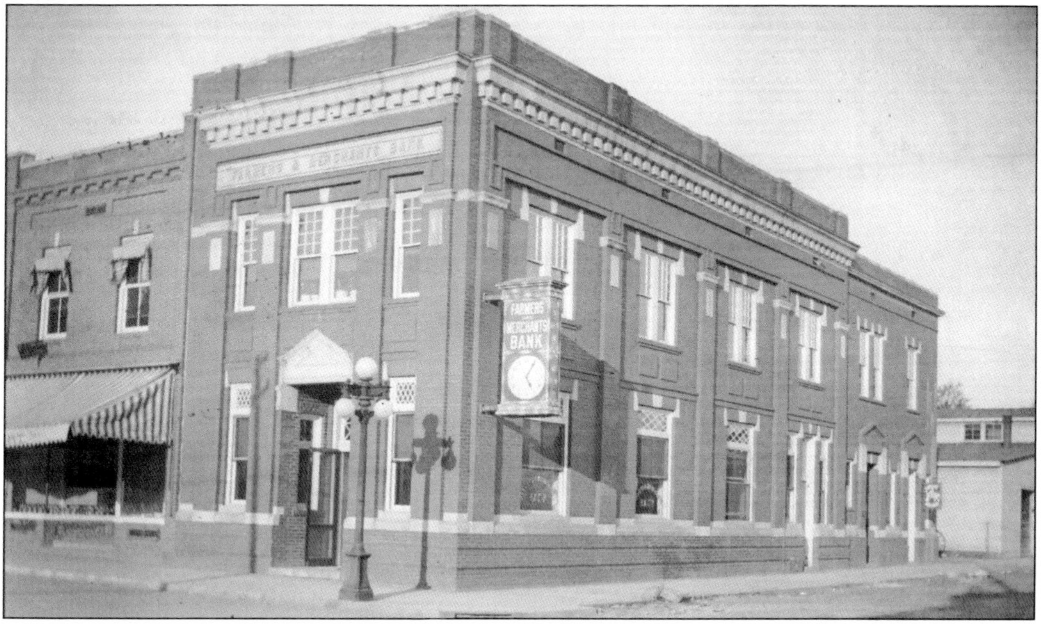

The Farmers & Merchants Bank was located on the southeast corner of Fourth and Chestnut Streets in the old LaFayette Mutual Life Insurance Company building. The officers in 1915 were T.A. McNeill Sr., president; R.R. Barnes, vice president; L.E. Whaley, vice president; and K.M. Barnes, cashier. The directors were D.H. Britt, W.M. Bridger, A.P. Caldwell, C.B. Skipper, M.W. Floyd, J.E. Carlyle, and George L. Thompson. (Courtesy of Historic Robeson, Inc.)

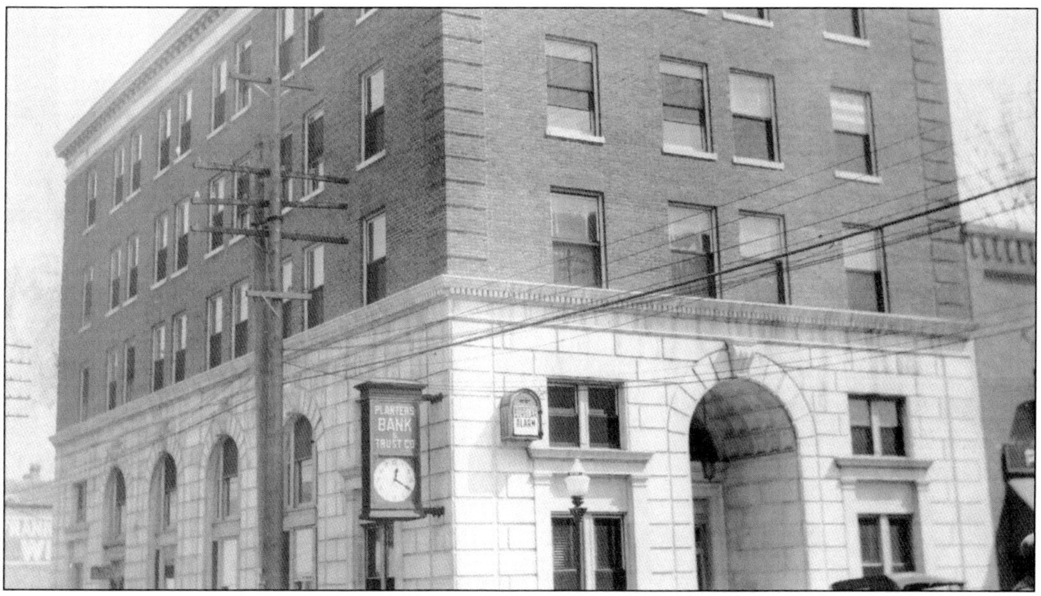

The Planters Bank & Trust Company was organized in 1916 and took over the operations of the Farmers & Merchants Bank. The new bank was under the leadership of former cashier K.M. Barnes as president. Other officers were vice presidents Robert C. Lawrence and Aaron Weinstein; secretary and treasurer George E. Rancke Jr., counsel Horace E. Stacy Sr., and trust officer George L. Thompson. They soon built a new structure across the street, but the bank closed during the Depression. (Courtesy of Historic Robeson, Inc.)

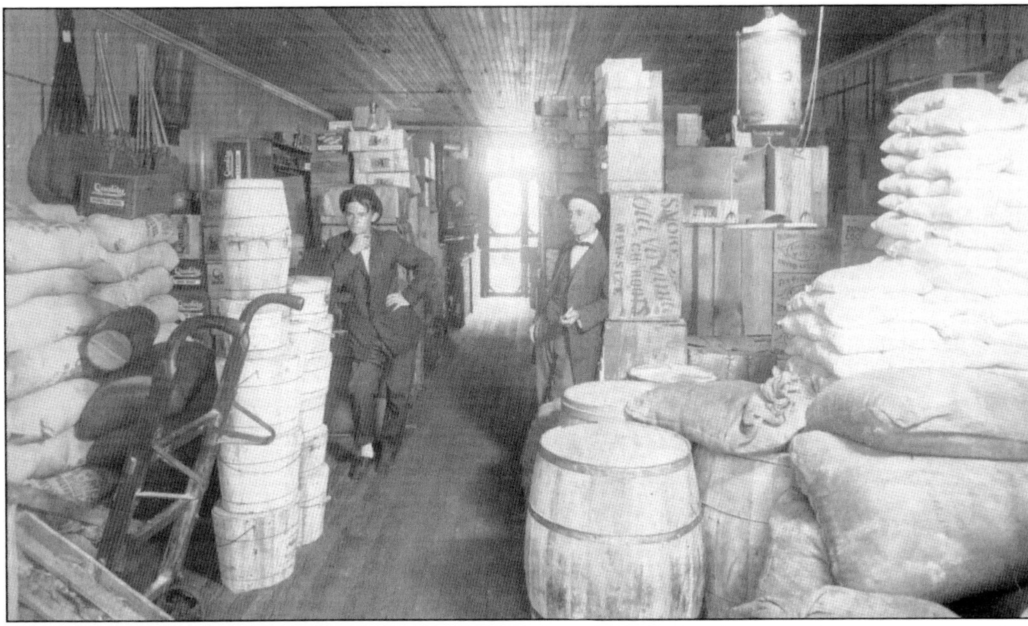

This photograph shows the interior of Whitfield & French, a wholesale grocer that was organized on March 1, 1905, by George M. Whitfield and George Godwin French. It was located near the depot on Elm Street. When French died, Whitfield bought out his late partner's share of the business. In later years, French's son Berry Godwin French operated the French Allen Fuel Company with partner Pit Allen across Elm Street from this store. (Courtesy of Brad Thompson.)

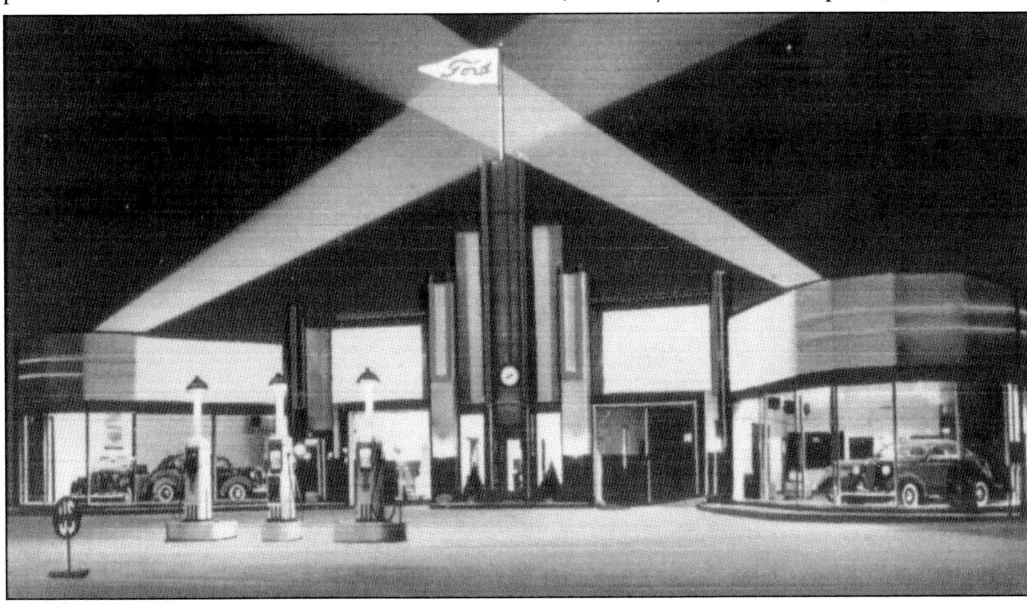

Thomas M. Burney & Son, Inc., consisted of builder Thomas Matthew Burney and his engineer son Russell Thomas Burney. In 1938, the firm designed and built the Norment Motor Company on West Fifth Street for Clint Norment. The high Art Deco–style building, which featured large plate-glass windows and terrazzo flooring, was called their greatest modern work. The Pittsburgh Plate Glass Company featured the building that year in its advertising. (Courtesy of the Hubbard-Tyner Collection.)

Three

Hotels and Restaurants

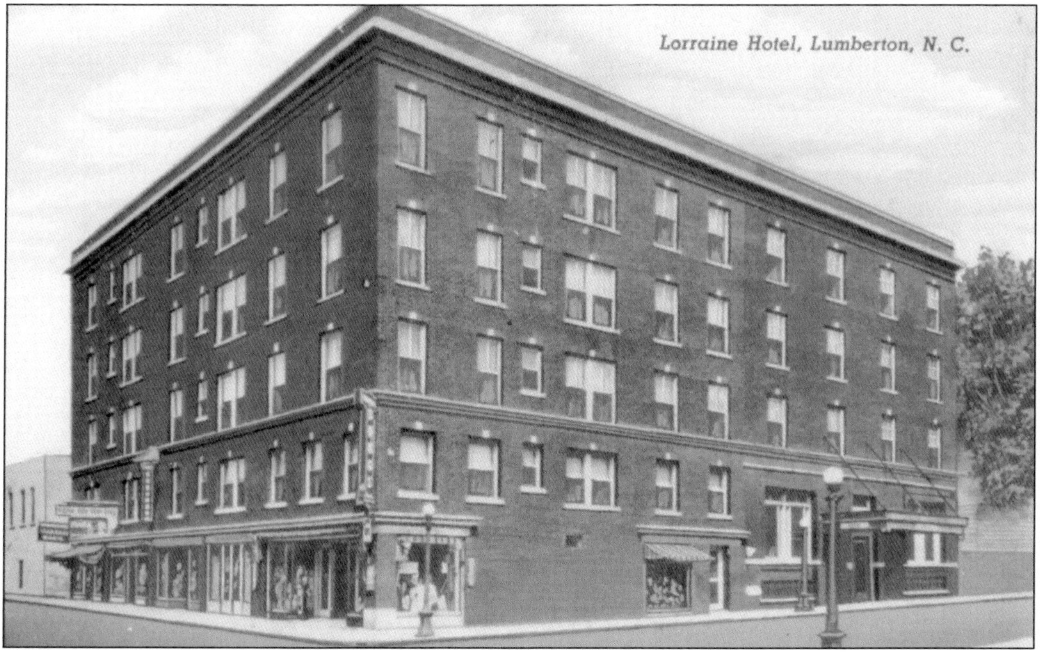

A group of local businessmen formed the Lumberton Hotel Company to build a first-class hotel in downtown. Located on Chestnut Street beside the courthouse, it opened informally on December 14, 1916. Of the total cost of $60,000, about $5,000 was used to furnish it. There were 44 bedrooms—15 with tubs and 15 with showers. The hotel closed in 1961, and the lot is now part of the courthouse parking. (Courtesy of the Hubbard-Tyner Collection.)

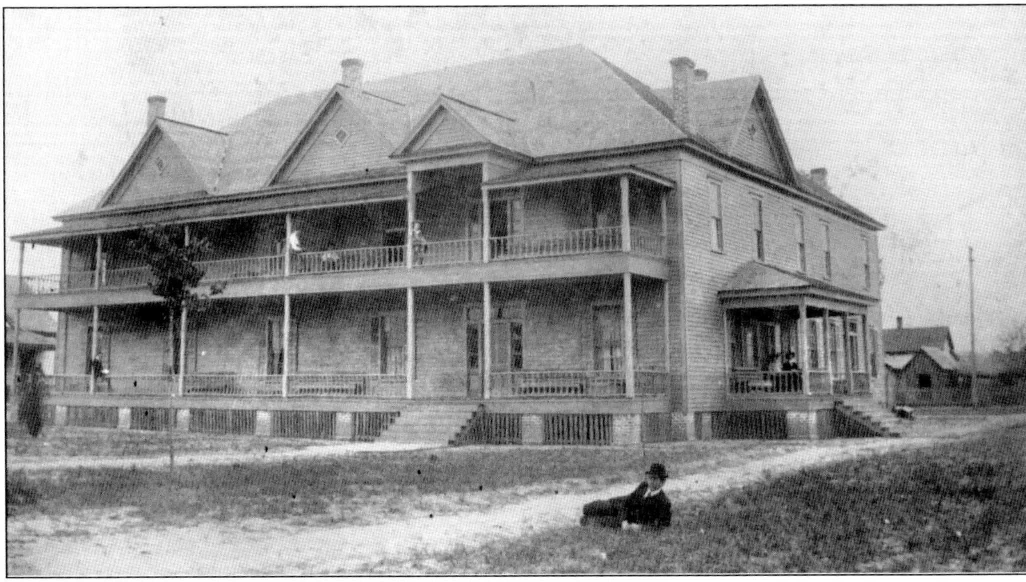

This wonderful, large, wooden building was originally the dormitory of the Robeson Institute, which was located on the corner of Walnut and Eighth Streets. After the school was purchased and converted to Lumberton Graded School, the old dormitory was used as a hotel for several years. (Courtesy of Brad Thompson.)

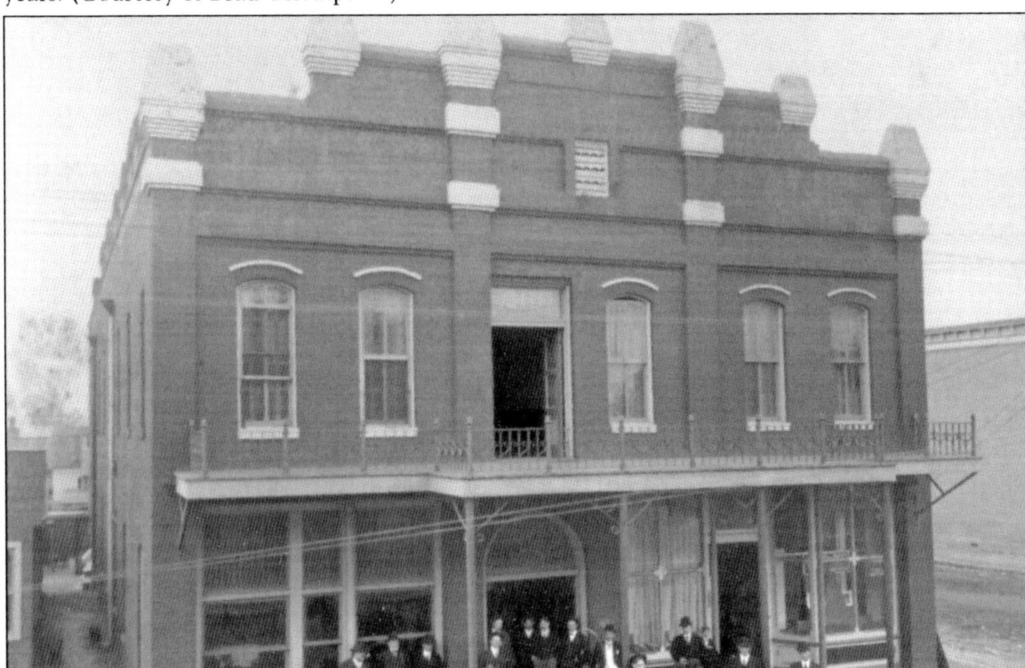

The Merchant's Hotel was owned by N.A. Jones and was operating by 1893 on the corner of Elm and Third Streets. The hotel was purchased in 1903 by Angus Wilton McLean and S.A. Edmund, who remodeled the property and reopened it as the Waverly Hotel. The Waverly was torn down in 1913 to build the Bank of Lumberton (later Southern National Bank). (Courtesy of Godwin/French Collection, Robeson Remembers, Robeson County History Museum.)

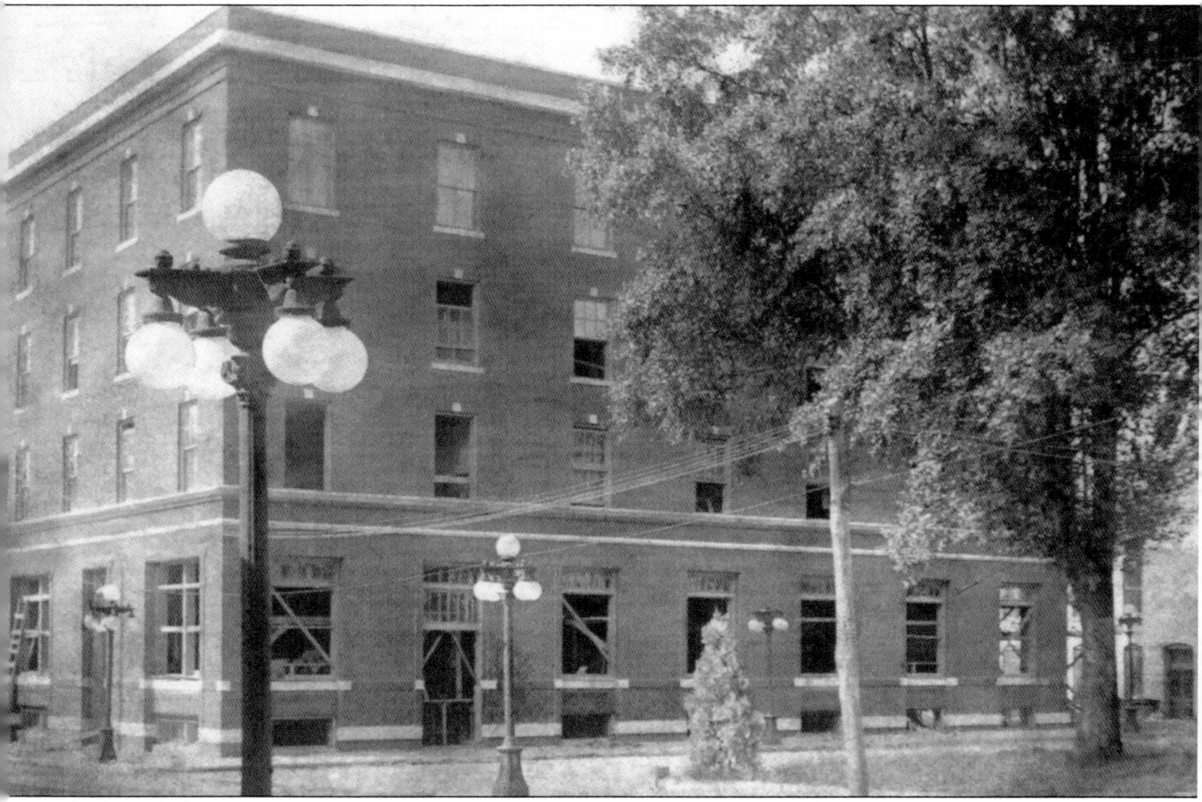

The board of directors of the Lumberton Hotel Company in 1916 offered $5 to the person who came up with the best name for the hotel. Among the hundreds of suggestions were Gough, National, Union, White House, Hotel Vashti, Cherokee Inn, Jerusalem, the Argyle, Lumbee Hotel, Hotel Robeson, Lumberton Enterprise, McLean, Mayflower, Lumbertonian, MacLumbee, Lumbee Queen, Lumbee Robeson, the Willis, Proctor, Carlyle, Bob Lawrence, Goodyear, Stonewall, Bee-Gee, Varser, St. Regis, St. Julian, Lumberton Center, Traveler's Home, Mackabee-Lumbee, Robeson Victory, Cityview, Bon Rest, Lorrain, Savoy, Majestic, Faultless, Everybody's, Motel Mac, Great Southern, and Hotel Bob White. In the end, they named it the Lorraine, adding an *E* to one of the suggestions to keep from having to pay out the $5 prize. (Courtesy of Tom Parker.)

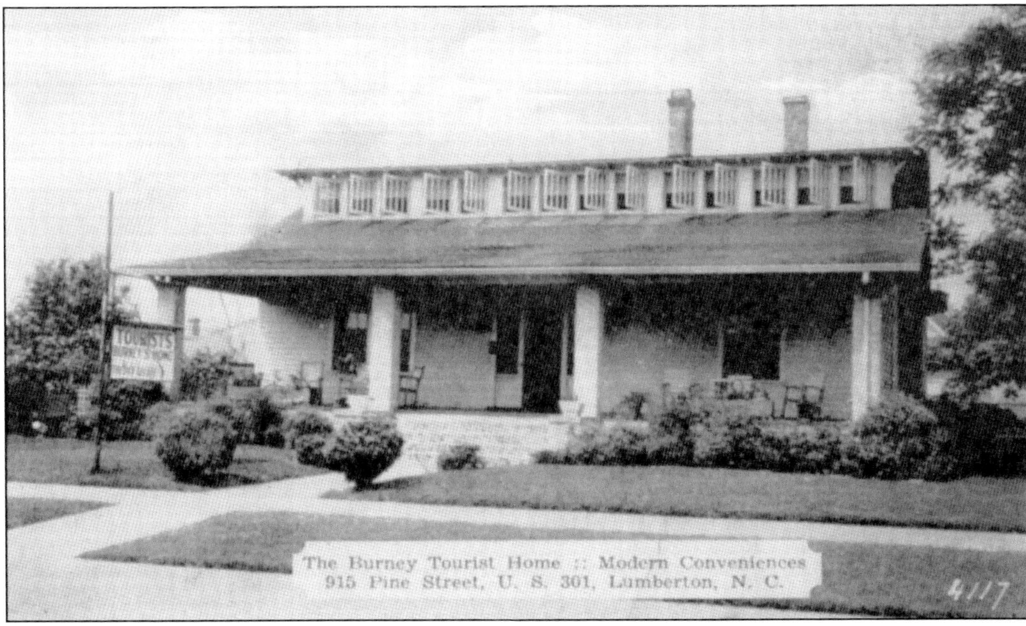

This bungalow-style home was constructed by local builder Thomas Matthew Burney in 1916 as a home for him and his wife, Mary Emily "Mollie" Russell. They were parents of Russell Thomas, Mary Pauline "Polly," Doris Elizabeth, Loris Fay, and Cleo. In October 1929, Mollie began operating a tourist home in the house. (Courtesy of the Hubbard-Tyner Collection.)

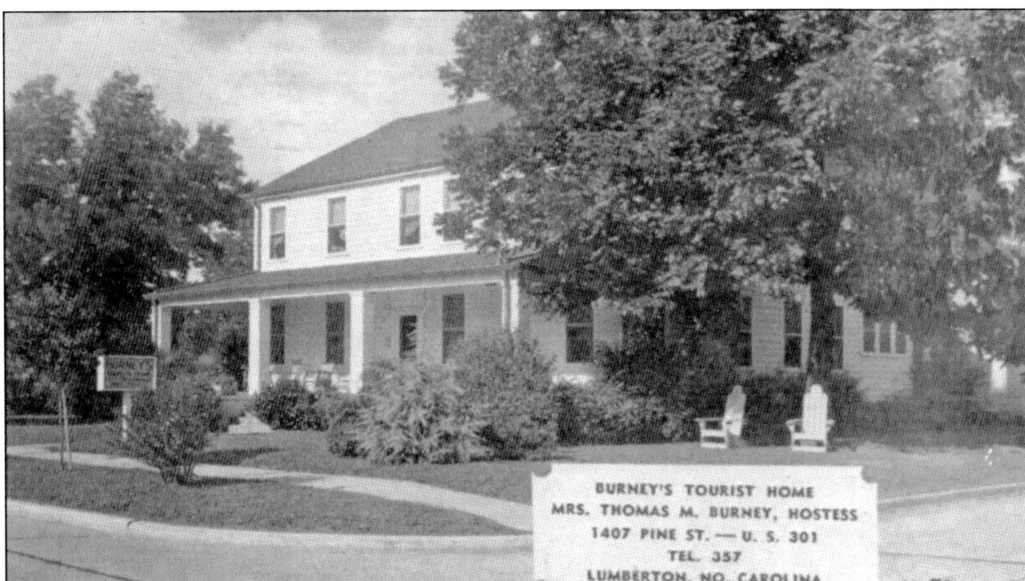

After his wife had operated the tourist home for eight years in the bungalow house, Thomas Matthew Burney remodeled it into this large two-story home. Mollie Burney ran the tourist home until her death, and afterwards, her daughter Polly continued its operation. Located on Highway 301 in downtown Lumberton, this tourist home was located on the same block as the Skinner Tourist Home. A favorite stop for men in the tobacco business, it never had an empty room during the tobacco market. (Courtesy of the Hubbard-Tyner Collection.)

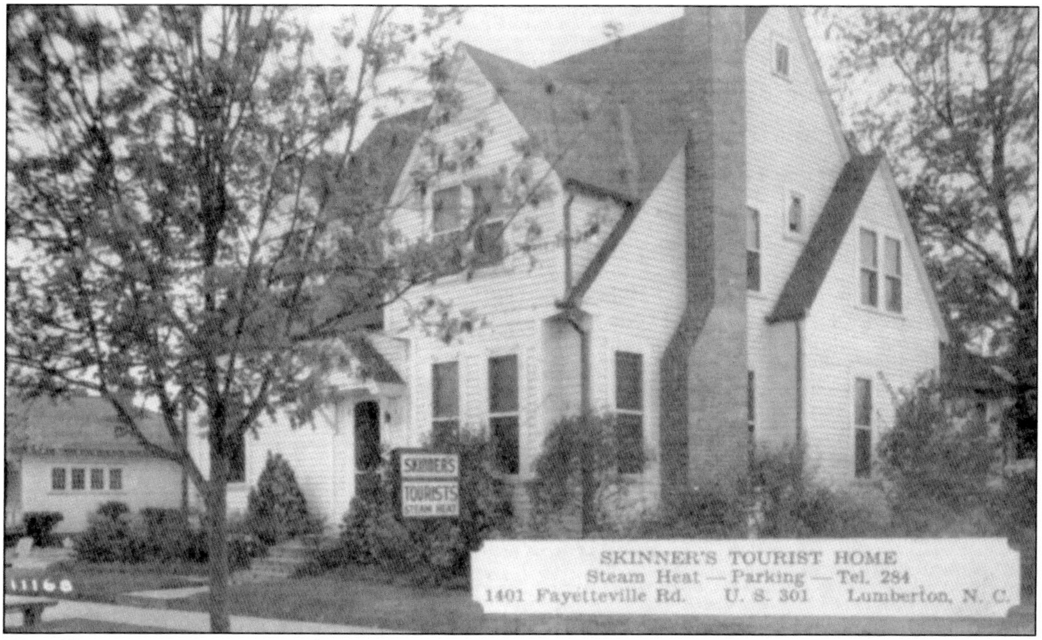

The Skinner Tourist Home, located on Highway 301, had its start as a boardinghouse for young military grooms and brides that flocked to Robeson County during World War II. Later, it not only served the traveling tourist but also the large crowds that came to Lumberton as part of the tobacco market. (Courtesy of the Hubbard-Tyner Collection.)

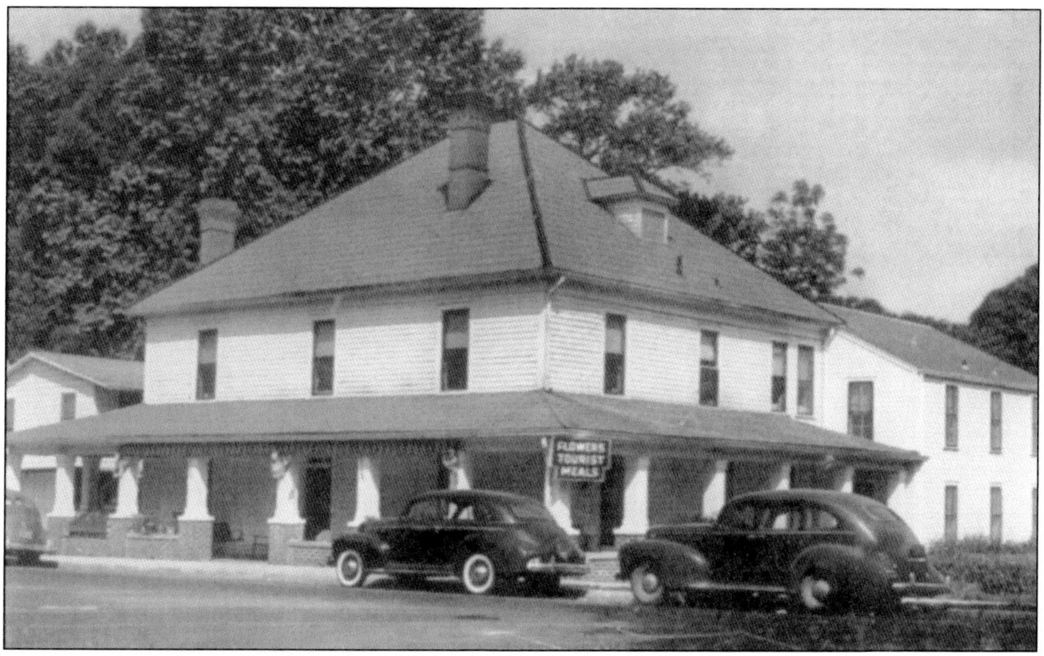

The Flowers Tourist Home was located in downtown Lumberton in what was once a fashionable residential section but is now all commercial property. It stood on Elizabethtown Road and was demolished to make way for a parking lot for the county office building. (Courtesy of the Hubbard-Tyner Collection.)

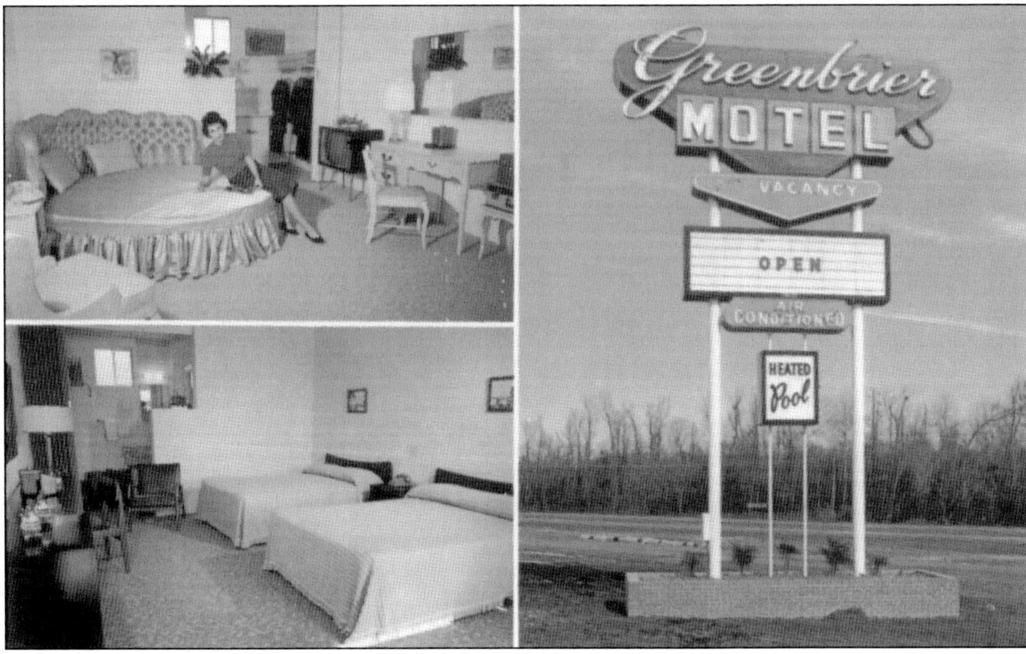

The Greenbrier promoted itself as the newest and most ultramodern motel in the Lumberton area. Located on Highway 301, it had 50 units offering travelers comfort in air conditioning, thermo-controlled heating, in-room television, and a heated swimming pool. Johnson's Restaurant was located next door. The Greenbrier's bridal suite offered a circular bed, which it claimed was the talk of the Southland. (Courtesy of the Hubbard-Tyner Collection.)

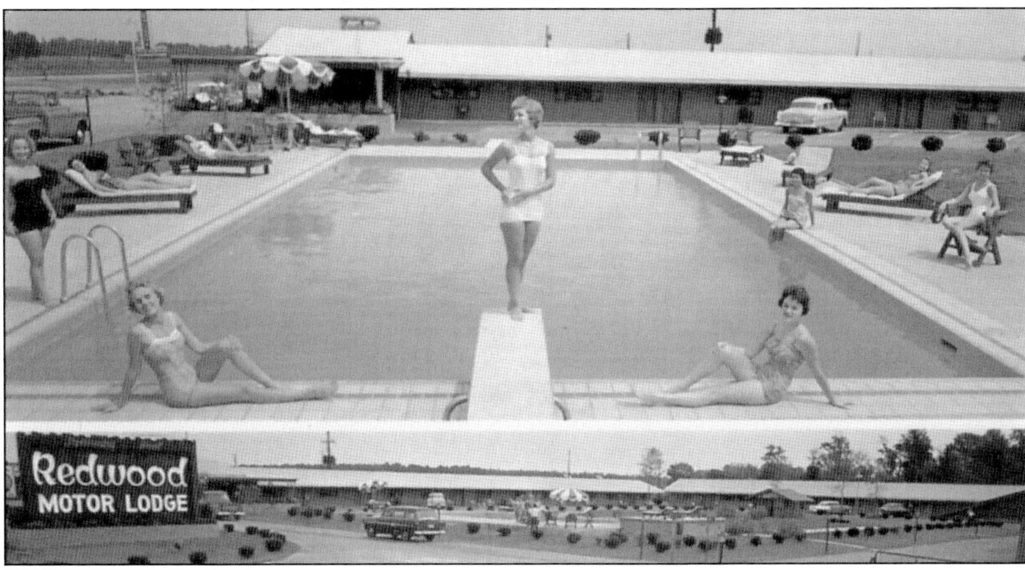

The Redwood Motor Lodge was recommended by Quality Courts, Duncan Hines, and the American Automobile Association (AAA). It had 40 spacious guest rooms with air conditioning and central heat. Each room also had a tile bathroom with a tub and a shower, as well as television and telephone. The 50-foot pool served to draw visitors to the Redwood Motor Lodge, which was located two miles north of Lumberton on Highway 301. Next door was Blanchard's Restaurant. The Redwood was owned by William and Virginia Bauer. (Courtesy of the Hubbard-Tyner Collection.)

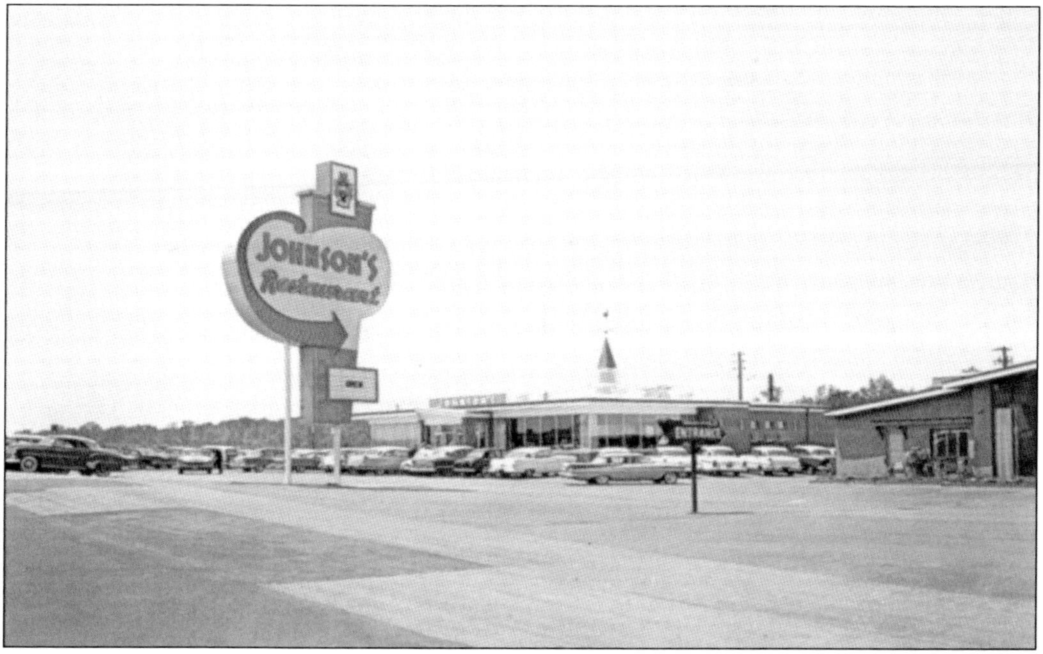

Johnson's Restaurant, located at the intersection of Highways 301 and 211 alongside the Greenbrier Motel, was not the usual highway food joint. It offered charcoal steaks, seafood, and Long Island duck in an atmosphere that included soft organ music. (Courtesy of the Hubbard-Tyner Collection.)

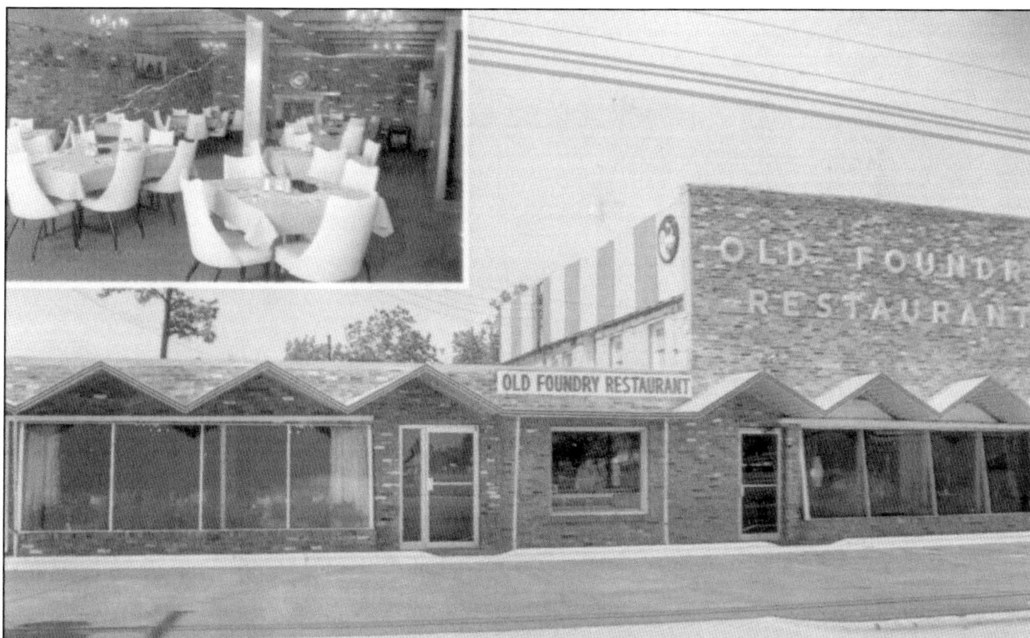

The Old Foundry Restaurant was opened by Hubert, Hilton, and Dobbs Oxendine in 1946 on the site of the Old Iron Foundry on West Fifth Street. It was located a quarter mile east of the Pembroke exit of Interstate 95, just south of Lumberton. (Courtesy of the Hubbard-Tyner Collection.)

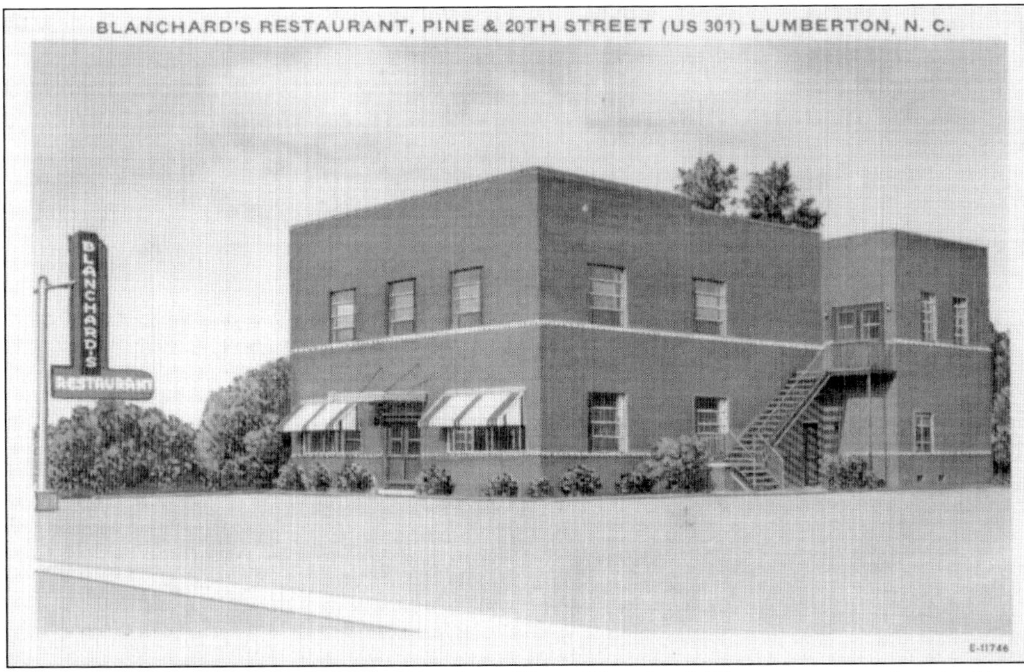

Blanchard's Restaurant was owned by Claude and Janie Blanchard. This restaurant advertised itself as a source for wonderful food in the heart of tobacco land. Located on Pine Street, which was part of Highway 301 heading into downtown Lumberton, it was known for its peanut pie. Patsy Hester, a waitress, remembers that they had customers from all over eastern North Carolina for the Sunday-night buffet. Faye Walters D'Ippolito played the piano in the upstairs banquet room for many events. (Courtesy of the Hubbard-Tyner Collection.)

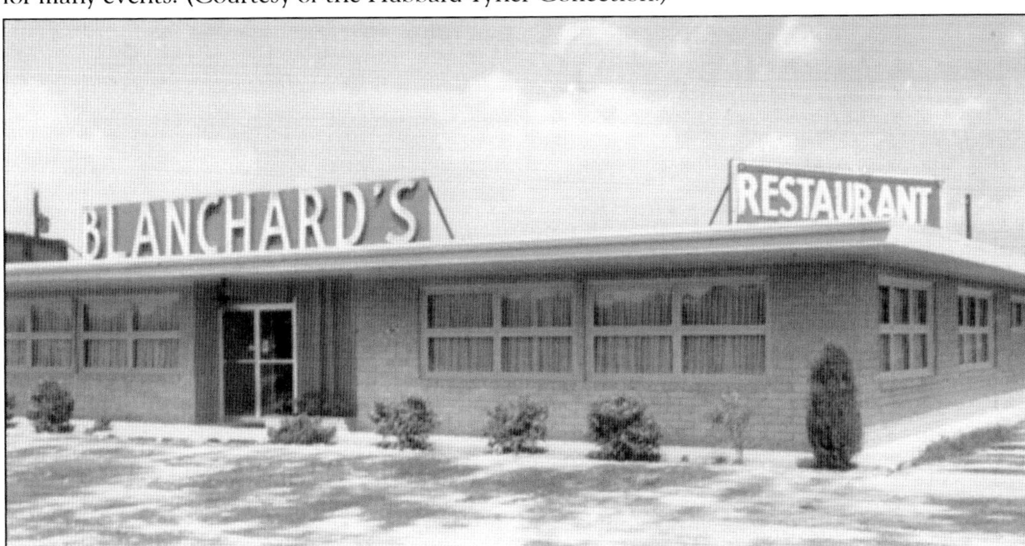

Blanchard's Restaurant moved from its Pine Street location to a new building on Interstate 95 to be part of the hotel row. It was located beside the Redwood Motel Lodge and featured two private party rooms. On May 8, 1978, John and Ruth Ann Baker McLellan opened John's Restaurant, a haven to not only travelers but also to the citizens of the county. John's closed in 2007, and the building was demolished. (Courtesy of the Hubbard-Tyner Collection.)

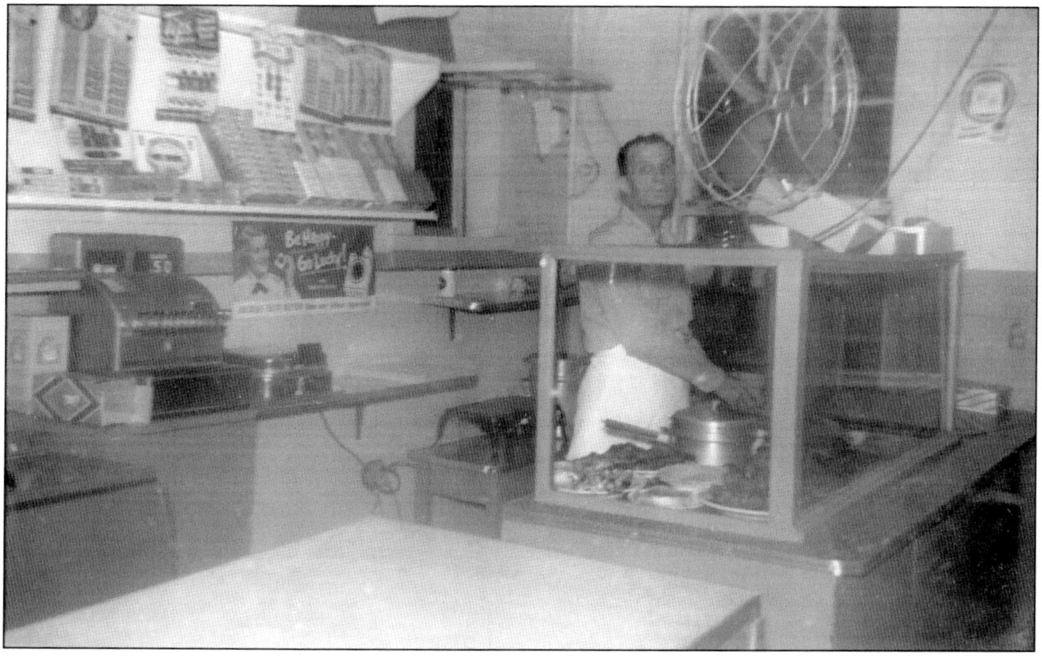

Jerome and Colleen Stallings worked at East Side Grocery and Café before opening Stallings Grill on Second Street. This photograph of Jerome Stallings was taken in the early 1950s. Many remember that the grill was the only place to go for great hot dogs. A customer could go in on Saturday night and come out with a sack full for $2. (Courtesy of Mitchell Prevatte.)

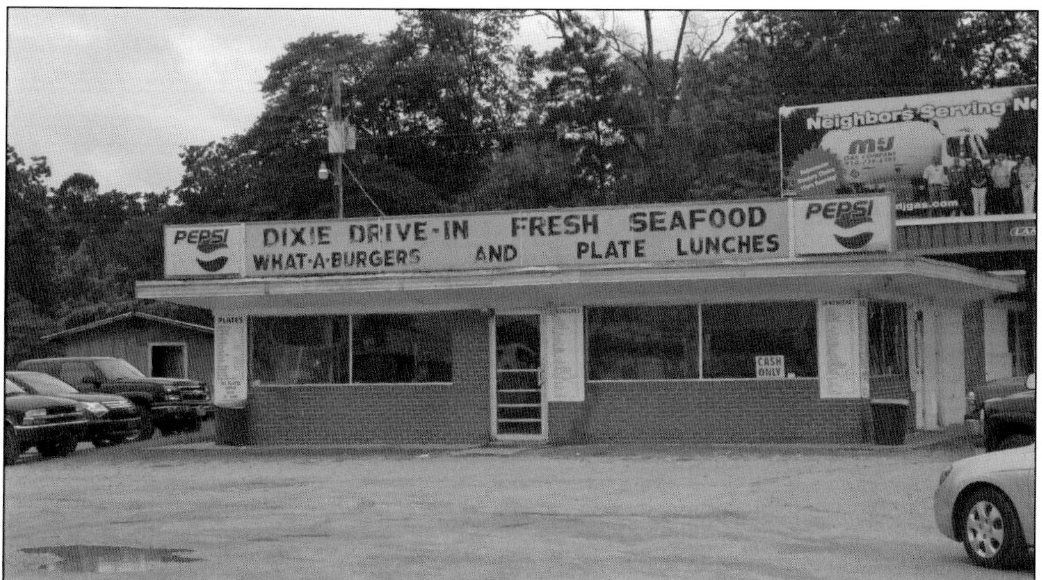

The Dixie Drive-In sits on the corner of Second Street and Roland Avenue; although there is no paved parking lot, there is still curb service with carhops who come out and take orders. The Brown Derby previously occupied this spot and was operated by Howard and Nita Stevens. Bob Carr built the present building, and the Stevens family took it over in 1963. The Stevenses' sons, George, Tony, and Steve Stevens, work together to operate the Dixie Drive-in. (Courtesy of the Hubbard-Tyner Collection.)

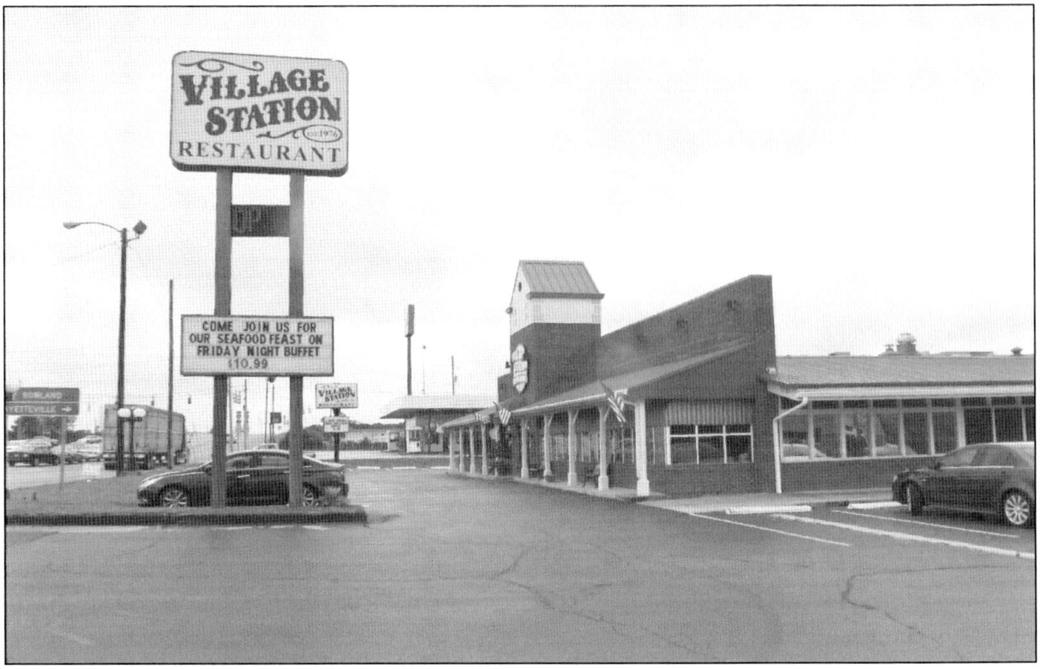

The Village Station, owned by Arnold West, has become a mainstay on Roland Avenue. Several years ago it moved across the street, taking over the former Western Sizzlin. (Courtesy Hubbard-Tyner Collection.)

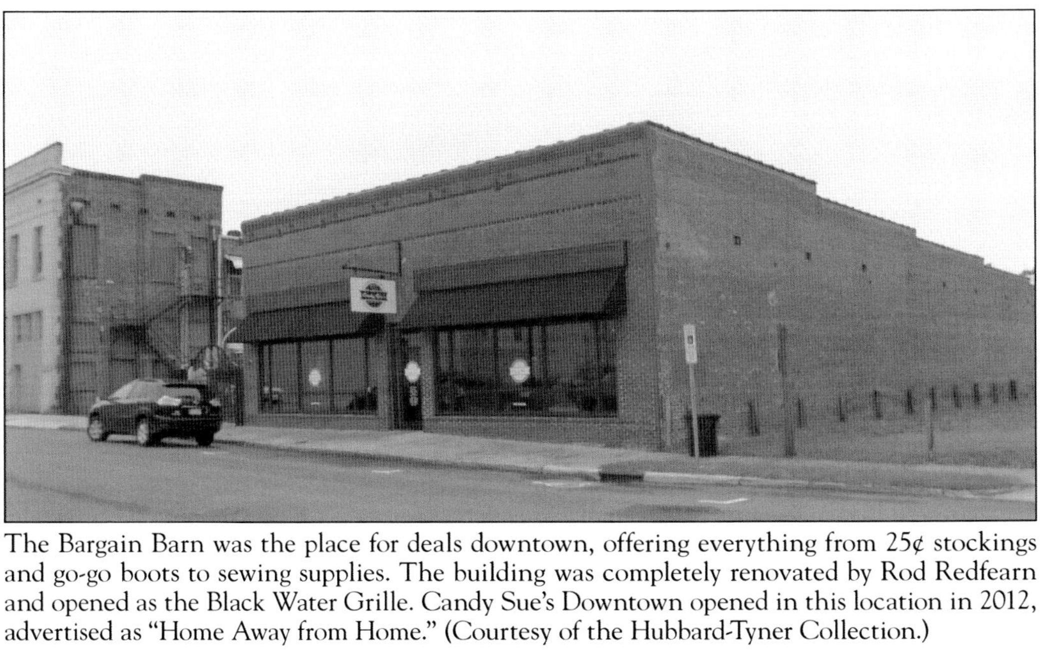

The Bargain Barn was the place for deals downtown, offering everything from 25¢ stockings and go-go boots to sewing supplies. The building was completely renovated by Rod Redfearn and opened as the Black Water Grille. Candy Sue's Downtown opened in this location in 2012, advertised as "Home Away from Home." (Courtesy of the Hubbard-Tyner Collection.)

Four

Around Town

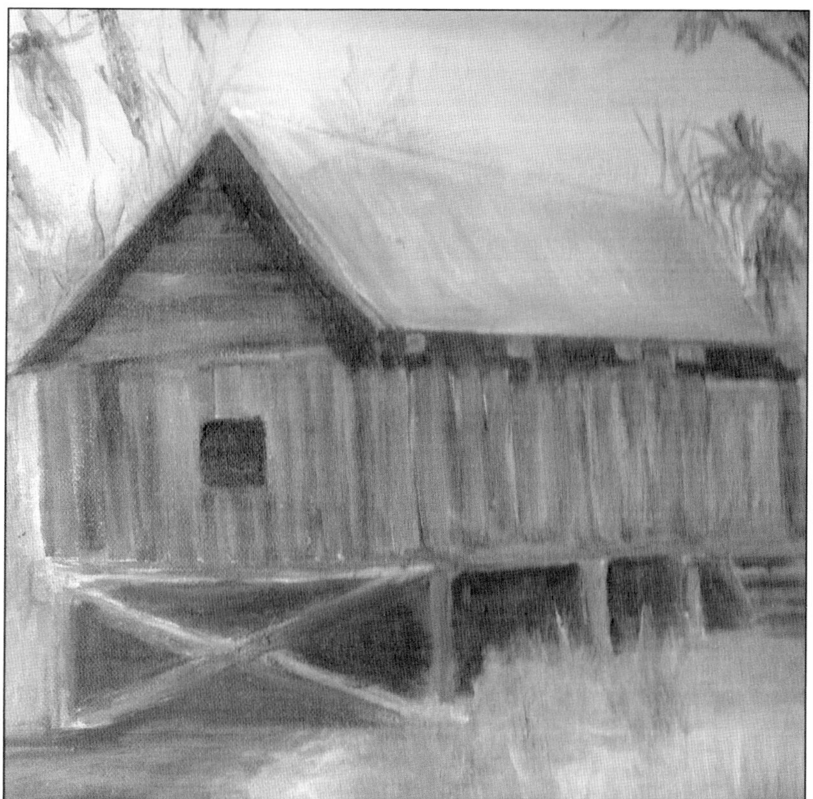

This painting by Miriam Pittman depicts the Lennon's Mill House, originally built by John Hawthorne Sr. around 1800. The mill was later owned by the Warwick family before being purchased by the Lennons. The millpond is one of the famous Carolina bays and covers 1,500 acres. (Courtesy of Robeson County History Museum.)

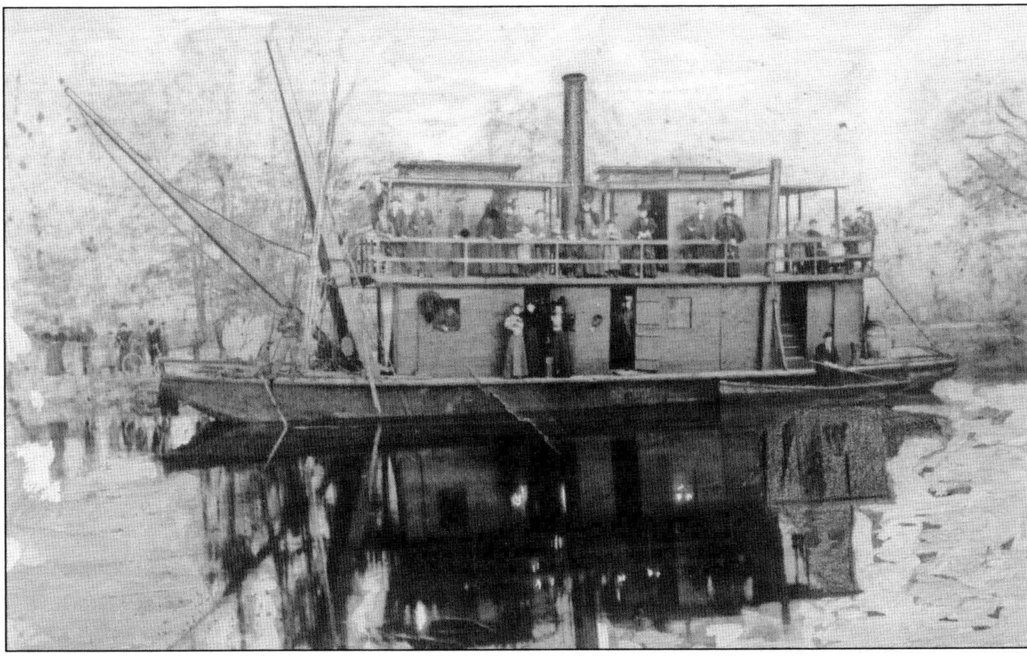

This photograph was originally owned by Elizabeth Wishart, daughter of W.S. Wishart, and possibly shows the *Kitty B*, which was known to travel the waters of the Lumber River. This 60-foot, flat-bottom, square-ended boat more than likely was used to carry logs down the river during the week and for pleasure-seekers on the weekends. (Courtesy of Historic Robeson, Inc.)

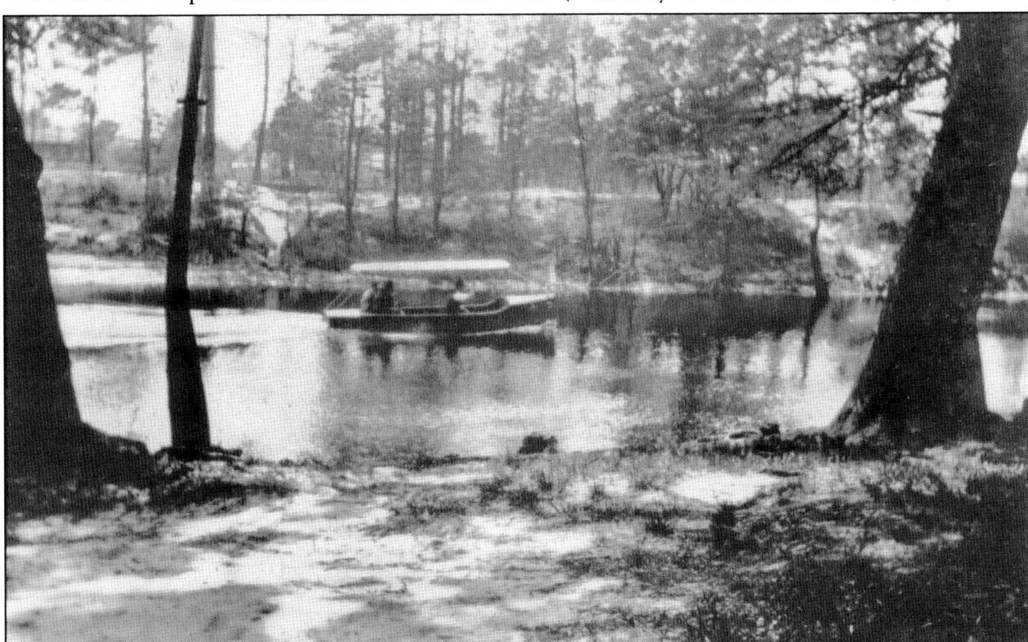

In the late 18th and the 19th centuries, lumbering and naval stores were very important to the region, and the river was a vital route for transporting their products. Logs that were 100 feet long were rafted downriver in the late 1800s to Georgetown, South Carolina. Lumberton itself was an important turpentine and timber town. (Courtesy of Historic Robeson, Inc.)

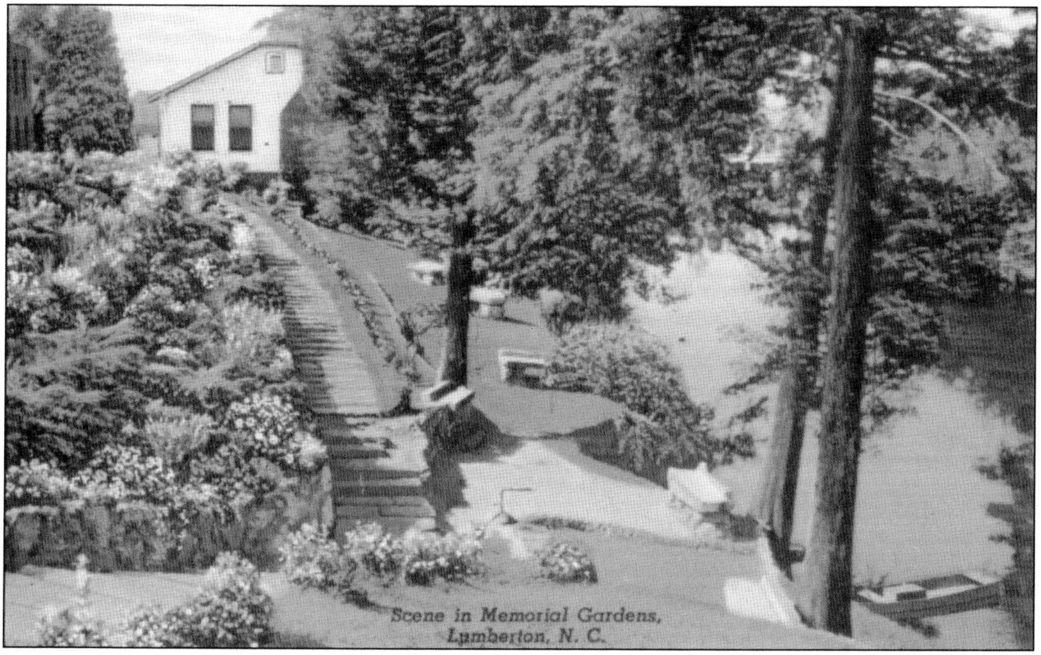

For years, one of Lumberton's most beautiful spots was the American Legion Memorial Gardens, located where Third Street connects with Water Street. Located at the top of the garden was the American Legion hut. The 48-by-100-foot wooden edifice was built in 1932 for the American Legion Post No. 42. The garden was one of the favorite projects of Kate Britt Biggs and Annie Ruth Caldwell Baker. (Courtesy of the Hubbard-Tyner Collection.)

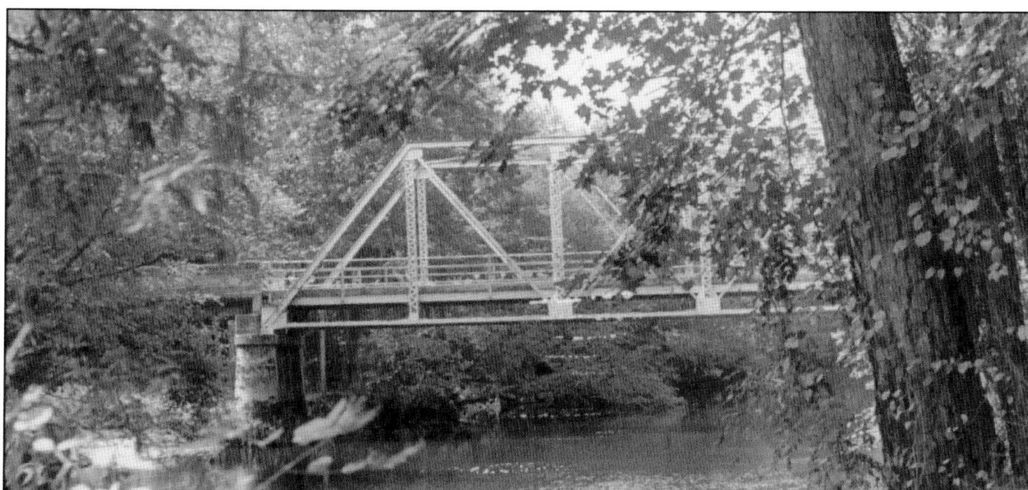

A favorite quote about the Lumber River appeared in John Charles McNeill's *Argus*: "Writing about the Lumber River, to a man who has spent his summers in dalliance with her, is like writing about his sweetheart. She is coquettish, as subject to change, as teasing as any girl that goes; and no human angel ever possessed more variable hues and tints and shadows in her misty eyes than this unconscious flirt." This wonderful iron bridge, typical of those installed in the early 1900s, was located over the Lumber River just outside of Lumberton, near the Robeson County Health Department. (Courtesy of Historic Robeson, Inc.)

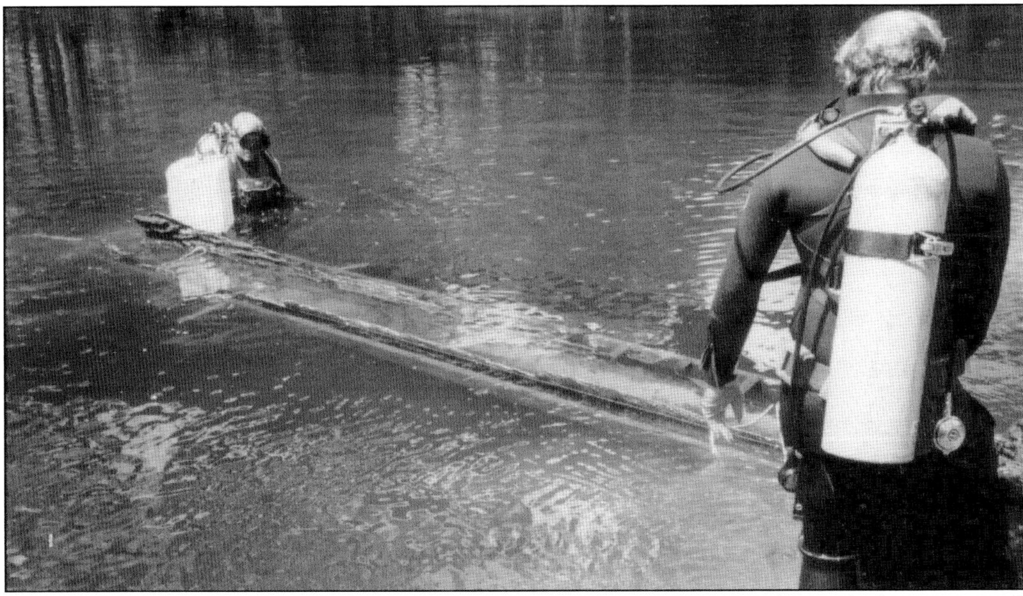

According to poet John Charles McNeill (1874–1907), the Indian name "Lumbee," which was originally used for the river, came from an Indian word that means "black water." Early European surveyors and settlers called it Drowning Creek, and it appears as such in Colonial records of 1749. Legislative action in 1809 changed the name to Lumber River. In May 1985, Paul Valenti, a scuba diver and historian, found a yellow-pine canoe dating back to 930 A.D. (Courtesy of Paul Valenti.)

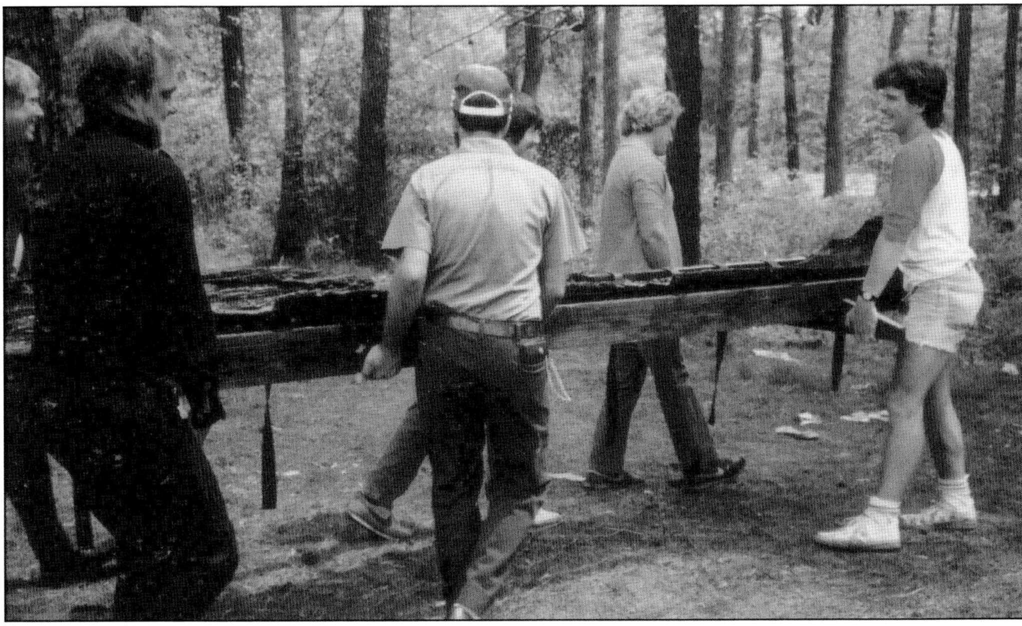

The North Carolina Department of Cultural Resources confirmed that the canoe was the oldest found in the state. "I really wasn't sure just what it was," Valenti explained. "It was wedged up against some trees and wasn't easy to recognize." He decided it was an Indian artifact and marked the area so that he could bring archaeologists back to examine the canoe. It has been preserved at the Native American Resource Center at the University of North Carolina at Pembroke. (Courtesy of Paul Valenti.)

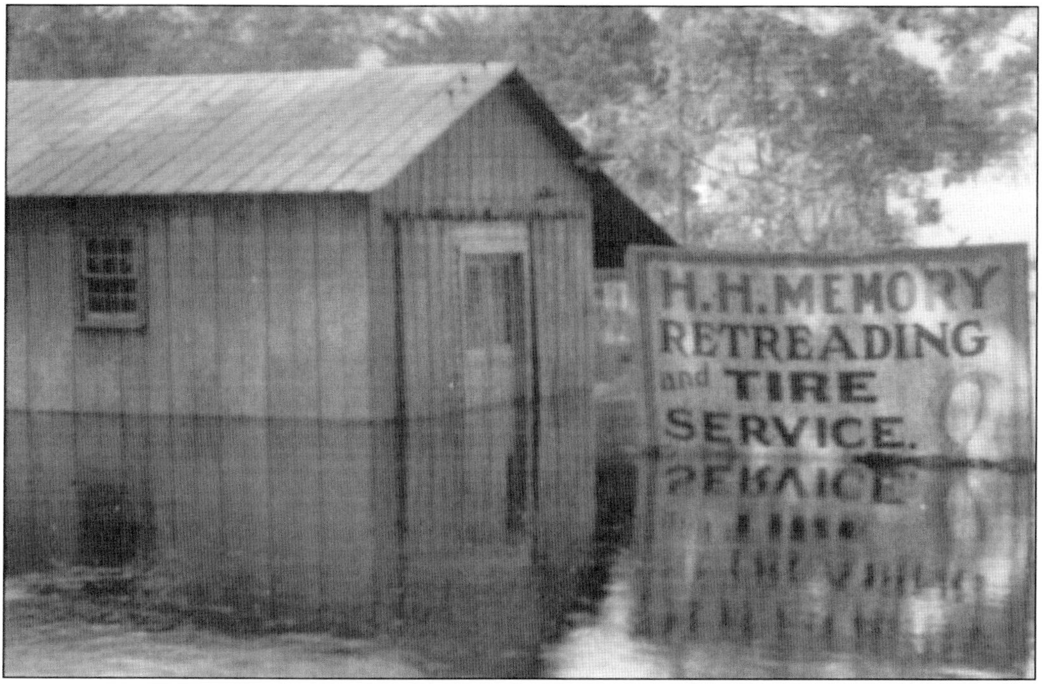

The Lumber River is not always peaceful and enjoyable. In September 1945, the river left its banks, causing havoc to downtown Lumberton. Here is shown H.H. Memory's tire service, which was located across from the jail on Elizabethtown Road. (Courtesy of Historic Robeson, Inc.)

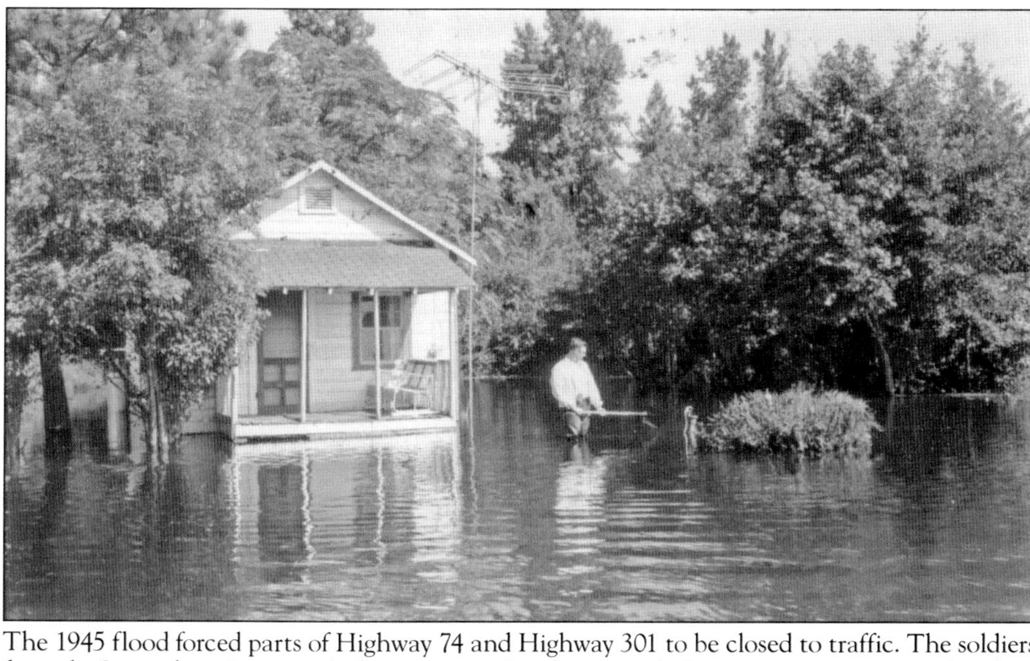

The 1945 flood forced parts of Highway 74 and Highway 301 to be closed to traffic. The soldiers from the Laurinburg-Maxton Airbase came to Lumberton to help rescue citizens trapped in their homes. The base also provided cots and field kitchens to be used by those who had to abandon their houses. This was not the first time that Lumberton suffered from large floods; it was also hit in 1918 and 1928. (Courtesy of Historic Robeson, Inc.)

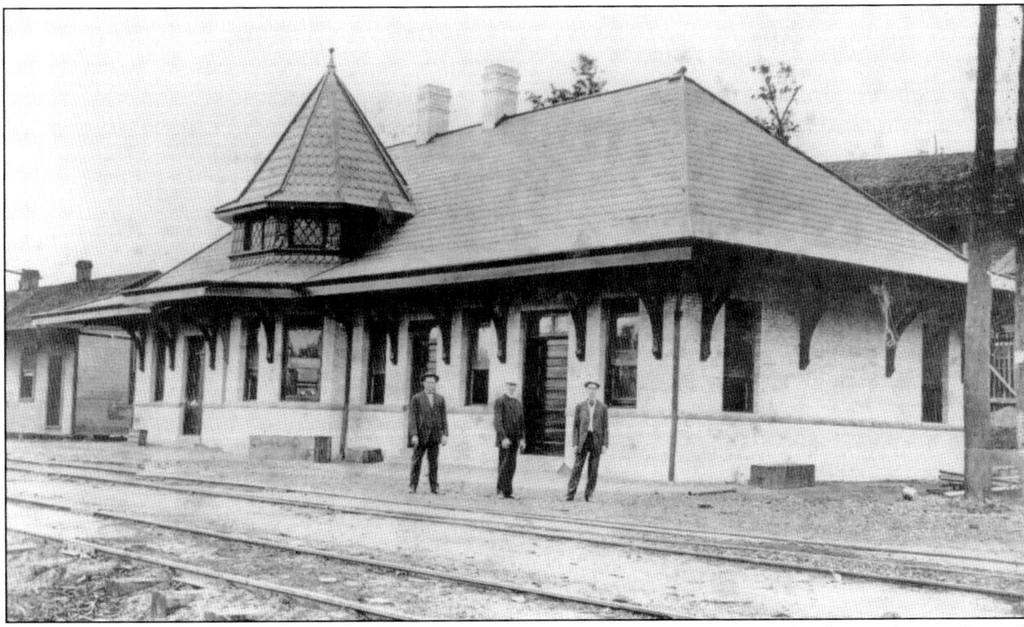

Shown here is the Lumberton Depot of the Seaboard Air Line Railway, which was located south of First Street between Elm and Chestnut Streets. This area of town was a busy and bustling place with multiple trains coming through every day. The depot was demolished in 1946 to make way for the M.H. McLean Wholesale Grocery. (Courtesy of the Carolina Collection, UNC-Chapel Hill.)

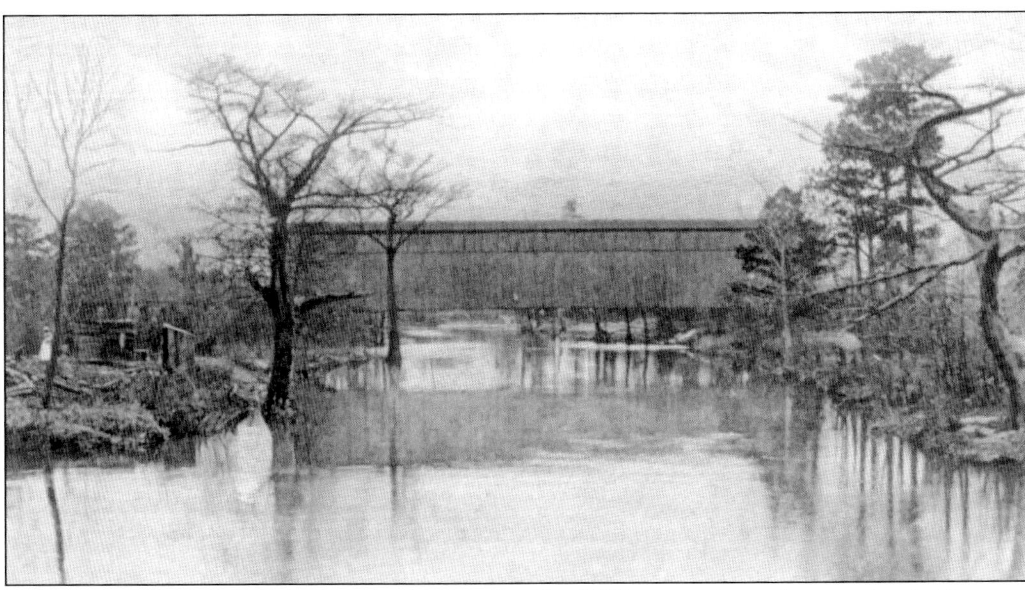

This covered railroad bridge was built after the Civil War to replace the wooden bridge near the depot that was burned by Sherman's troops when they marched through Lumberton in March 1865. According to the January 11, 1909, issue of the *Robesonian*, this structure was being replaced by a steel bridge after having been in service since 1880. (Courtesy of the Hubbard-Tyner Collection.)

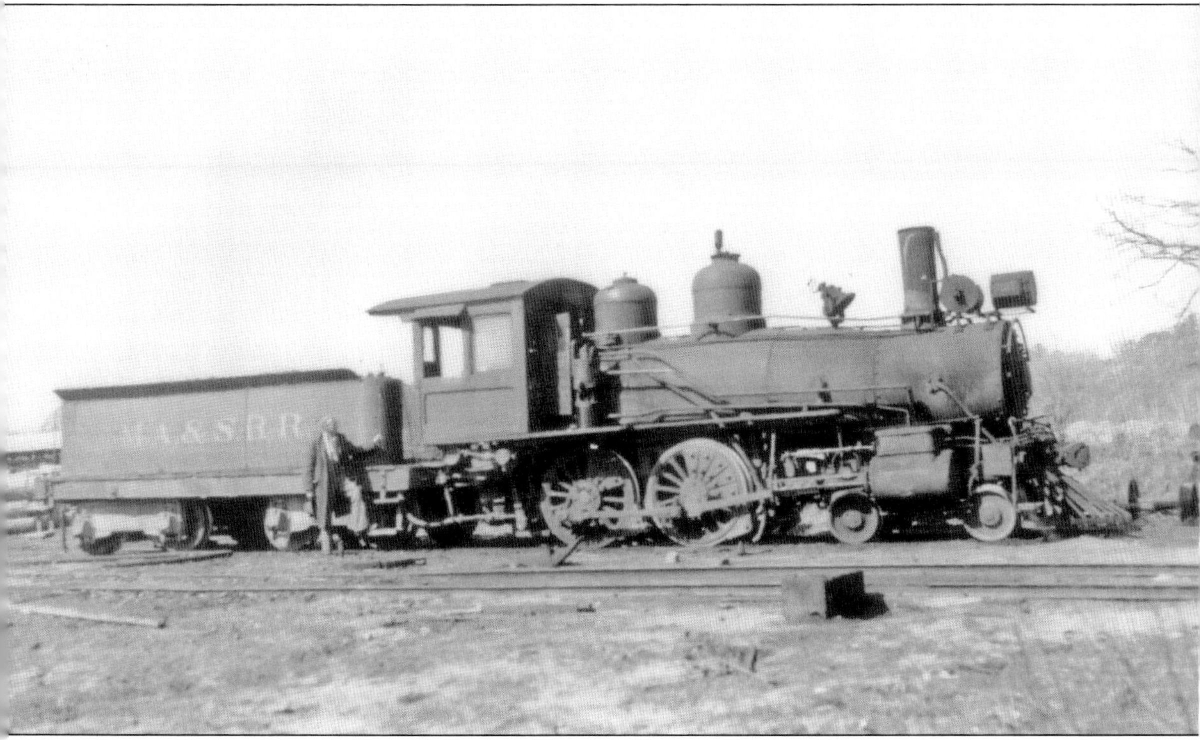

The Virginia & Carolina Southern Railroad was incorporated in 1907. Angus Wilton McLean was president and general counsel, while J.F.L. Armfield was vice president and general manager. It had 65.8 miles of track, and the route included stops in St. Pauls, Elizabethtown, Lumberton, and Hope Mills. The railroad had four locomotives, seven freight and passenger cars, and three gasoline motorcars. This image shows a railroad worker taking time out to pose for a traveling photographer. (Courtesy of the Carolina Collection, UNC-Chapel Hill.)

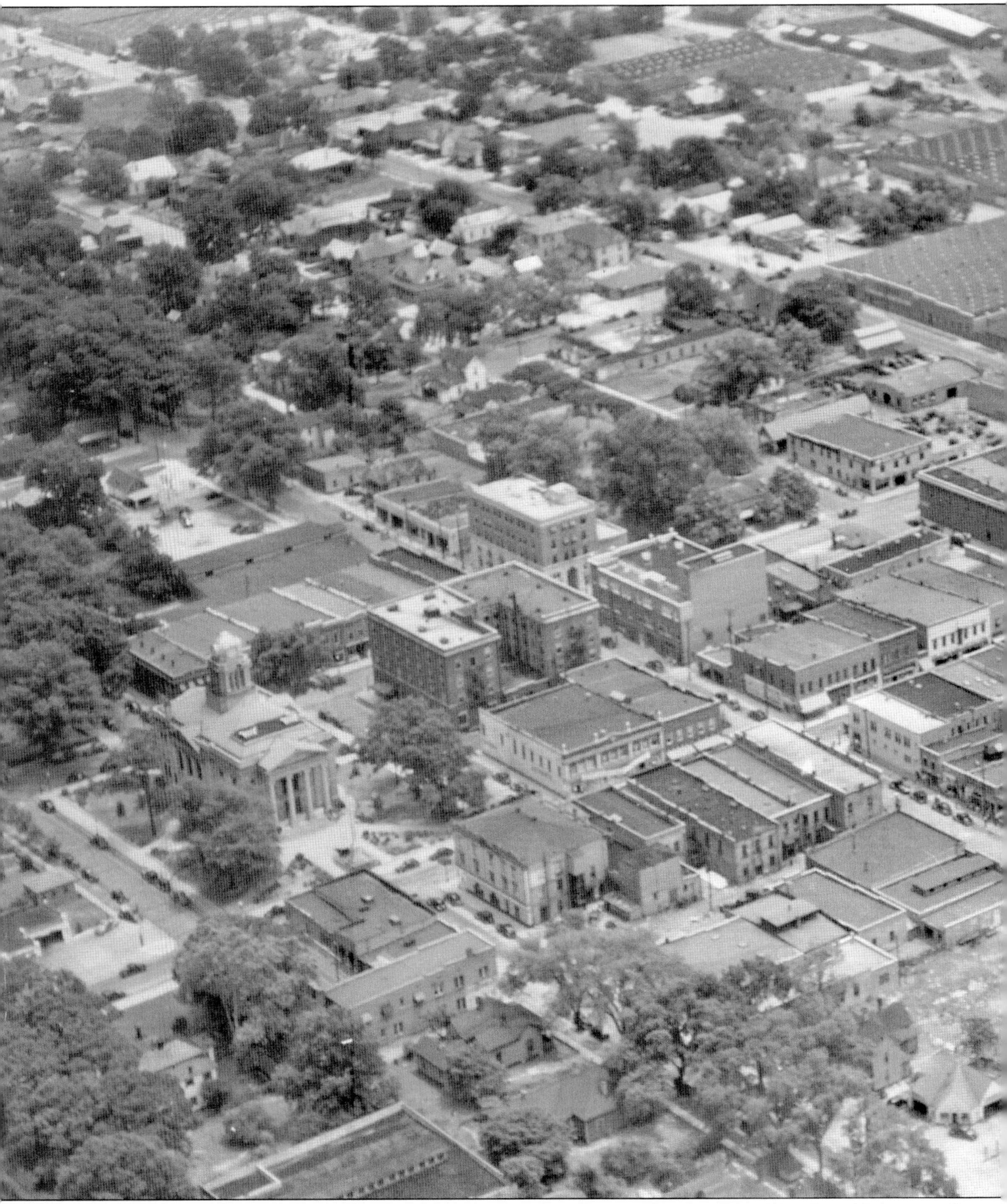

This aerial view of downtown was taken sometime before 1945, as indicated by the old depot still standing in the upper right-hand corner. The depot was demolished in 1945 to make way for M.H. McLean Wholesale. The next block, which is now home to the Robeson County Public Library, was at that time a city park that honored World War I and II soldiers. Also visible are many of the

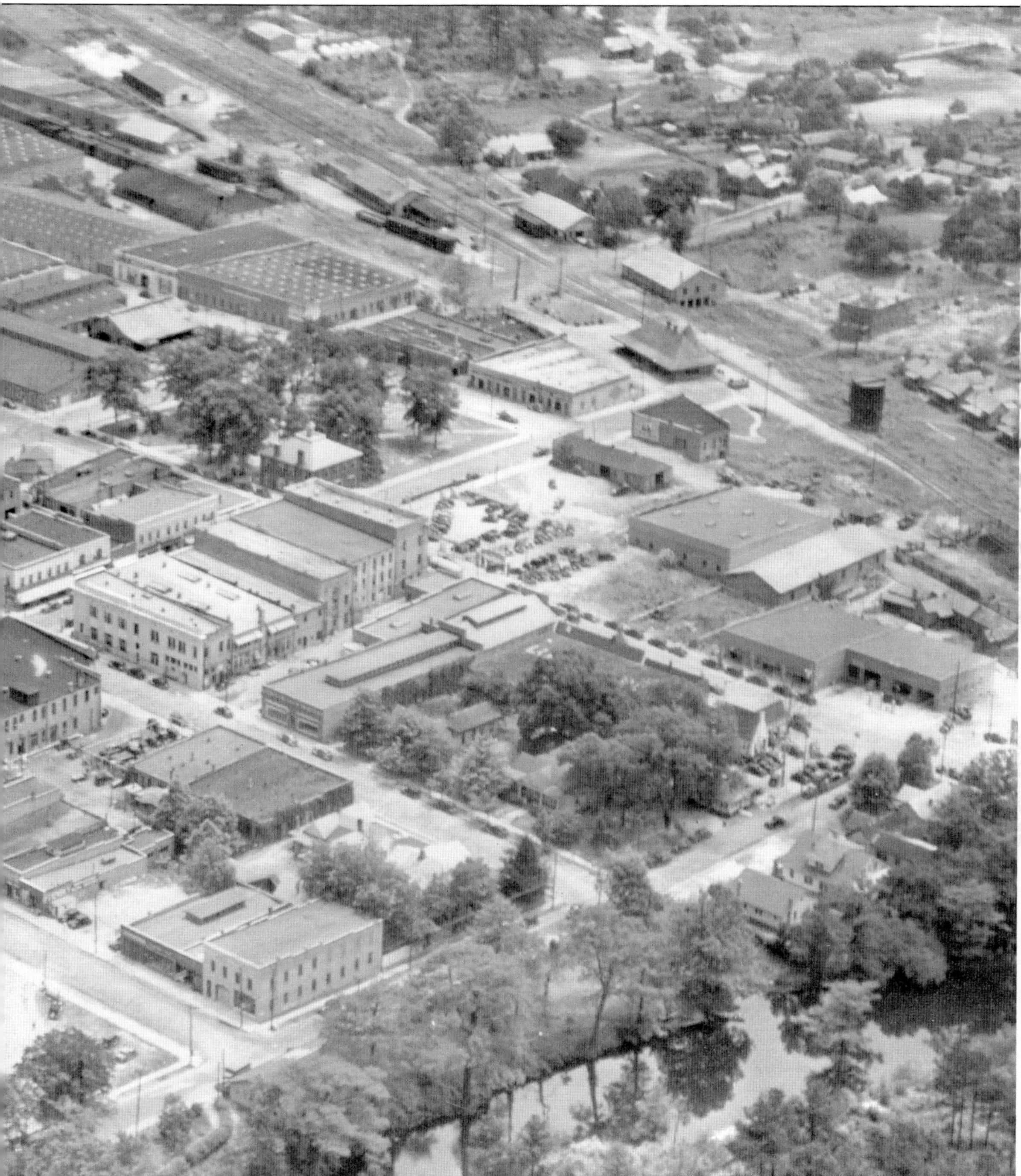

old homes that were located in the central business section, which included the Carlyle (corner of Fifth and Water Streets), Linkhaw (corner of Third and Fifth Streets beside Bargain Barn), and Gough (corner of Third and Chestnut Streets) businesses. The beautiful third courthouse can also be seen, surrounded by large trees. (Courtesy of the Robeson County Public Library.)

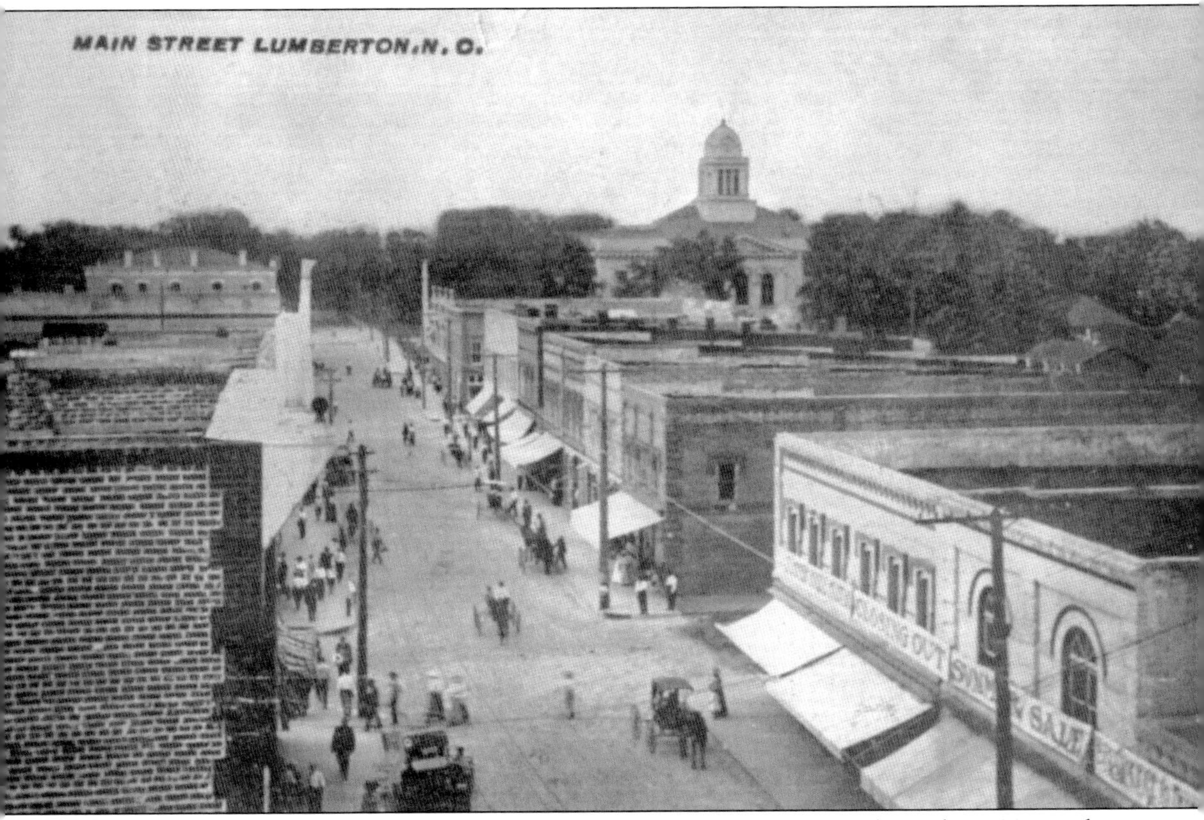

The wonderful aerial photograph of Lumberton's Main (now Elm) Street shows the 1908 courthouse in the background and a great view of the busy, wide dirt street with wagons and buggies. The shops lining the street drew not only Lumberton residents but shoppers from around the county. Caldwell & Carlyle is shown on the right-hand side in the area where the plaza is located. (Courtesy of the Hubbard-Tyner Collection.)

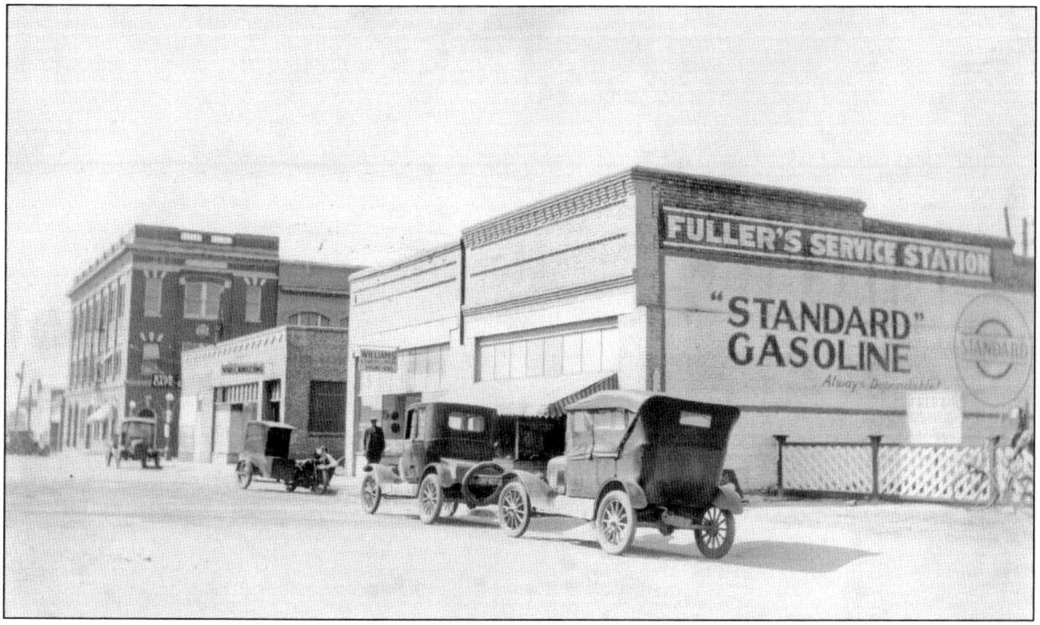

This view of Second Street between Elm and Chestnut Streets shows Fuller's Service Station, Williams Laundry and Dry Cleaning, and the Star Café. Williams was owned by brothers M.W. and Dewey Williams. Note that in front of the laundry is a motorcycle with a tall enclosed sidecar used to make deliveries. (Courtesy of Historic Robeson, Inc.)

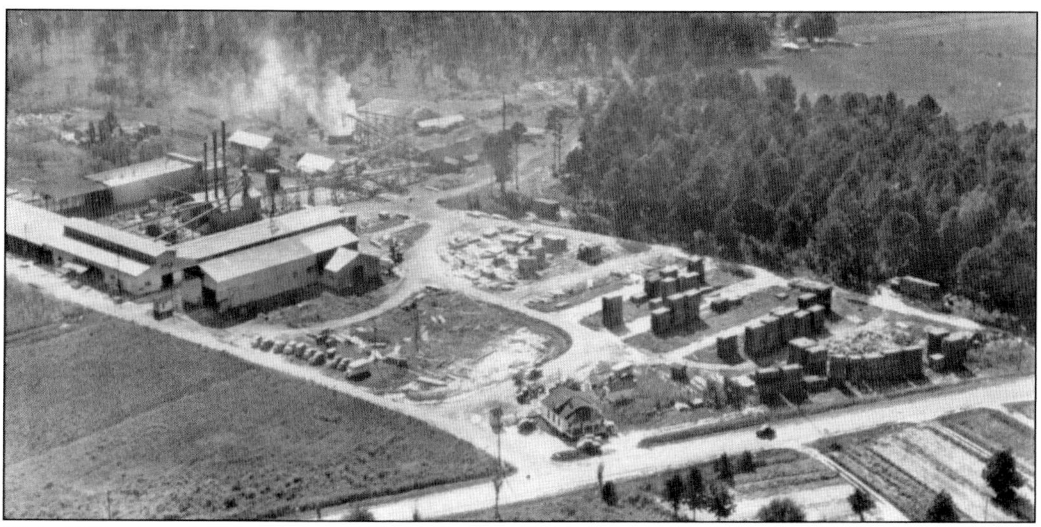

This 1951 view shows the Lumber River Manufacturing Company, which was owned by W. Scott Shepherd and located on Roland Avenue in the area where McDonald's now stands. The company, which incorporated in 1949, specialized in southern pine and cypress and produced one million feet of lumber a year. Shepherd was married to Margaret McLean, daughter of Gov. Angus Wilton McLean. (Courtesy of Historic Robeson, Inc.)

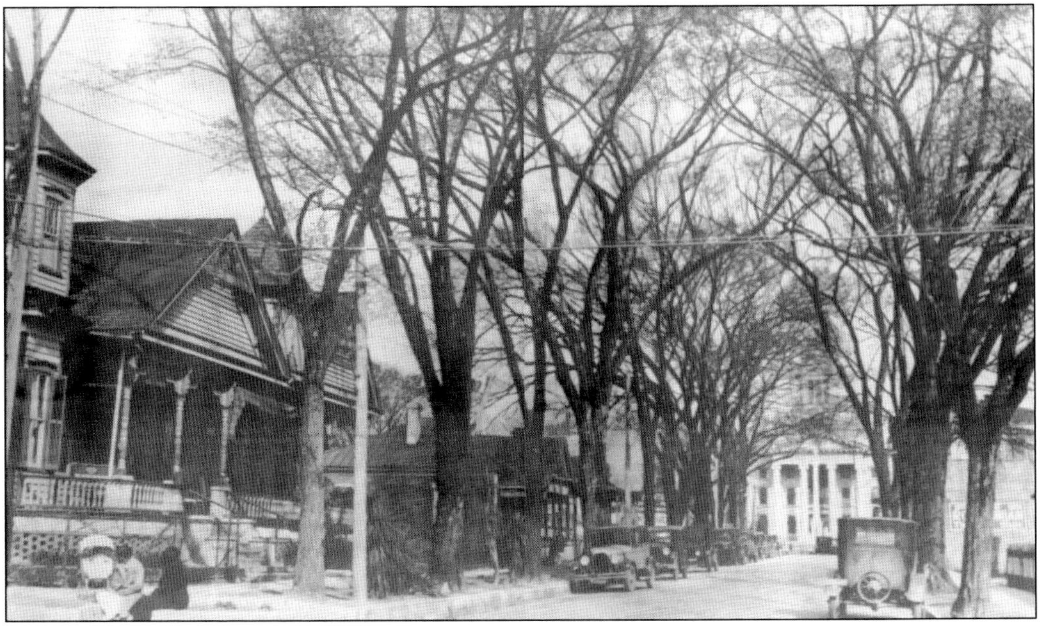

In the early 1900s, Fifth Street between Water and Elm Streets was still the site of many family homes. On the corner was the home of William Watts and Lillian Carlyle. Other families on the street included Harris and Maude Dunie (he operated a dry goods on Elm Street); B. Frank and Mary Davis (he was a clerk at the company store of Lumberton Cotton Mill); and Van and Florrie Squires (who was a bicycle dealer). (Courtesy of Brad Thompson.)

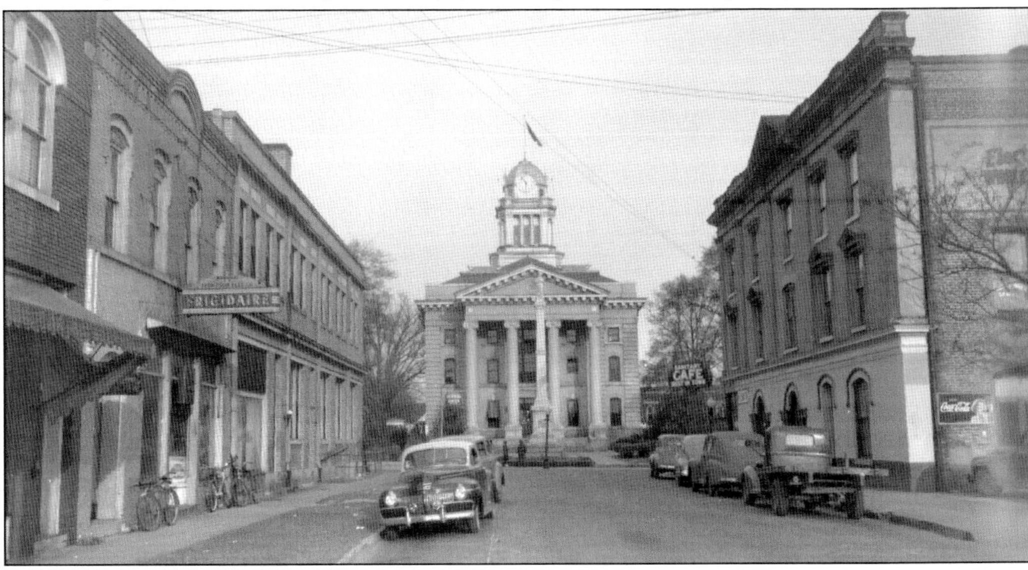

By the time of the 1956 city directory, the block was home to the following businesses: Court Square Hardware Company; Sanitary Café; Thompson Electrical Co.; City Sport & Repair Shop; Jefferson Standard Life Insurance; Lennon Electrical Co.; Lumberton Manufacturing Co., Inc.; Gillespie Photograph Studio; Twin State Parts Co.; WTSB Radio Station; surveyor William Stone; Freeman Printing Company; Norment Motor Co.; the *Robesonian*; and lawyers David M. Britt, John C. Campbell, J.C. Ward, Neill L. Britt, and F. Ertel Carlyle, who was also representing the county as a member of Congress from the 7th District. (Courtesy of Brad Thompson.)

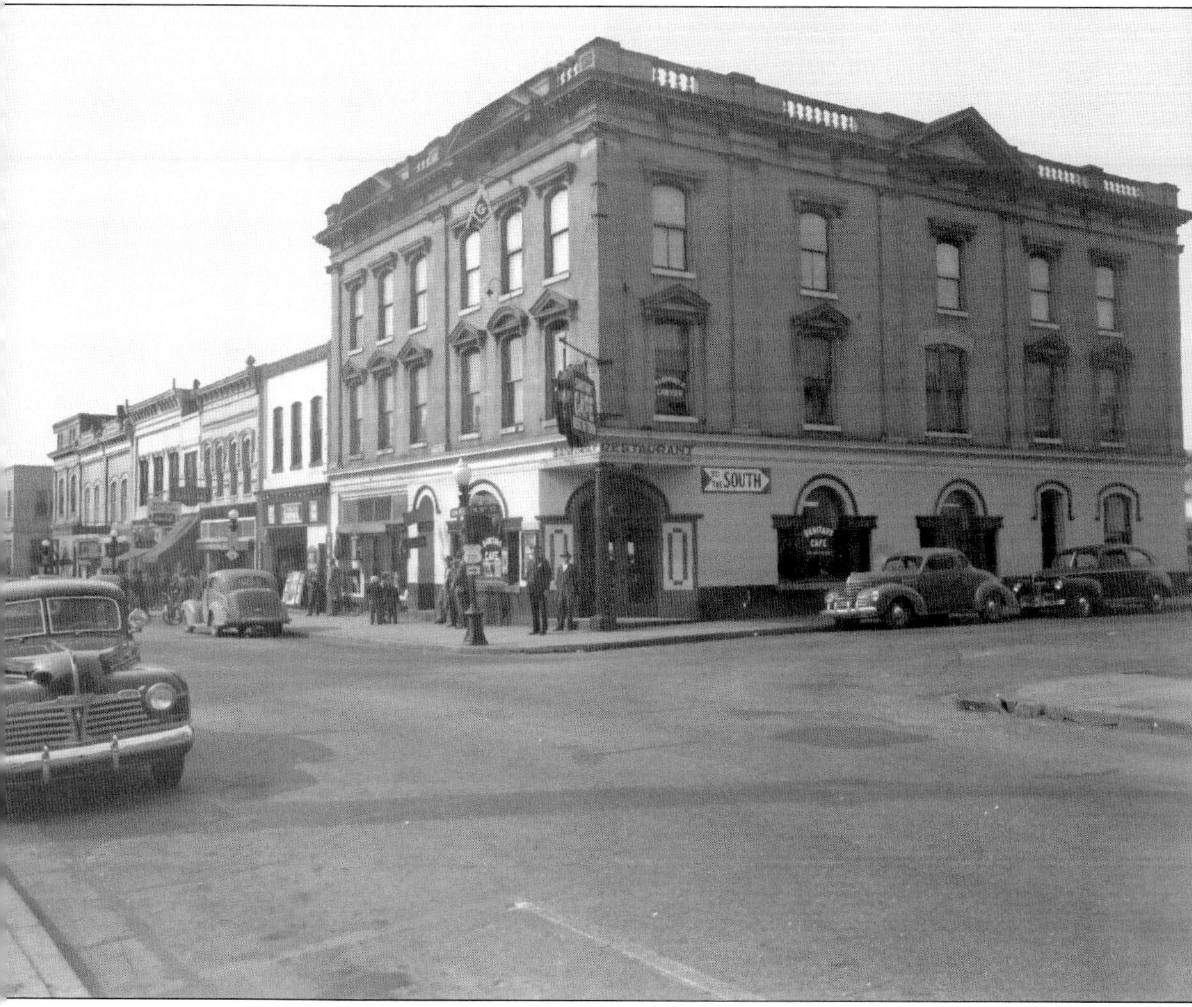

In this photograph of Elm Street is the old First National Bank of Lumberton building. The bank was established on September 14, 1904, and the officers in 1910 were George B. McLeod, president; A.R. McEachern, vice president; H.M. McAllister, cashier; and R. McA. Nixon, assistant cashier. At the time of this image, the building was the home of James Adams's Sanitary Café ("Best in town for good things to eat"), and on an upper floor was St Alban's Masonic Lodge. Adams was a native of Cyprus and had immigrated to the United States in 1916. The building later housed the Court Square Hardware Store and now is home to Bowen & Berry Attorneys and Elegant Portraits Carolinas. Next door was the Pastime Theatre (advertising 18¢ shows), then Lumberton Drug Store and Redmond's Fruit Store. (Courtesy of Brad Thompson.)

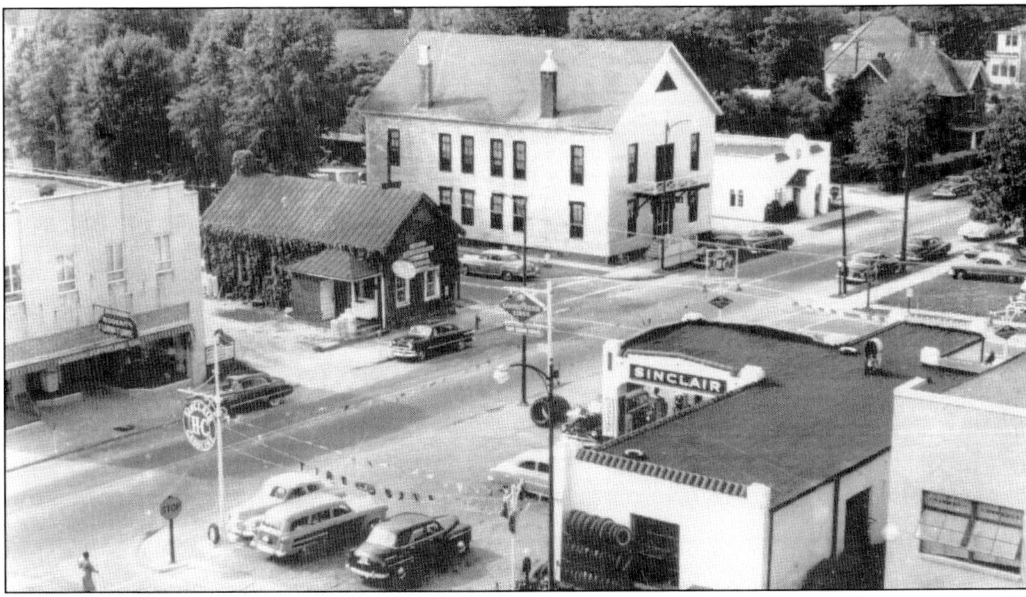

This photograph from the late 1950s was taken from the courthouse. Across the street are the Modern Furniture Store, the Proctor Law Office, and the Lumberton Opera House. The Proctor Law Office is owned by Historic Robeson and, believed to date to 1840, is the oldest building in Lumberton. Attorney Edward Knox Proctor purchased the building in 1869 and, until the 1930s, it served as law offices for Proctor, Lawrence & McIntyre. The name of the firm changed over the years as lawyers joined and left. Lumberton's first telephone and waterworks are said to have been installed on the lot in 1893. (Courtesy of Brad Thompson.)

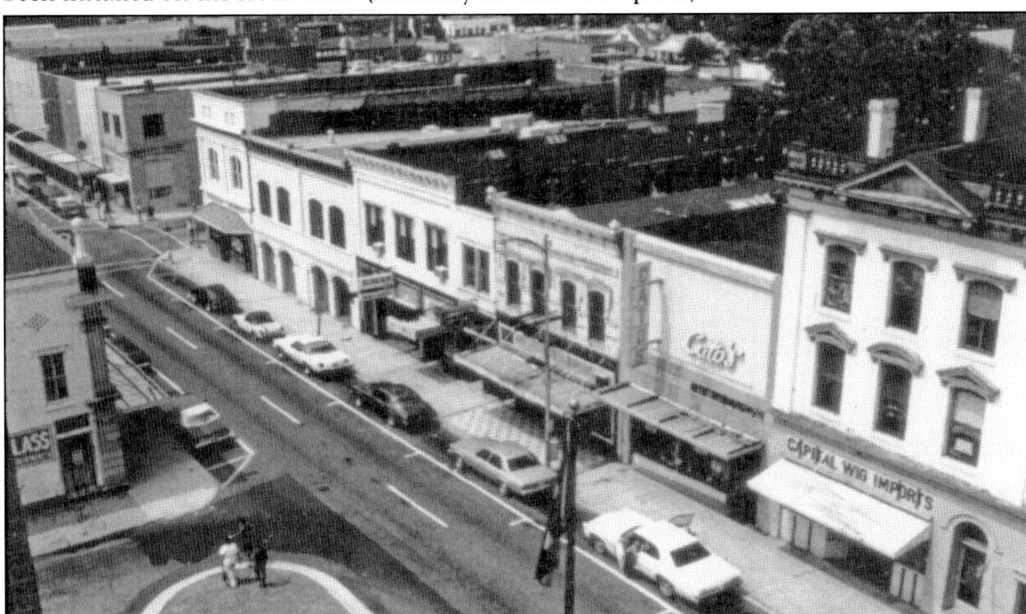

This 1970s photograph of the 400 block of Elm Street was taken from inside the courthouse. On the right side are Capital Wig Imports, Cato's, Singer Store, and Hedgepeth Pharmacy. On the left, Rayless Department Store is housed in the old White & Gough Store, which was the third brick structure built in downtown. (Courtesy of Frances Phillips.)

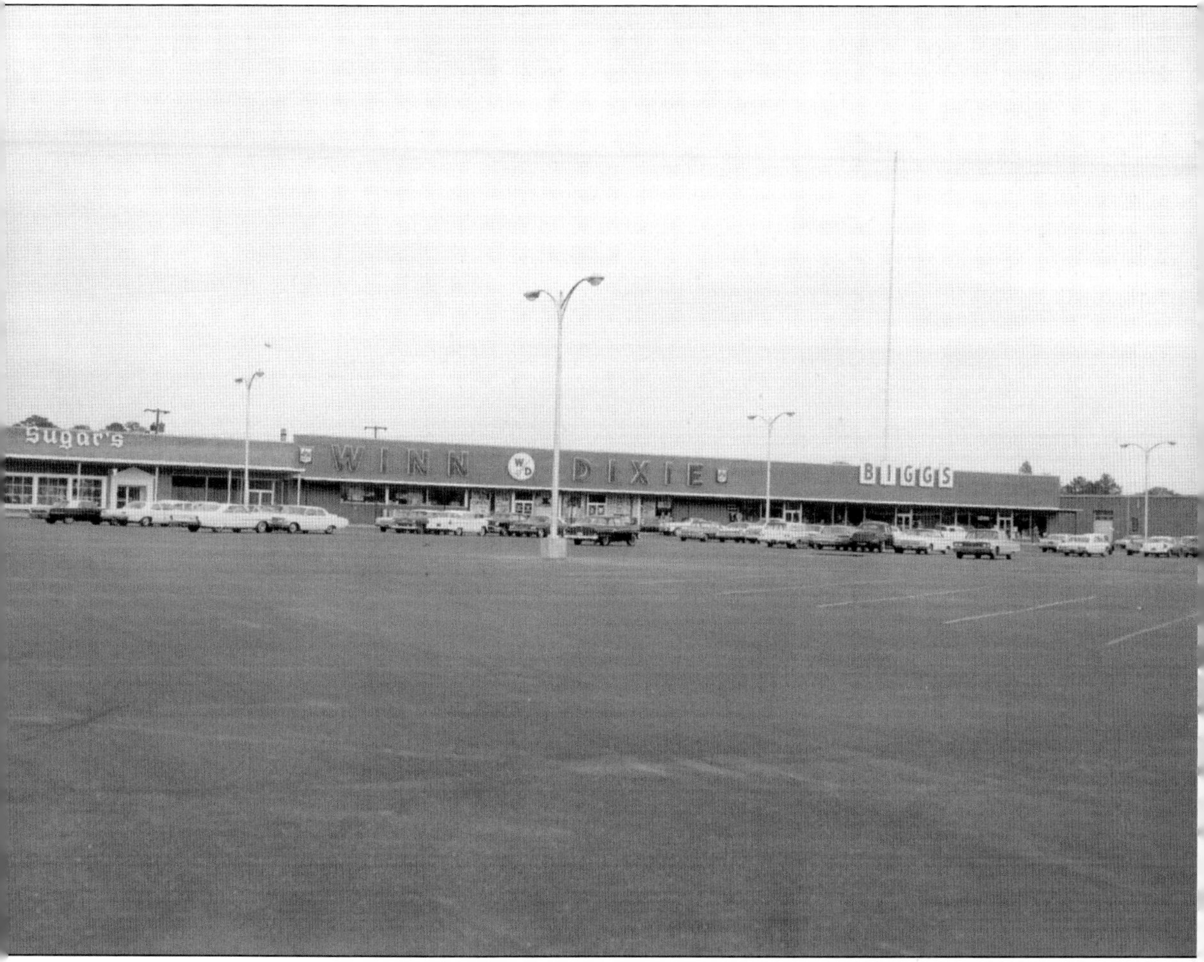

Kenneth M. Biggs, son of Confederate veteran Ebenezer Biggs and his wife, Ellen Carlyle, was born in Saddletree. He married Mamie Duckett, daughter of Robeson Institute principal Prof. John Duckett, and got a job as a bookkeeper for Caldwell & Carlyle. In 1903, with a personal loan from Angus Wilton McLean, he started a mercantile business, which grew by leaps and bounds because of his high business ethics. He has been the organizer and director of so many Lumberton corporations that a list of his directorates would sound like a roster of the town's business organizations. He was the first president of the chamber of commerce in 1936 and the longtime director of the National Bank of Lumberton. The K.M. Biggs store prospered over the years and in the 1960s, it moved out of downtown to a lot near Roland Avenue on Elm Street. The new shopping center featured the Biggs store, Winn-Dixie, and Sugar's Men's Store. The complex was enlarged and converted over the years and is now Biggs Park Mall. (Courtesy of Brad Thompson.)

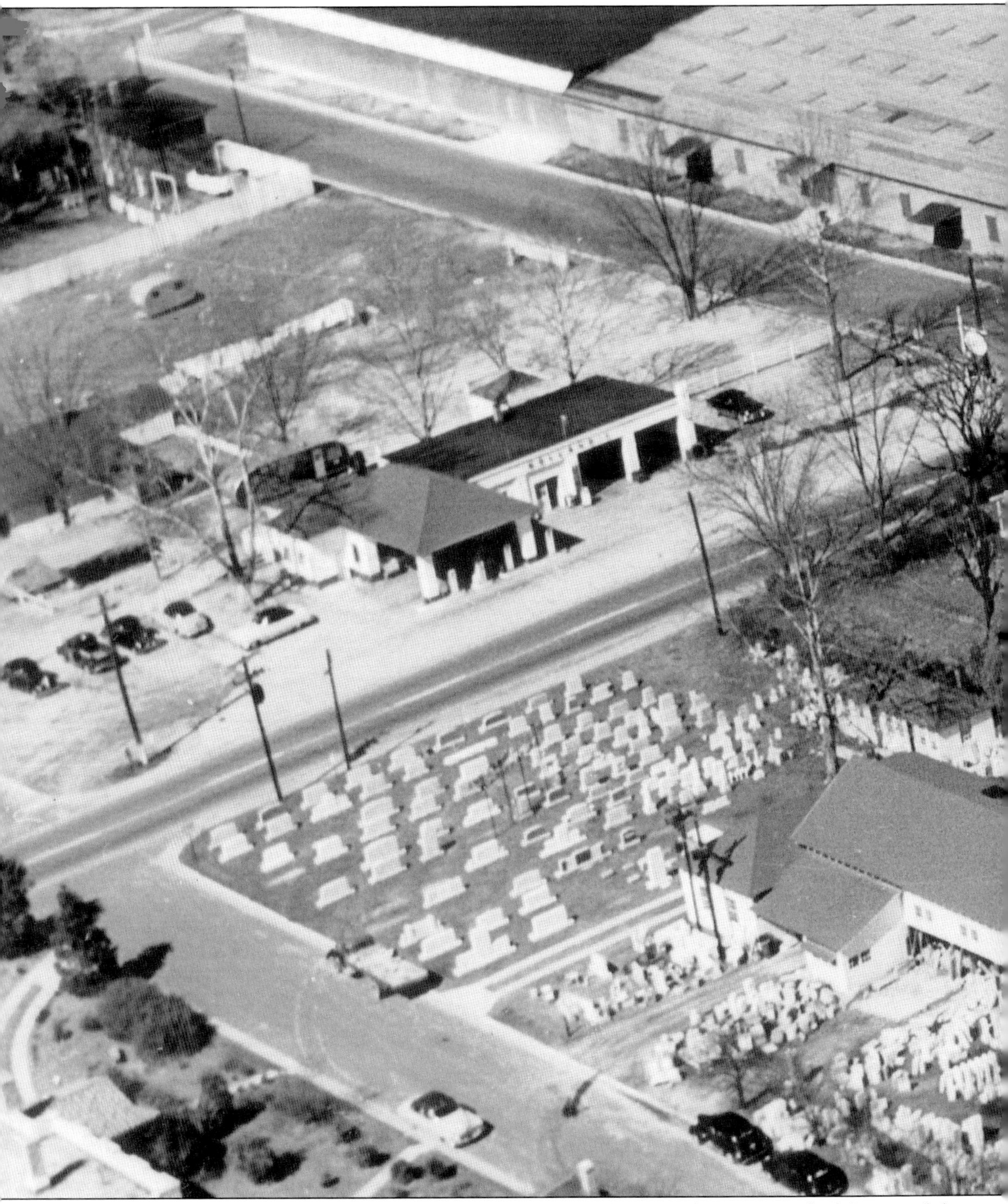

This aerial image of Pine and Cedar Streets at Twentieth Street shows a wonderful view of the yards of Southern Marble Works, which were covered with not only completed marble and granite monuments but also large stacks of stone ready to be cut by master stonecutters. To the left can be seen the granite home of James Cooper, one of the owners of Southern Marble Works. The

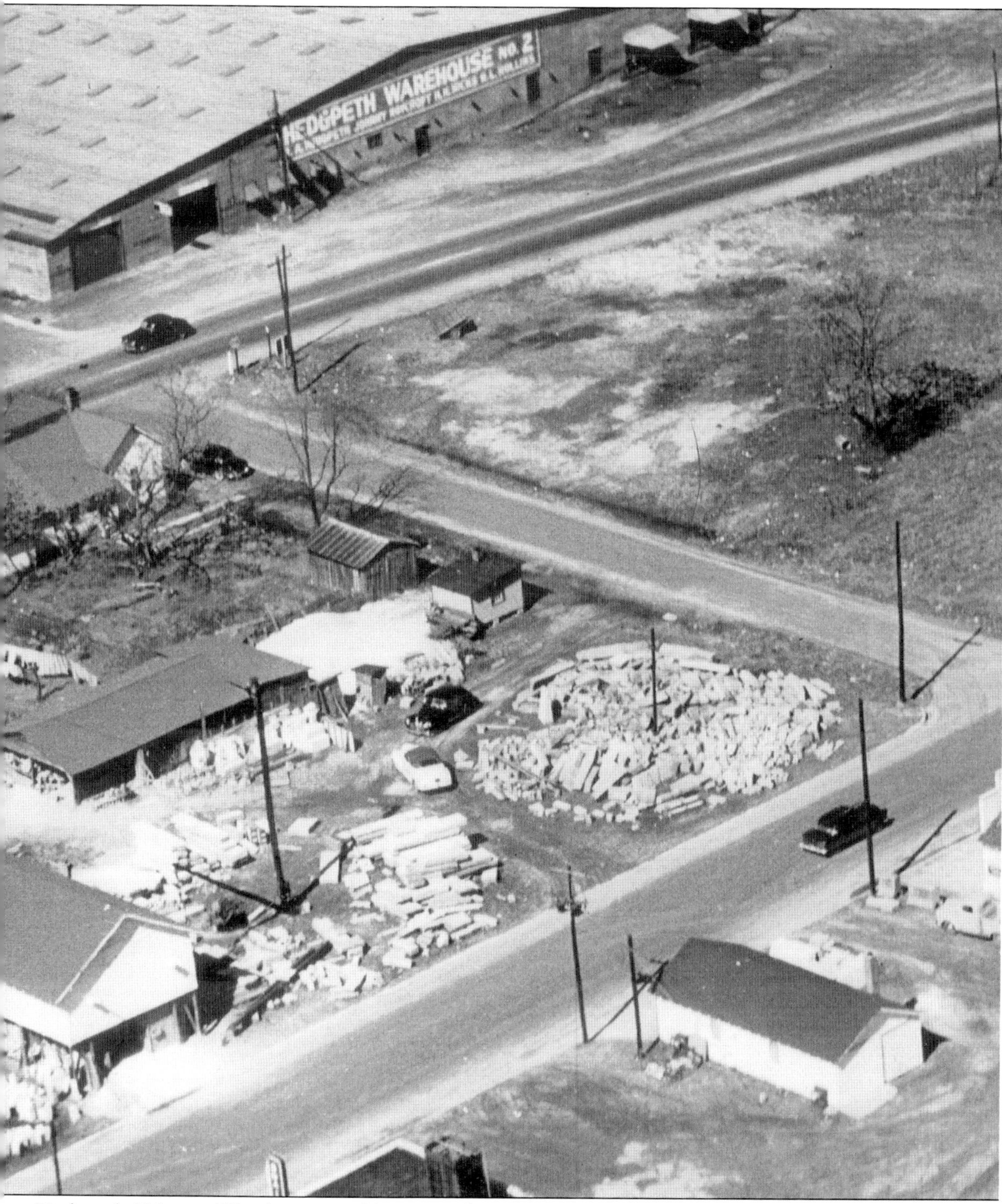

Hedgpeth Tobacco Warehouse, visible across the street, was owned by Romulus A. Hedgpeth, H.H. Hicks, R.L. Rollins, and Johnny K. Roycroft. It has since been demolished, and the property is now home to a shopping center owned by K.M. Biggs, Inc. (Courtesy of Cooper Collection, Robeson Remembers, Robeson County History Museum.)

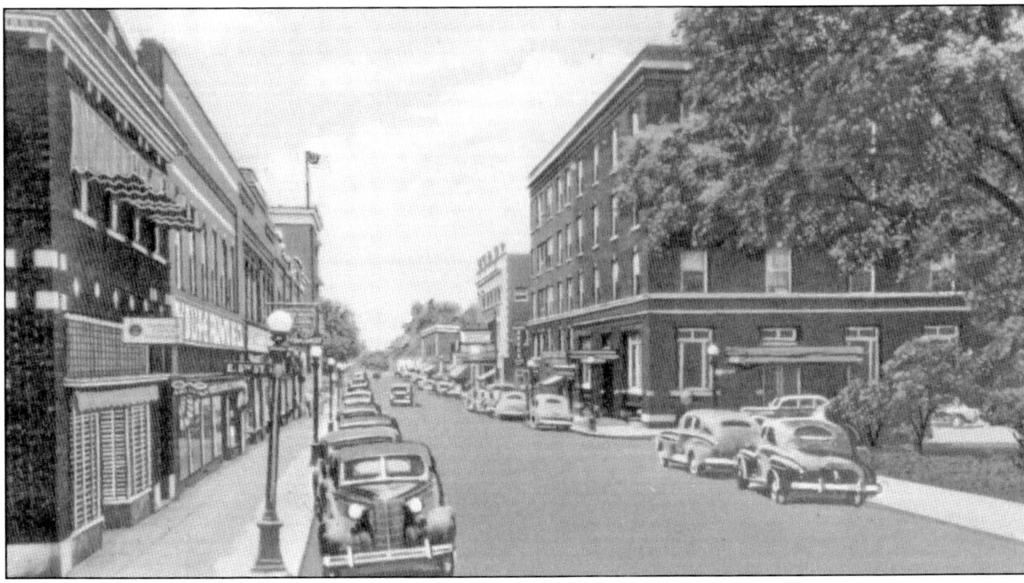

Chestnut Street has always been an important retail center in Lumberton. Longtime businesses on this street were the Lorraine Hotel, McDuffie Furniture, Sellers Sporting Goods, Merrimac Music Company, and the Carolina Theatre. At its south end is the beginning of the tobacco market, which in its prime sold millions of dollars worth of flue-cured tobacco every year. (Courtesy of Brad Thompson.)

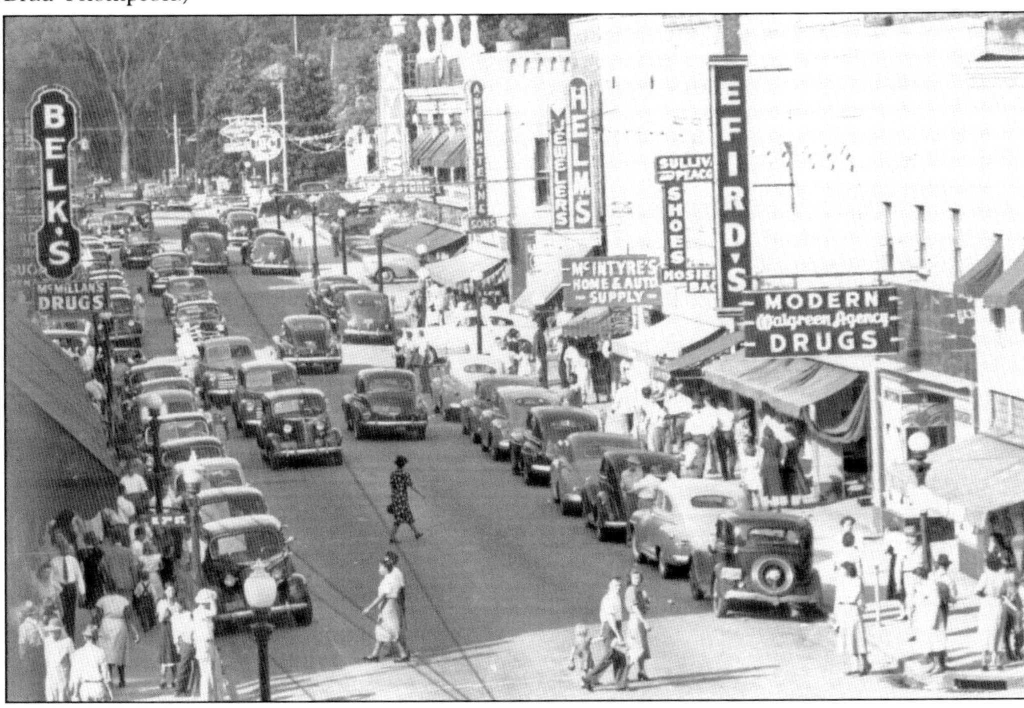

A great view of Elm Street from the corner of Third Street shows Belk-Hensdale Department Store, Modern Drugs, Efird's Department Store, McIntyre Home & Auto Supply, Sugar's Men's Store, McMillan Drug Store, Aaron Weinstein & Sons Department Store, and Rayless Department Store. (Courtesy of Brad Thompson.)

Five

HOUSES OF WORSHIP

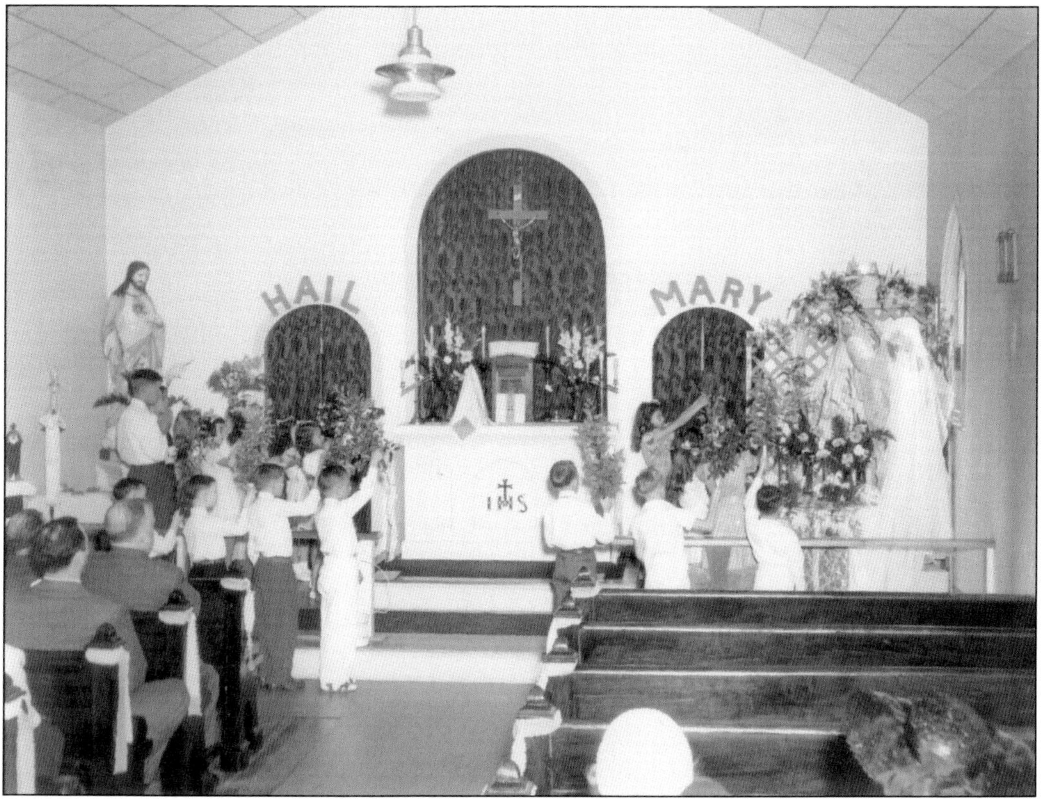

This is a celebration of May Day at St. Francis De Sales Catholic Church. May is a month in which Mary, the mother of Jesus, is celebrated. An older girl is chosen as May Queen and gets to place a crown on the head of a statue of Mary. This is always a special day for the Catholic Church. (Courtesy of Gillespie Studio Collection, Robeson County History Museum.)

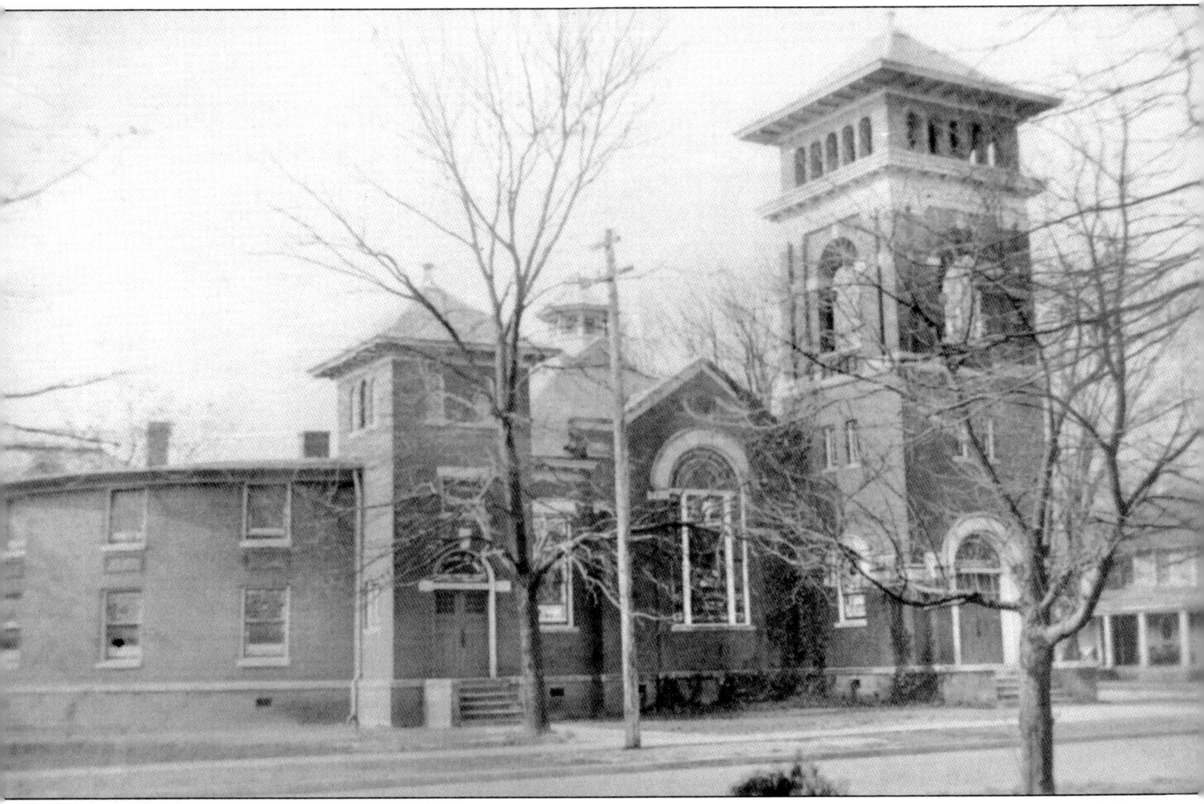

Chestnut Street United Methodist Church is the oldest church in town and is considered the "Mother Church of Lumberton." On March 11, 1787, Bishop Francis Asbury—the first Methodist bishop in America—preached at Robeson County's new courthouse. It is believed that the Methodist Church of Lumberton was organized between 1787 and 1803. The first building was located on Water Street. In 1878, a second church was built on the corner of Seventh and Chestnut Streets. This is the third church building, built in 1913, it was demolished in 1956. (Courtesy of Historic Robeson, Inc.)

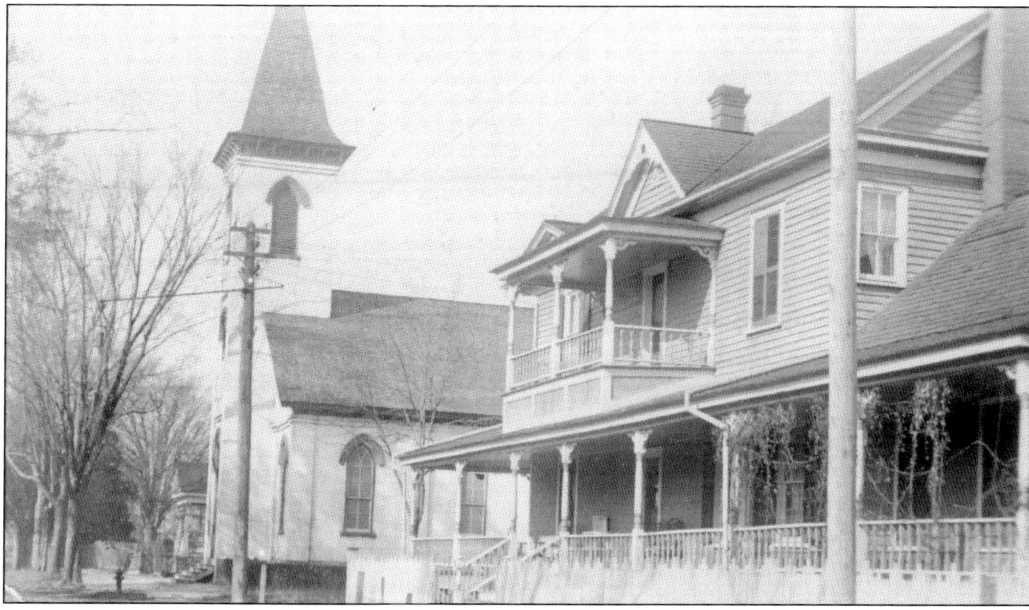

First Baptist Church was the offspring of the Lebanon, Antioch, Back Swamp, Mount Elim, Orrum, and other Baptist congregations in Robeson County. On July 1, 1855, elders Haynes Lennon and D.B. Ayers, together with other Baptist churches, convened to constitute the Baptist church in Lumberton, of which Lennon became the first pastor. Pictured here is the second church building, which was erected on the corner of Fifth and Walnut Streets in 1875. (Courtesy of the Carolina Collection, UNC-Chapel Hill.)

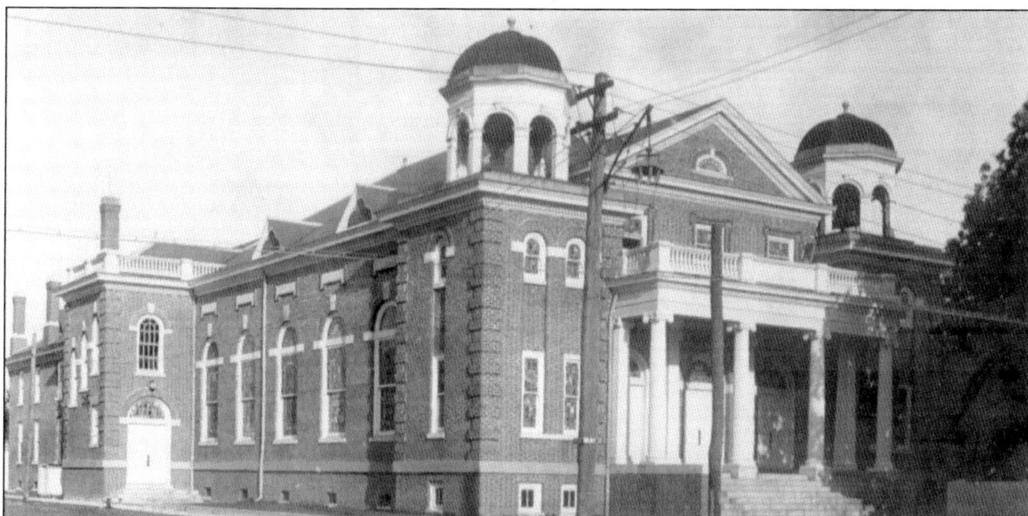

First Baptist Church's current building was completed on Thanksgiving Day 1910. Over the years, the congregation has added buildings and renovated the present sanctuary. First Baptist is the mother church of Sandy Grove Missionary Baptist Church, organized in 1873; East Lumberton Baptist Church, organized in 1907; West Lumberton Baptist Church, organized in 1915; North Lumberton Baptist Church, organized in 1918; Godwin Heights Baptist Church, organized in 1953; and Forest Acres Baptist Church, organized in 1990. (Courtesy of Kate Biggs Collection, Robeson County Public Library.)

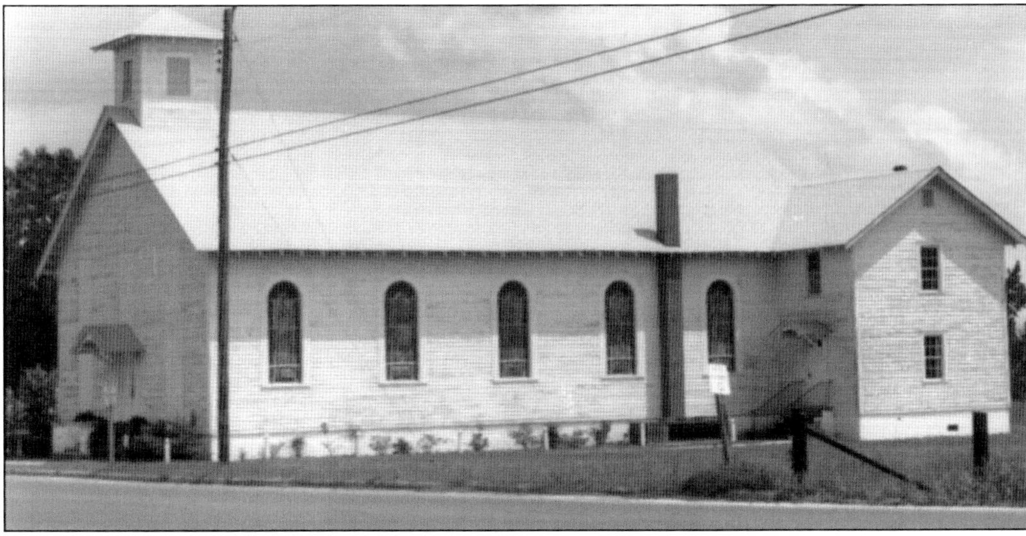

On October 10, 1915, Dr. Charles Greaves informed First Baptist that there was a need for a house of worship at North Lumberton. On April 6, 1918, a site was purchased for the church. Luther H. Caldwell was one of the organizers of the Sunday school at North Lumberton and was most active in the establishment of this church and in its work until his death on July 22, 1935. (Courtesy of Brad Thompson.)

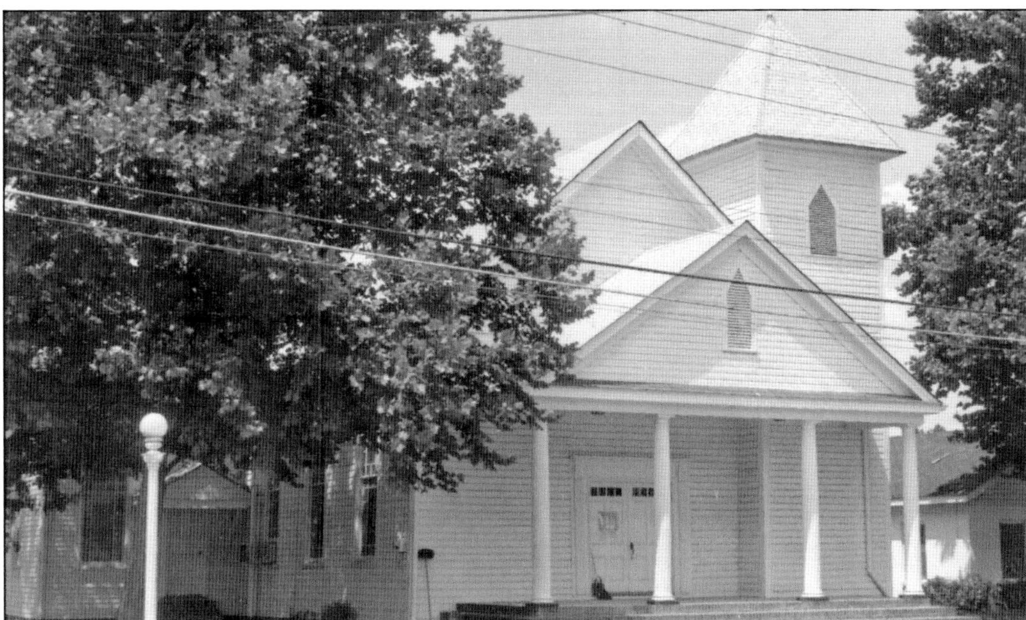

The minutes of First Baptist Church from November 27, 1908, contain the following entry: "As a result of Revival Meeting held by Brother Paul during the past week at West Lumberton, 9 members were added to the Lumberton Baptist Church." The following year, the church sponsored a Sunday school at West Lumberton. Land was donated by Jenkins Bennett, and the West Lumberton Baptist Church was dedicated on Sunday, May 5, 1918. (Courtesy of Brad Thompson.)

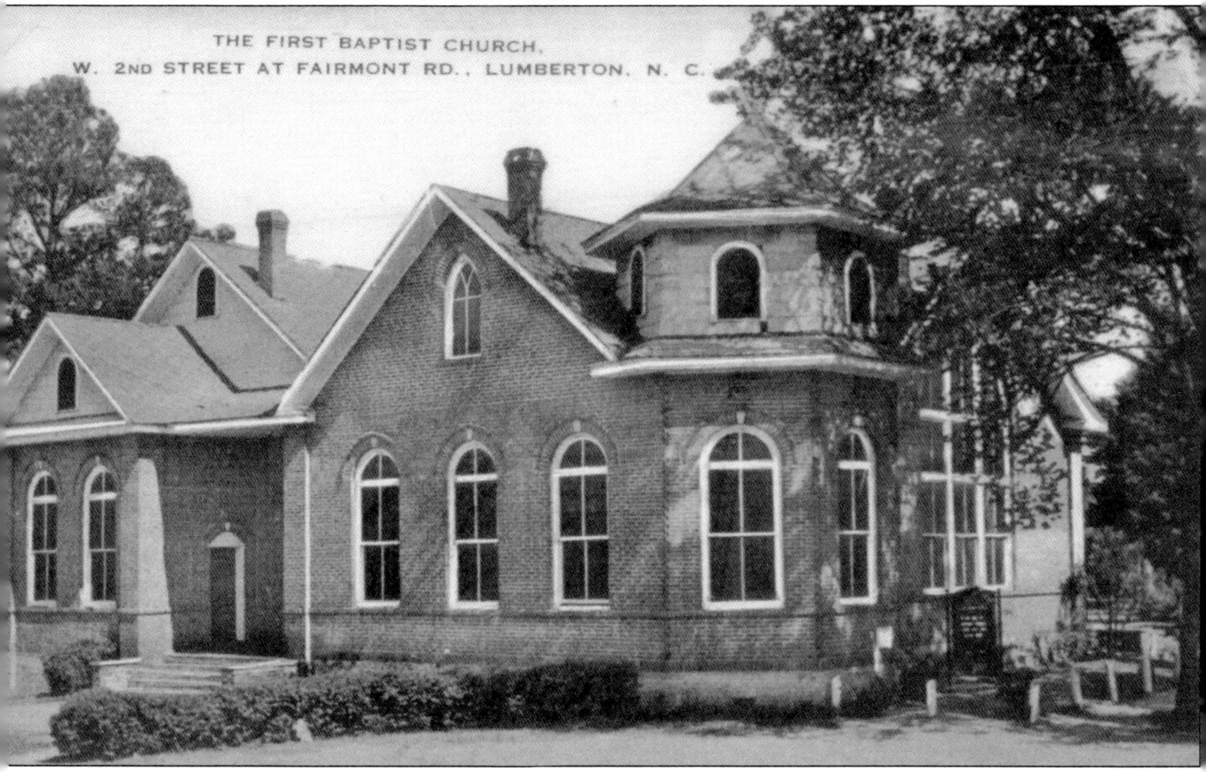

In 1922, First Baptist Church was organized on West Second Street at the corner of Fairmont Road (now Martin Luther King Jr. Drive) as the result of a desire to unite the congregations of St. John and Providence Missionary Baptist Churches. Rev. E.B. Turner served as its pastor for 57 years, and this African American church has provided a shelter in the storm for the community throughout the years. (Courtesy of the Hubbard-Tyner Collection.)

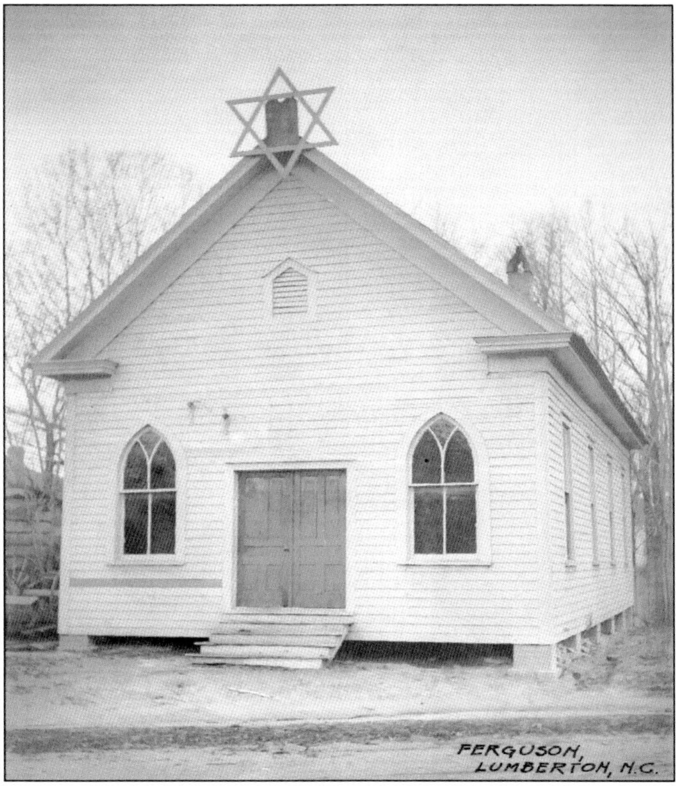

The first Beth El temple, a wooden structure, was built in 1908 on Water Street across from the jail. The land was donated by Aaron Weinstein. By the early 1950s, the original synagogue was in poor condition, and a new brick facility was built in 1954 farther down Water Street. In 1988, Temple Beth El was closed due to a loss of members. Shortly thereafter, the synagogue was sold and is currently used as a church. (Courtesy of Brad Thompson..)

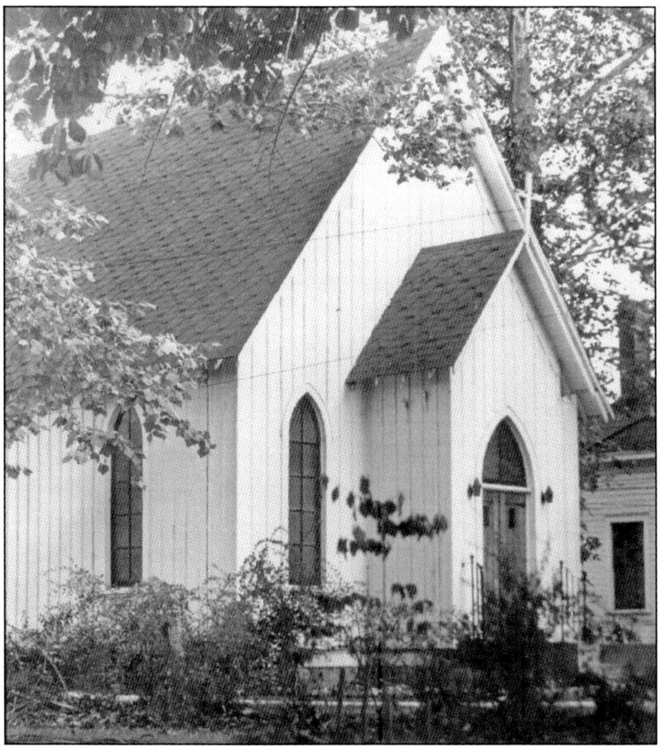

On June 12, 1912, nine men and women met with the Right Reverend Robert Strange in the home of John Q. and Ann Beckwith to organize an Episcopal church. A small, white, Gothic-style church was constructed of wood with dark oak furnishings, a reed organ, a seating capacity of 125, and a large pot-bellied stove. On Palm Sunday, March 28, 1915, the Right Reverend Thomas Campbell Darst consecrated Trinity of Lumberton as his newest mission. (Courtesy of Brad Thompson.)

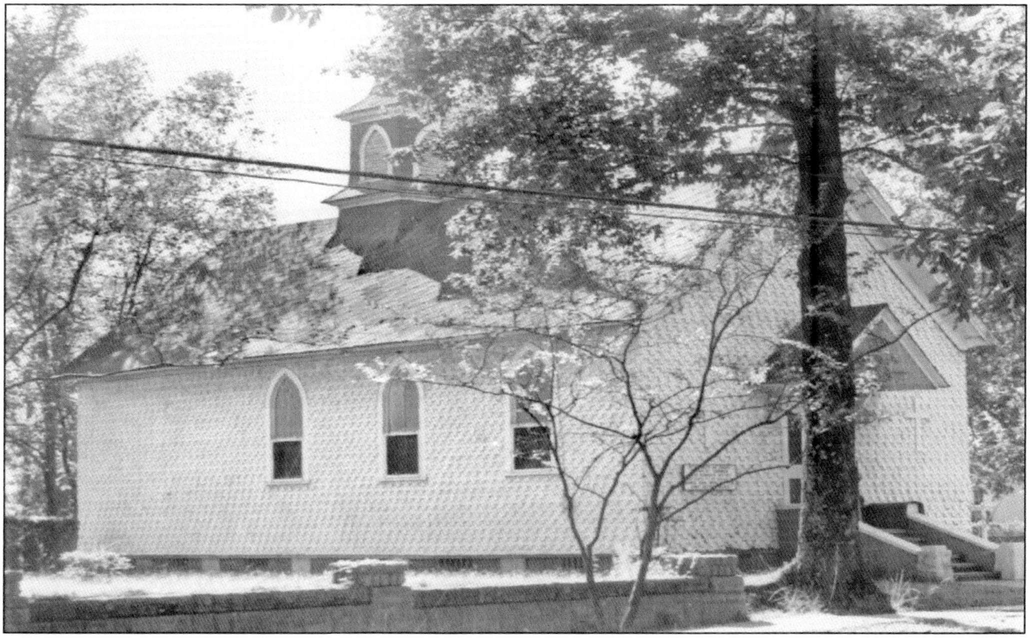

St. Francis De Sales Catholic Church had its beginning in 1870, with services taking place at the Redmond home and being officiated by priests who visited from Wilmington, the first being Father Moore. About 1910, under Father Hayden, church services began to be held in the opera house, and in 1917, this church was built on Fifth Street. An African American mission—the St. Madeleine-Sophie Mission—was started on Elizabethtown Road. The churches also maintained separate schools. Eventually, the parishes merged as St. Francis De Sales Catholic Church and moved into the new buildings on Elizabethtown Road. (Courtesy of Brad Thompson.)

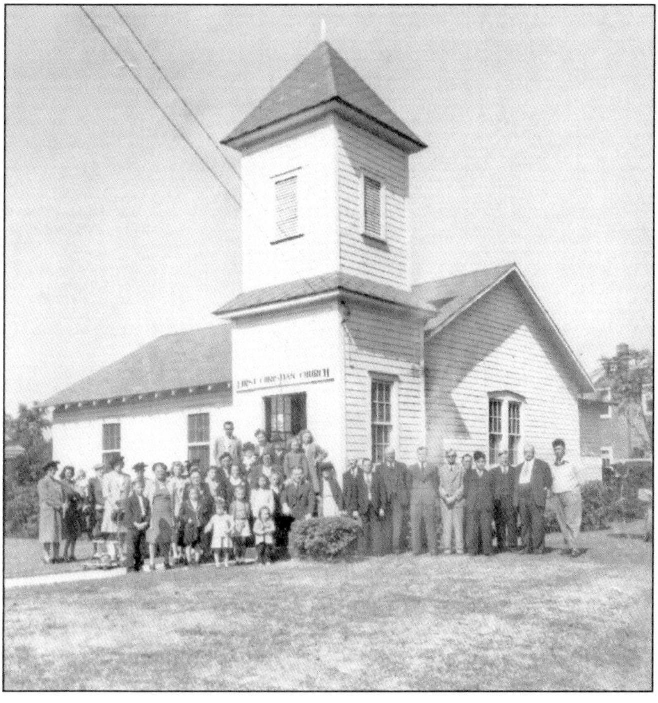

The Christian Church was organized with seven charter members in 1925 largely through the efforts of G.L. Canady and H.M. Beasly. They met in the old Presbyterian church on Fifth Street until it burned in January 1927. They then met in the Linkhaw building and the courthouse until this building was constructed in 1928 on the corner of Fifteenth and Barker Streets. The church ceased operation and the building is currently home to Robeson Family Counseling Center. (Courtesy of Jane Carroll Lee.)

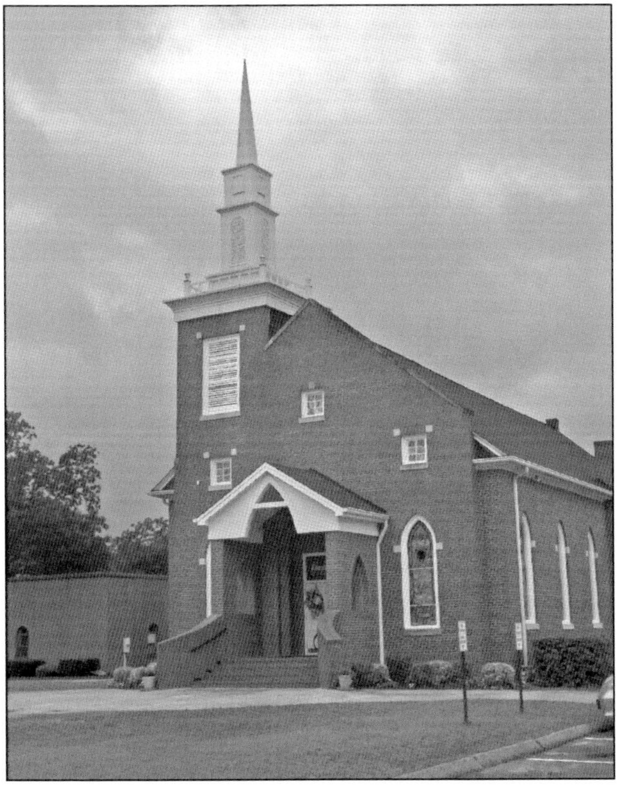

In 1873, a group of African Americans purchased a plot of land for a church—Sandy Grove—about 1.5 miles south of the Lumber River. Some of the known founders were Sandy and Rachel Smith, Eric and Florence Cobb, Pierce Powell, and Emanuel Fulmore. The current building was erected in 1940 as a wooden structure and was later covered in brick veneer. All of the existing black Baptist churches in the city grew from Sandy Grove. (Courtesy of the Hubbard-Tyner Collection.)

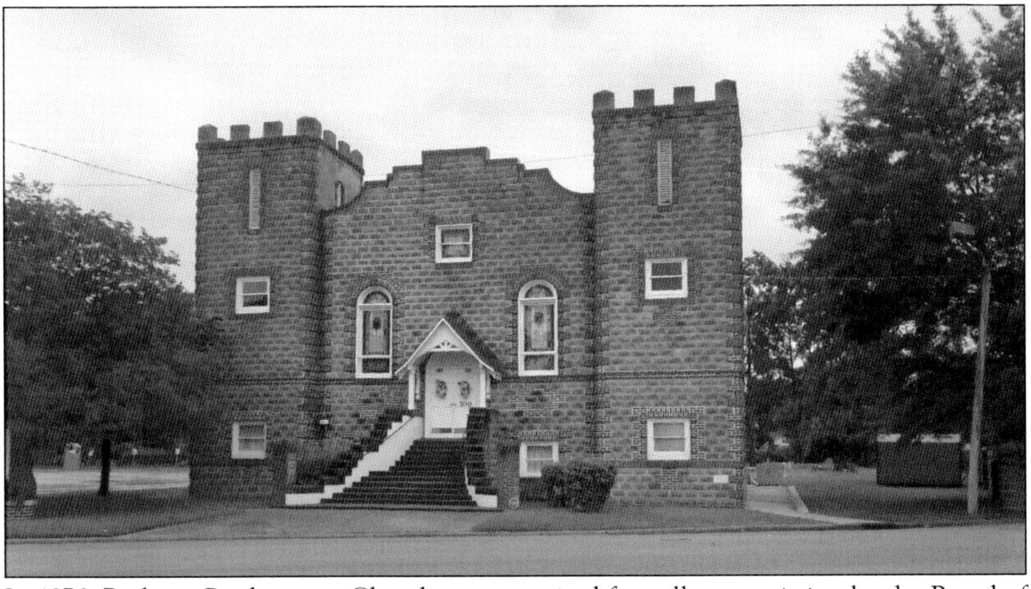

In 1876, Bethany Presbyterian Church was organized formally as a mission by the Board of National Missions of the Presbyterian Church, USA. In 1903, Dr. John Henry Hayswood was called as the pastor. During that year, Bethany School, later known as Redstone Academy, was established as an elementary and secondary school for African Americans. Dr. Hayswood and his wife, Mattie, labored to help the church and the school to grow. (Courtesy of the Hubbard-Tyner Collection.)

Six

Residences

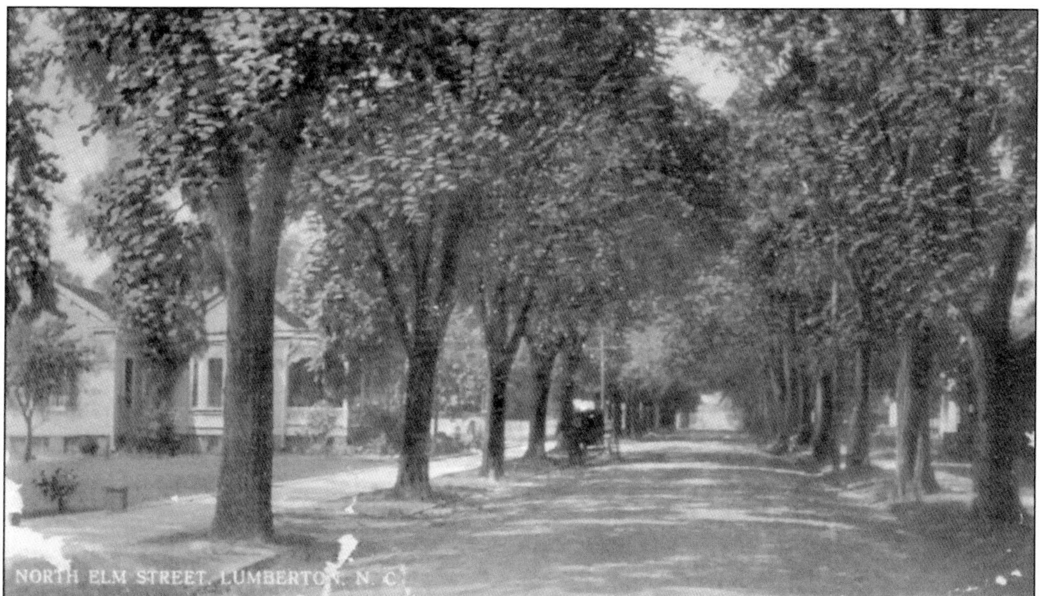

At the turn of the 1900s, a canopy of trees shaded the residential section of Elm Street. The street was chosen by many of Lumberton's leading citizens and businessmen as a site to build their homes. The home of Robert D. and Dovie Caldwell can be seen on the left. (Courtesy of the Hubbard-Tyner Collection.)

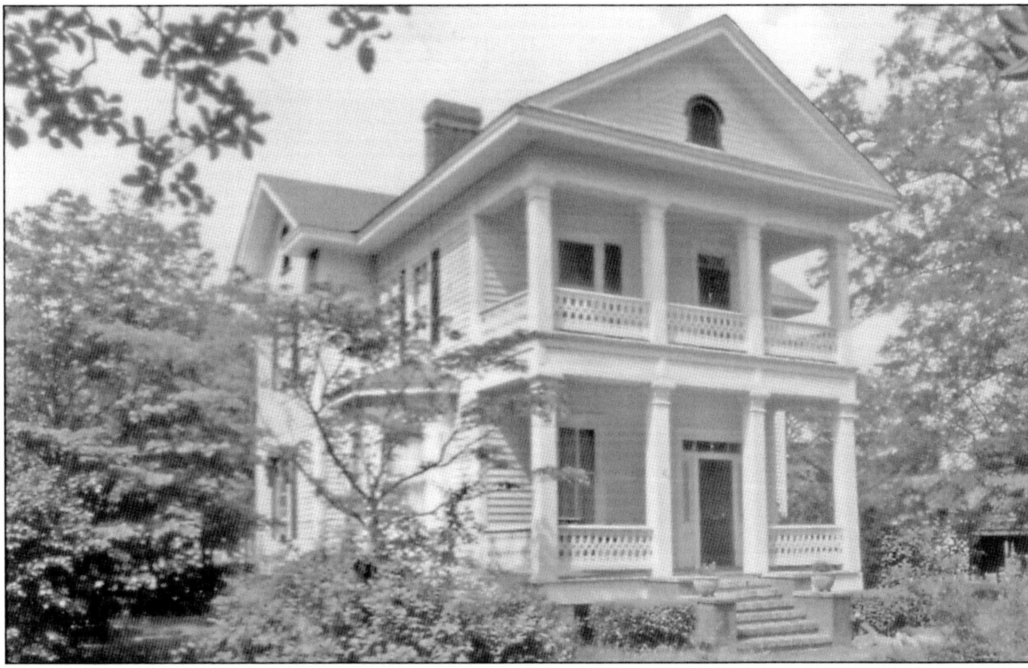

When this two-story transitional Greek Revival/Italianate–style home on Carthage Road was built in 1873 by Col. Alfred Rowland and his wife, Susan Blount, it was located on the outskirts of town. Richard and Lenore Taylor purchased the home in 1961. In front of the home, a heart-shaped bed of boxwood and azaleas is framed by a gravel walk outlined by dry-laid rock in the shape of a chalice. (Courtesy of Historic Robeson, Inc.)

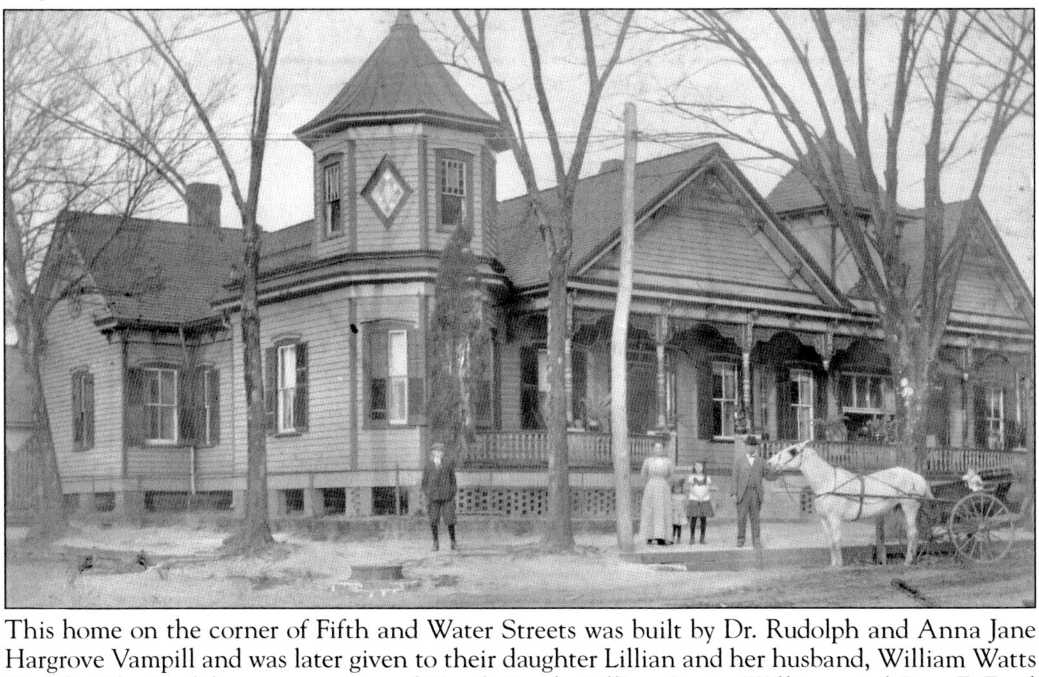

This home on the corner of Fifth and Water Streets was built by Dr. Rudolph and Anna Jane Hargrove Vampill and was later given to their daughter Lillian and her husband, William Watts Carlyle. The Carlyles were parents of Hazel, Sarah, Lillian, Janie, William, and Sen. F. Ertel Carlyle. (Courtesy of the Hubbard-Tyner Collection.)

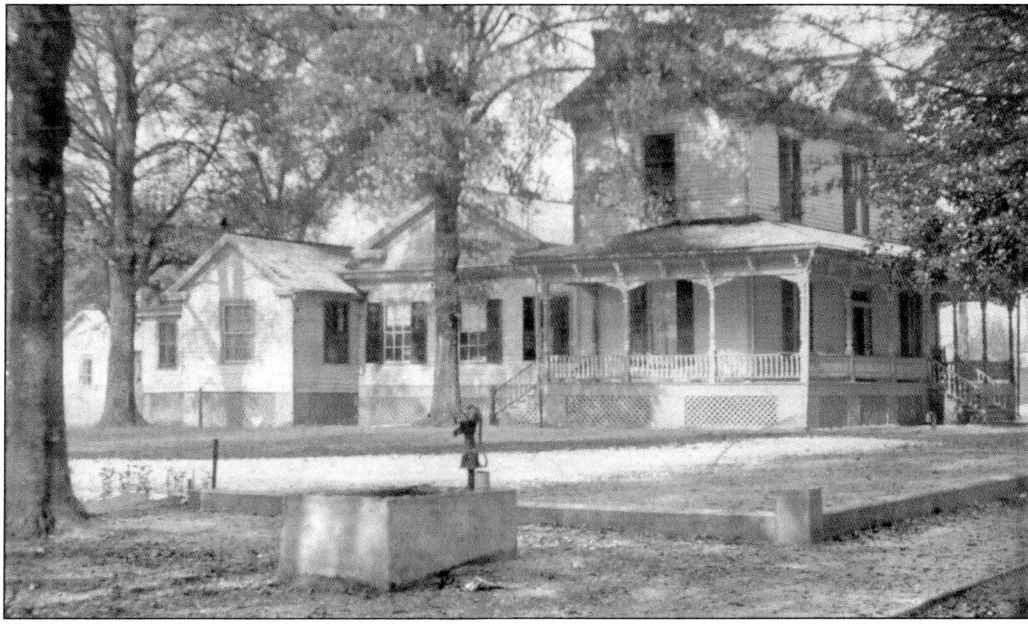

The home of Thomas A. Norment and his third wife, Mollie Rozier, was located at 907 North Elm Street and built around 1875. The couple were the parents of Clinton, Ruth (Mrs. Cutler Moore), and Mary Rozier (Mrs. Louis Stovall). The home was eventually demolished by Clinton Norment to build the Norment Apartments. The pump and concrete box were meant to be used for horses but became a favorite place for neighbor children to flock. (Courtesy of Historic Robeson, Inc.)

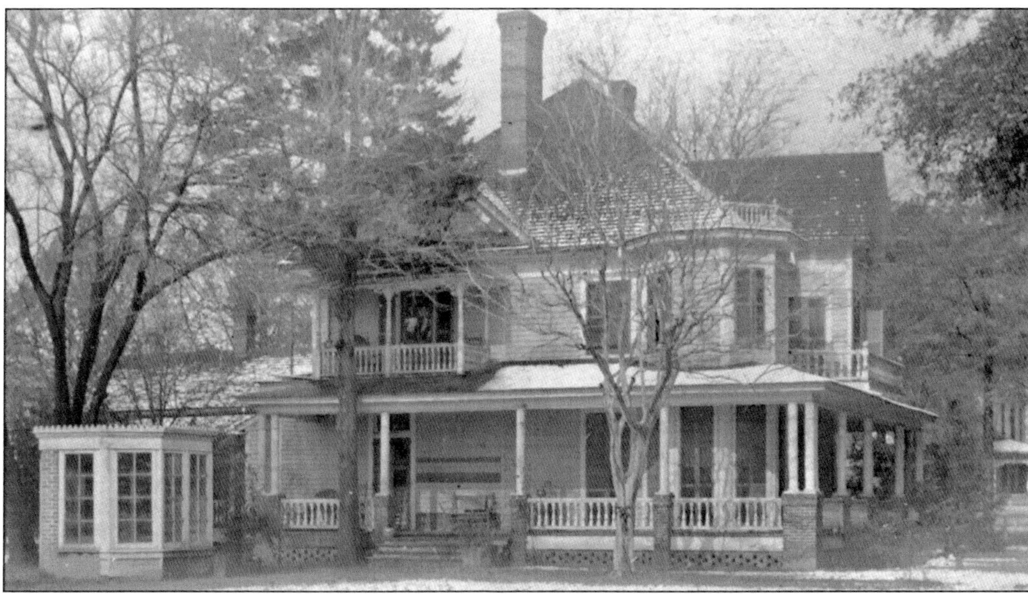

The home of Claude B. Townsend (1851–1940) and his wife, Susan A. Townsend (1848–1931), was located at 811 North Elm Street. Claude was a lawyer, county commissioner, clerk of court, and vice president of National Bank of Lumberton. He was also salutatorian of Trinity College's 1872 class. He and Susan were parents of Vivian, Claudia, and Clare Townsend. Clare was a gifted artist and violinist, and a life-sized statue marks her grave at Meadowbrook. (Courtesy of Historic Robeson, Inc.)

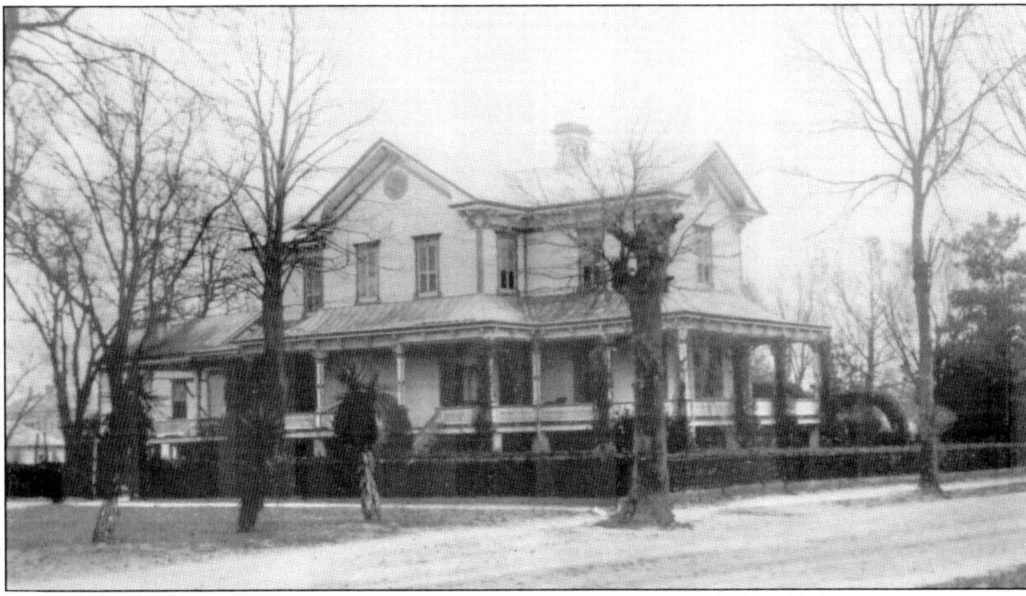

Alexander Hamilton MacLeod, who founded the First National Bank, and his wife, Emily Sarah Blount, built this home in 1876 on the corner of Chestnut Street and Elizabethtown Road. The home was purchased in 1926 by E.J. Britt, who updated and modernized it. It was demolished in 1973, and the site is now home to the Lumberton Housing Authority and the chamber of commerce buildings. (Courtesy of the McLeod Collection, Robeson Remembers, Robeson County History Museum)

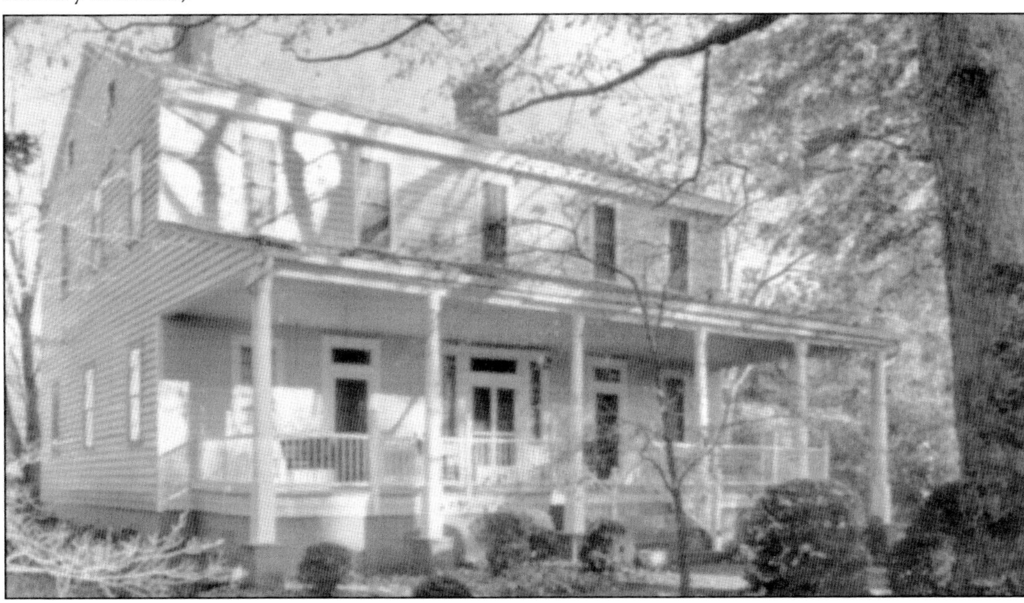

The Humphrey-Williams-Smith Plantation features a Greek Revival- and Tidewater-style residence completed in 1846 by Richard B. Humphrey on property that had been in his family since 1772. The home passed to his daughter and son-in-law Warren and Ann Eliza Williams in 1859, and to their children Robert, Ida, and Janie in 1908. In 1965, Charles Thomas Smith became the owner. The main house was listed in the National Register of Historic Places in 1973, and in 1988, the listing was expanded to include the outbuildings. (Courtesy of the Hubbard-Tyner Collection.)

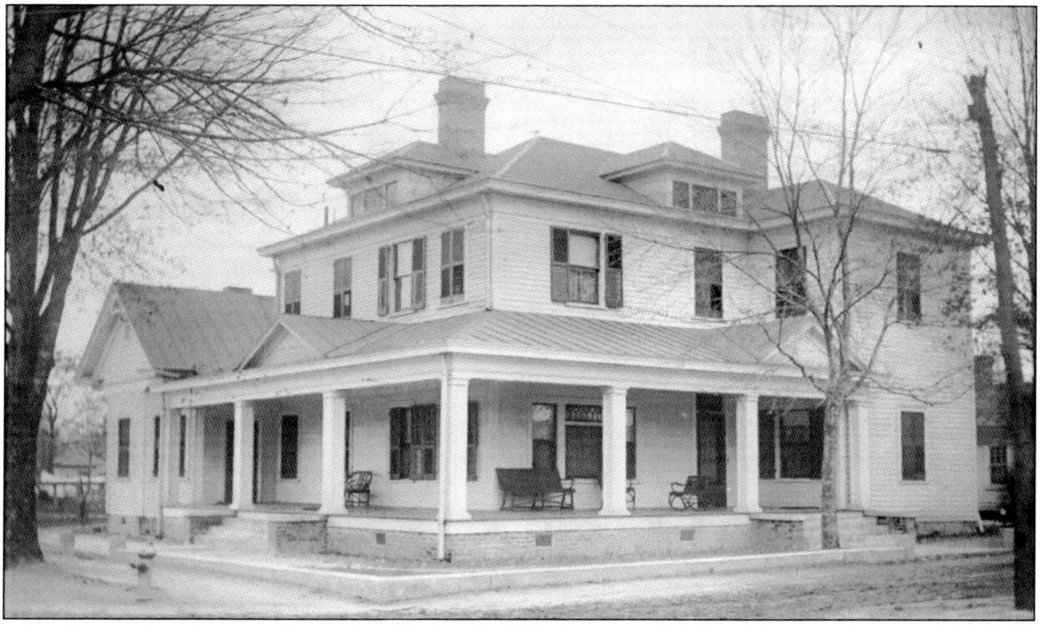

The Quitman Tolton Williams home is located on the corner of Ninth and Caldwell Streets. Williams moved to Lumberton in 1879, and three years later he married Emma Thompson. He founded Q.T. Williams Insurance in 1889, and his son Edwin Williams joined the firm in 1918. After the elder Williams's death in 1931, the firm merged with McLean's Insurance owned by A.T. McLean, forming Williams & McLean. (Courtesy of Historic Robeson, Inc.)

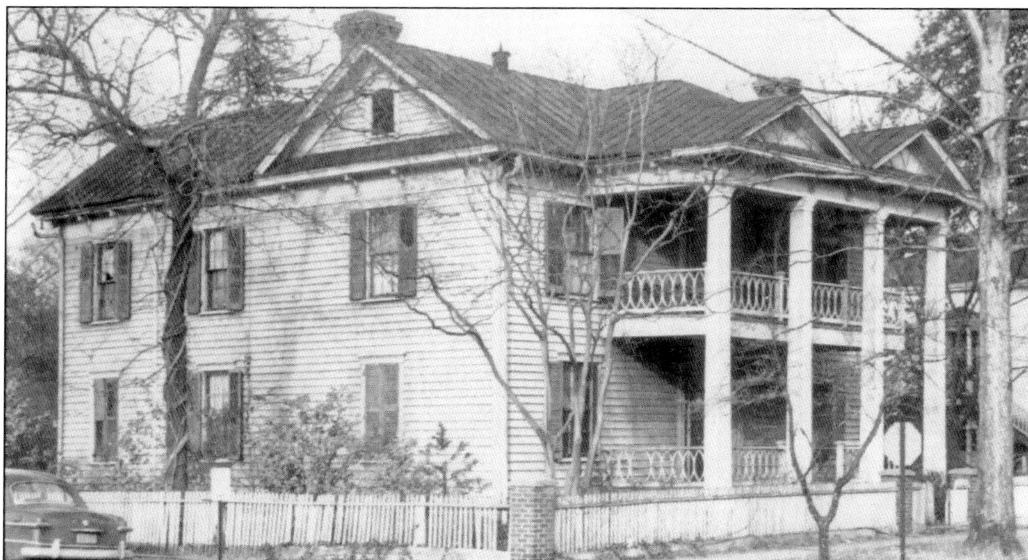

The John and Florence McAllister home faced Sixth Street at the corner of Chestnut Street. John was president of McAllister Hardware. Living with them in 1916 were sons Alexander, secretary-treasurer of the National Cotton Mills; Charles P., a merchant tailor; and John D., manager of McAllister Hardware; and John D.'s wife, Olive. Son Willis, secretary-treasurer of McAllister Hardware and Lumberton Motor Car Co., lived on the same block with his wife, Kate. (Courtesy of Brad Thompson.)

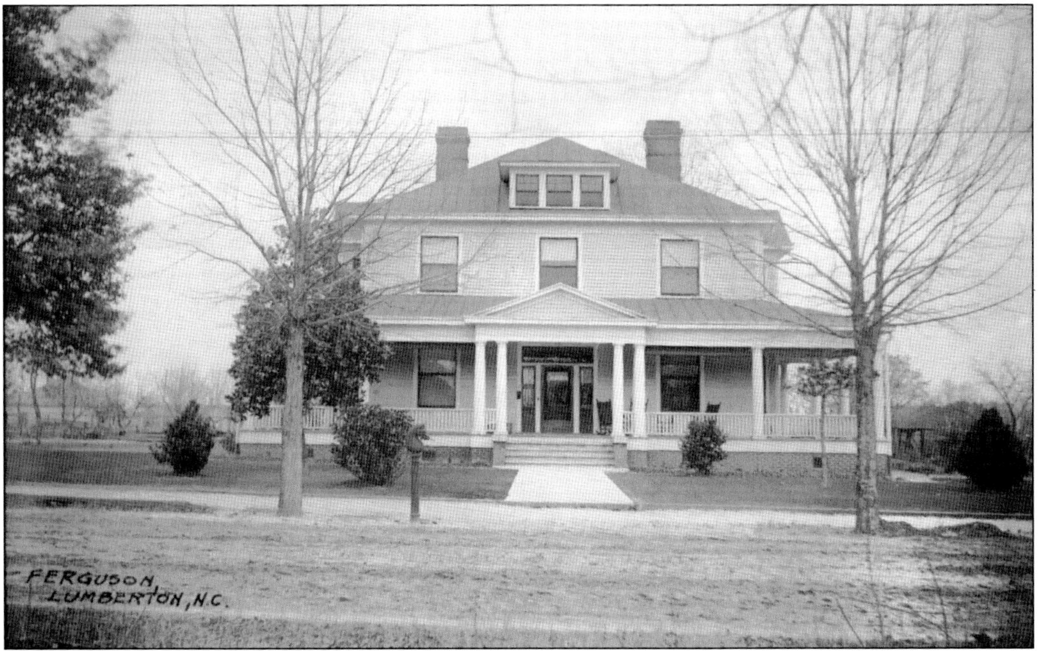

The home of John D. McMillan Jr. was at 606 Cedar Street. McMillan was the owner of McMillan Drugs, located at 313 Elm Street and founded in 1876 by his father, Dr. John D. McMillan Sr., a beloved physician of the horse-and-buggy days who rode the roads of Robeson day and night, winter and summer, upon his healing mission. (Courtesy of Historic Robeson, Inc.)

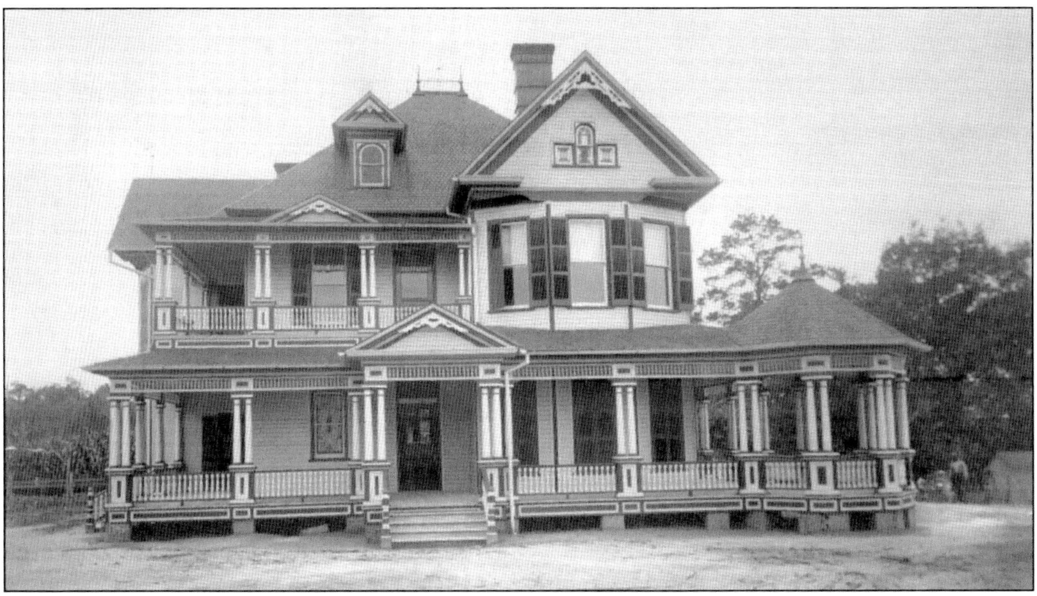

This two-story Queen Anne–style home was built in 1905 for Luther H. Caldwell and his wife, Nora Godwin, by Lumberton builder William Burney. Caldwell owned L.H. Caldwell Co., a general store on the corner of Third and Elm Streets. Christine Caldwell Thompson purchased the home in 1970 from her mother's estate, and in 1978, she had it placed in the National Register of Historic Places. The home was purchased by Brad Thompson and Andrew Fox on July 5, 2012 and they are in the process of restoring it. (Courtesy of Brad Thompson.)

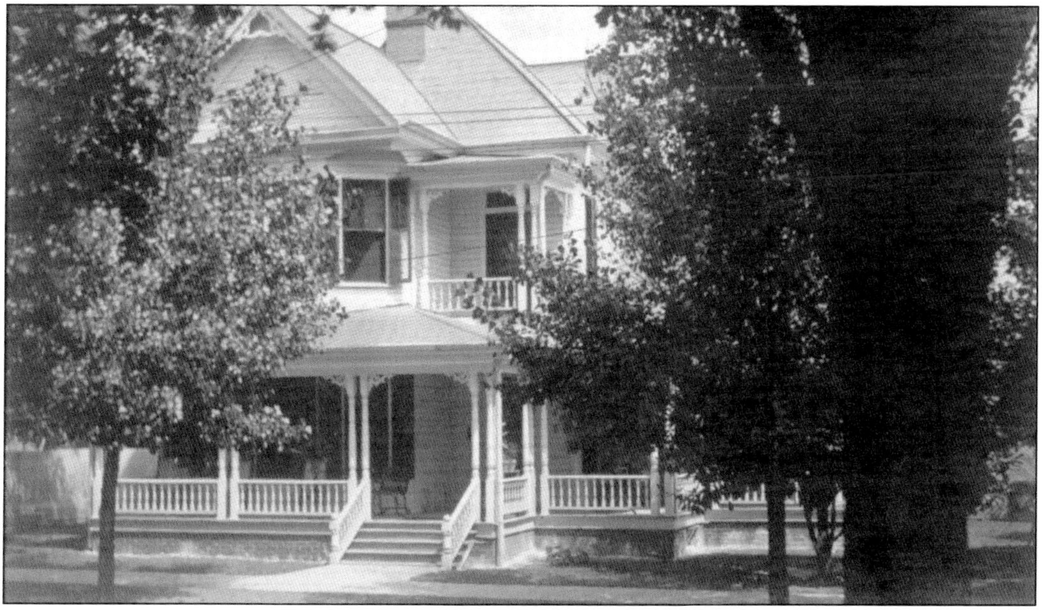

The home of Judge Lycurgus Rayner Varser and his wife, Lillie, was located at 209 East Fifth Street. While in the North Carolina General Assembly, Varser proposed a $75,000 allotment to the Indian Normal School (now UNC Pembroke) to construct the first brick building, now known as Old Main. He served as an associate justice of the North Carolina Supreme Court from 1924 to 1926 after being appointed by his former law partner, Gov. Angus Wilton McLean. (Courtesy of Historic Robeson, Inc.)

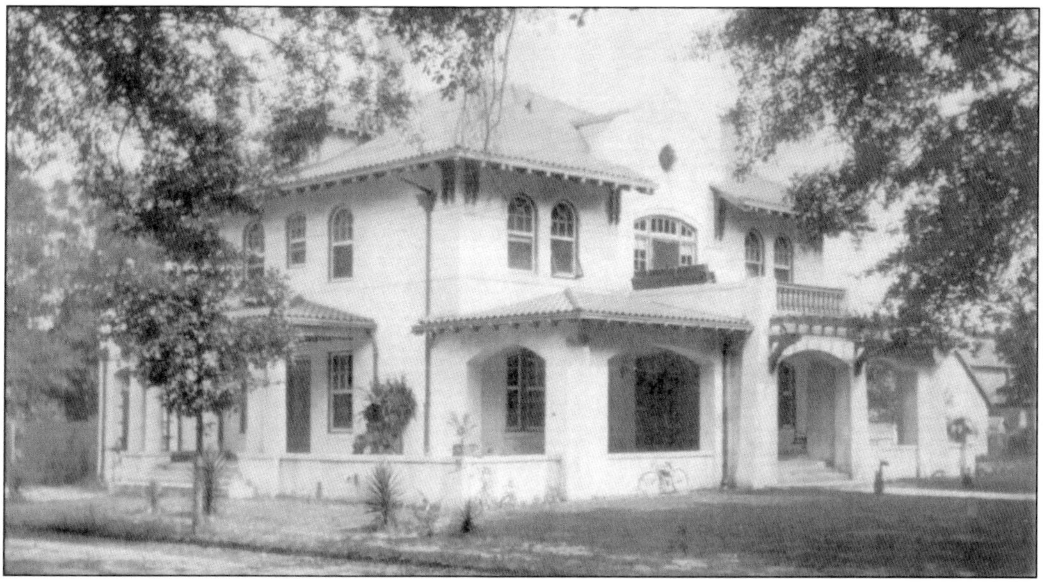

The Spanish-style home of Henry B. Jennings and his wife, Ada McLean (the daughter of Col. Neill Archibald McLean Jr. and Elizabeth Townsend), was located on the corner of Eighth and Elm Streets. Their son Dudley Lamont Jennings and his wife, Hoyland Livermore, lived in the home for many years. It was purchased by Biggs Funeral Home in 1970 and demolished to make a parking lot. Jennings was very active in the cotton-mill industry, owning the Jennings and Ada McLean Cotton Mills. (Courtesy of Brad Thompson.)

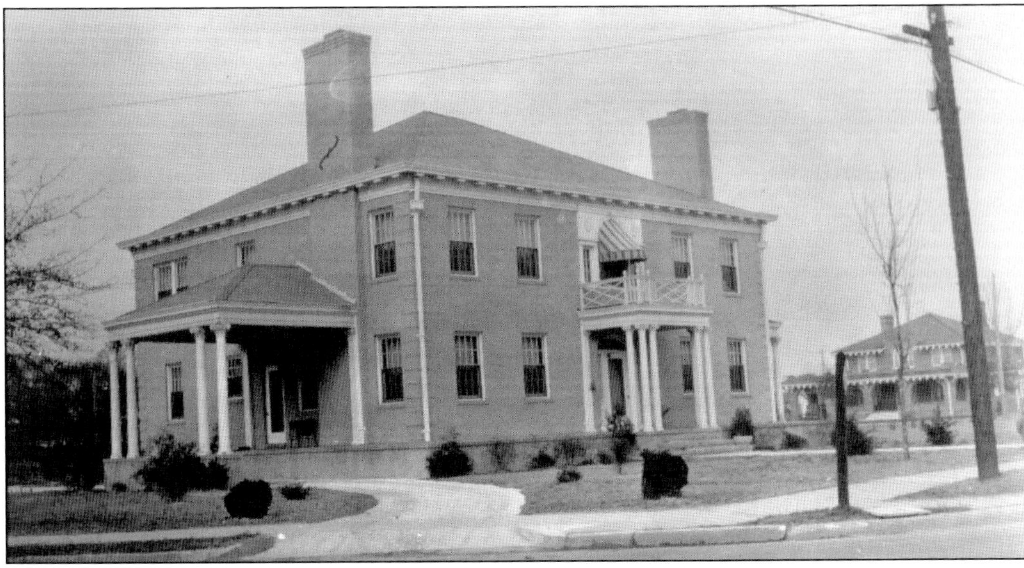

This Walnut Street home was built around 1918 for Lumberton lawyer and historian Robert Carbelle Lawrence and his wife, Emma Norwood. Lawrence moved to Lumberton in 1903 and became the law partner of Stephen McIntyre. He authored *The State of Robeson* and *Here in Carolina* in addition to writing historical sketches for the *Robesonian* and the *State* magazine. He died at Dorthea Dix Hospital in 1944 at the age of 67. (Courtesy of Historic Robeson, Inc.)

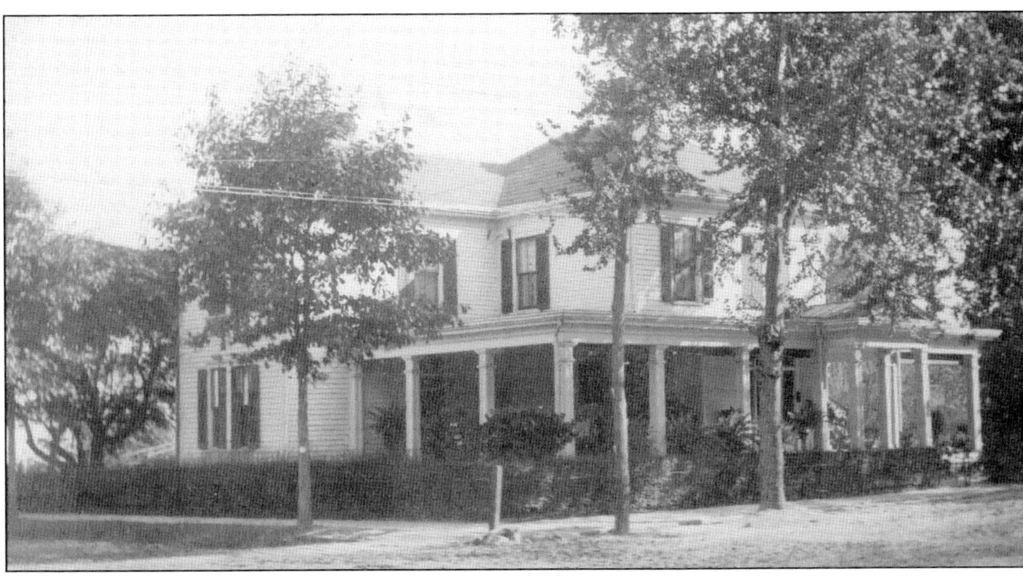

This is the home of Stephen and Minta McIntyre, which was located at 512 North Walnut Street. They were the parents of Mildred, Lillian, Robert A., and Stephen. He came to Lumberton and was in law practice with Edward Knox Proctor Jr. He was a North Carolina senator from 1899 to 1903. He served for many years as deacon and men's Sunday school teacher at First Baptist. (Courtesy of the Hubbard-Tyner Collection.)

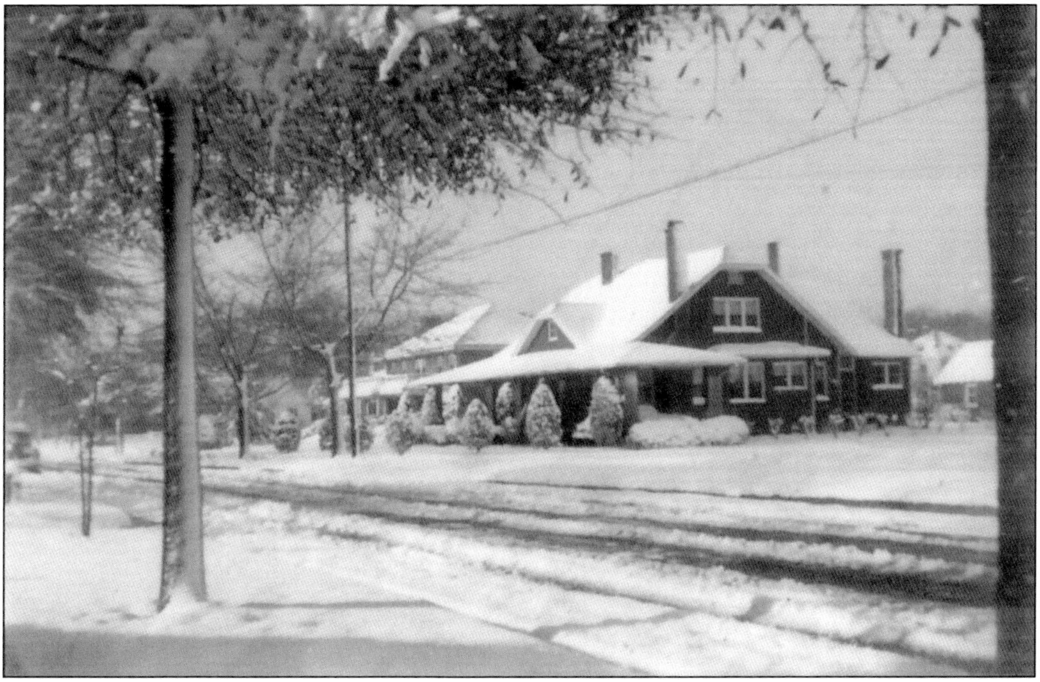

This Walnut Street home was built by W.H. Gray in 1928 for his wife, Mary. In 1931, Don and Sarah McGill purchased the home, and in 1933, it was sold to William and Ada Pittman Best. Merle and Ann Summers purchased it in 2001. This photograph was taken during a 1942 snowstorm. (Courtesy of Merle and Ann Summers.)

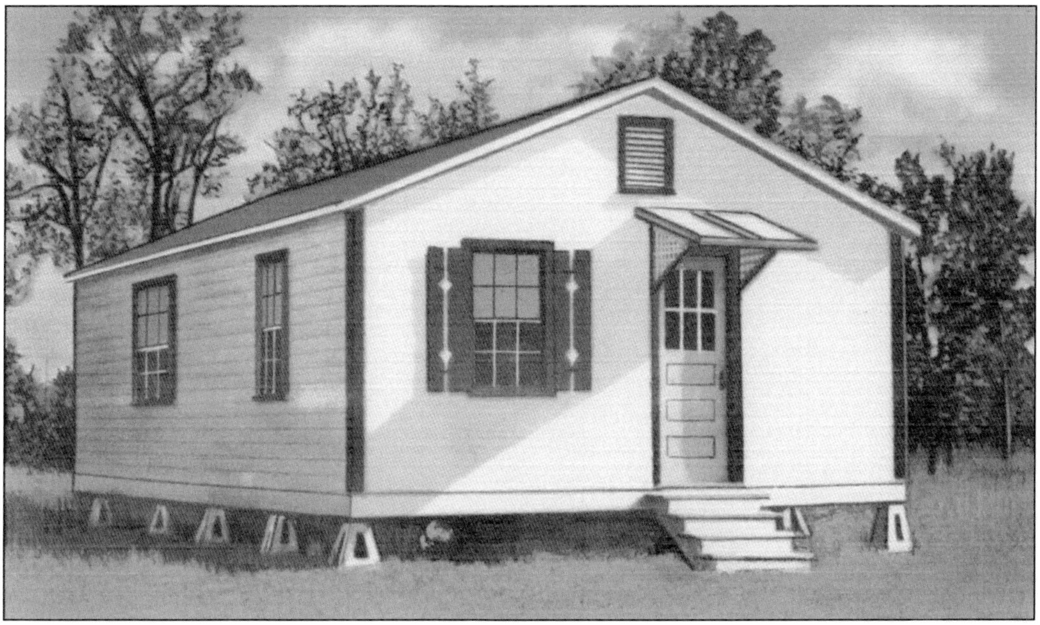

Advertising for the Domino Home began in October 1940 and focused on the benefits of owning one's own home rather than paying rent. The homes started at $440 and required only a small down payment and then a reasonable monthly payment. The prefabricated homes could be viewed at the company's plant on Elizabethtown Road. (Courtesy of the Hubbard-Tyner Collection.)

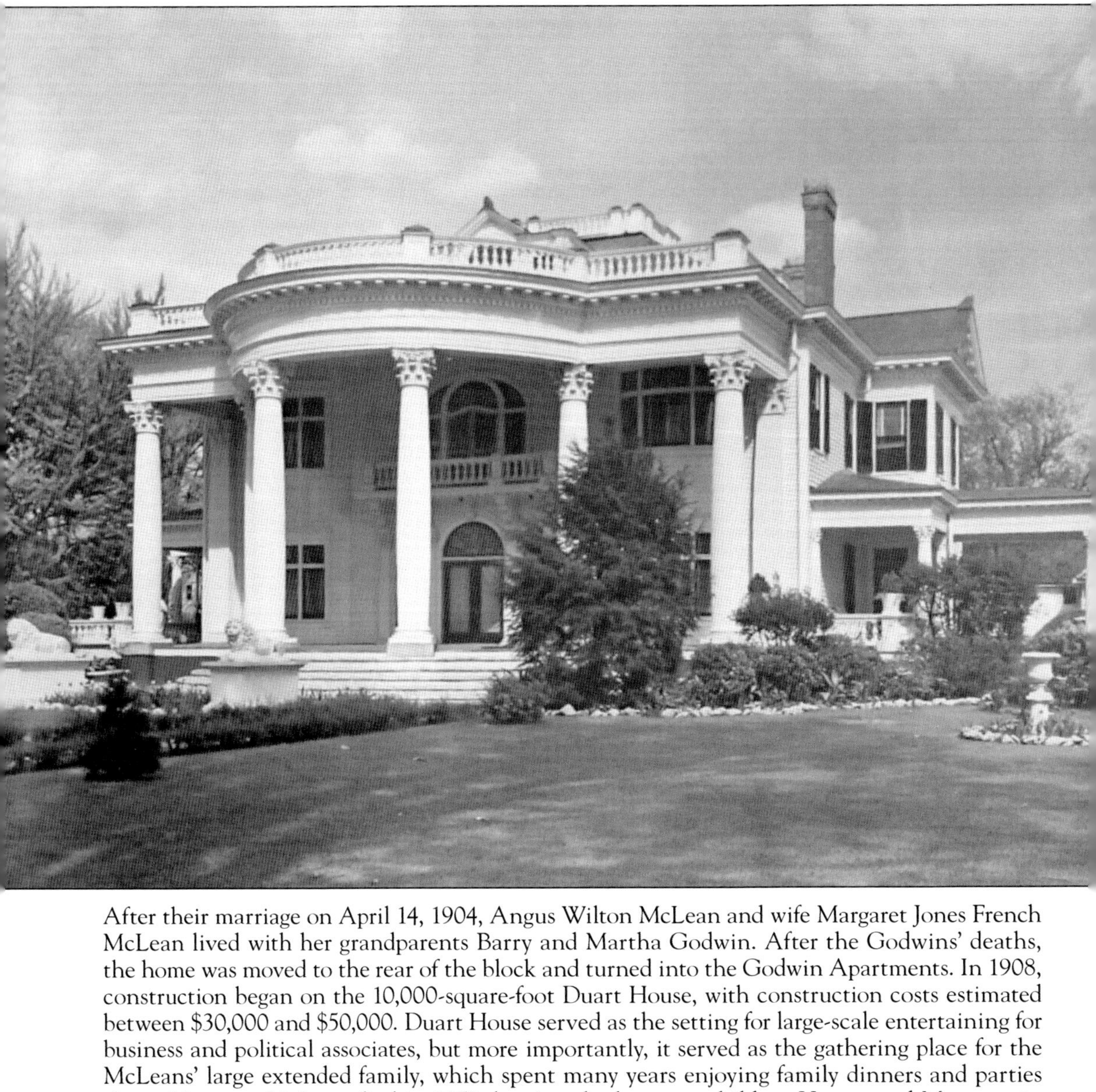

After their marriage on April 14, 1904, Angus Wilton McLean and wife Margaret Jones French McLean lived with her grandparents Barry and Martha Godwin. After the Godwins' deaths, the home was moved to the rear of the block and turned into the Godwin Apartments. In 1908, construction began on the 10,000-square-foot Duart House, with construction costs estimated between $30,000 and $50,000. Duart House served as the setting for large-scale entertaining for business and political associates, but more importantly, it served as the gathering place for the McLeans' large extended family, which spent many years enjoying family dinners and parties there. Margaret McLean died in 1959, leaving the home to children Hector and Margaret in the hopes that they would develop it into a business property. According to her will, her only wish was "that my yard and gardens not be turned into a parking lot as I would not like for my home to suffer this indignity." Two years later, Duart House was demolished, and in 1967, the headquarters of Southern National Bank, founded by Angus Wilton McLean, was built. (Courtesy of Marshall Shepherd.)

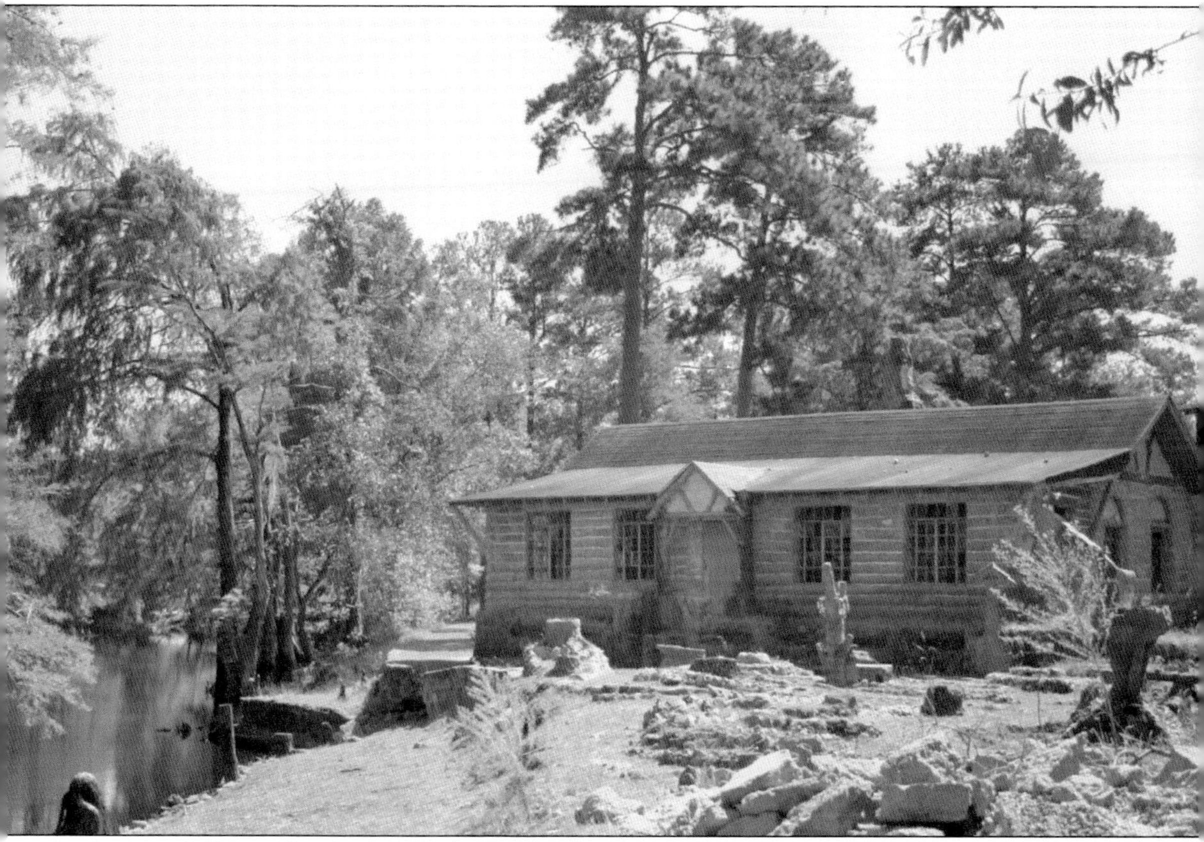

In the years following her husband's death, Margaret Jones French McLean desired a place where she could entertain in a more casual atmosphere than her main residence. Her answer was to build a home along the Lumber River on part of the National Cotton Mill property in West Lumberton. She chose German-born stonemason Christ Meyer as the builder for her river retreat. Meyer had come to America in 1905 and had become naturalized in 1929. In October 1939, he arrived in Lumberton and worked at the St. Frances de Sale Catholic Church. His masterpiece was to become known as "McLean Castle." The home has the appearance of a Bavarian mountain home, but it is constructed completely of cast concrete. The Castle served as a place to entertain the family for many years before being sold. (Courtesy of the Hubbard-Tyner Collection.)

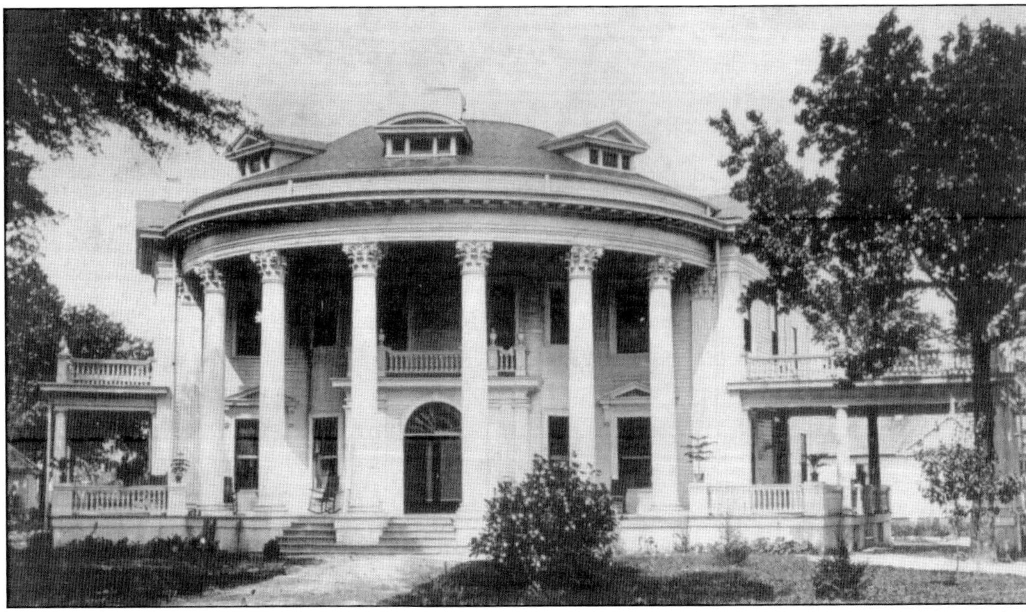

Albert Edward White and Ellen Fuller built this home in the triangular lot formed by Eighth Street and Elizabethtown Road at Chestnut Street. The front featured five columns seven feet around and twenty-five feet high. The Whites had one daughter, Vashti, who married Dr. Russell S. Beam and had one son, Russell S. Beam Jr. After the deaths of her husband and son, she married James Hall. (Courtesy of Brad Thompson.)

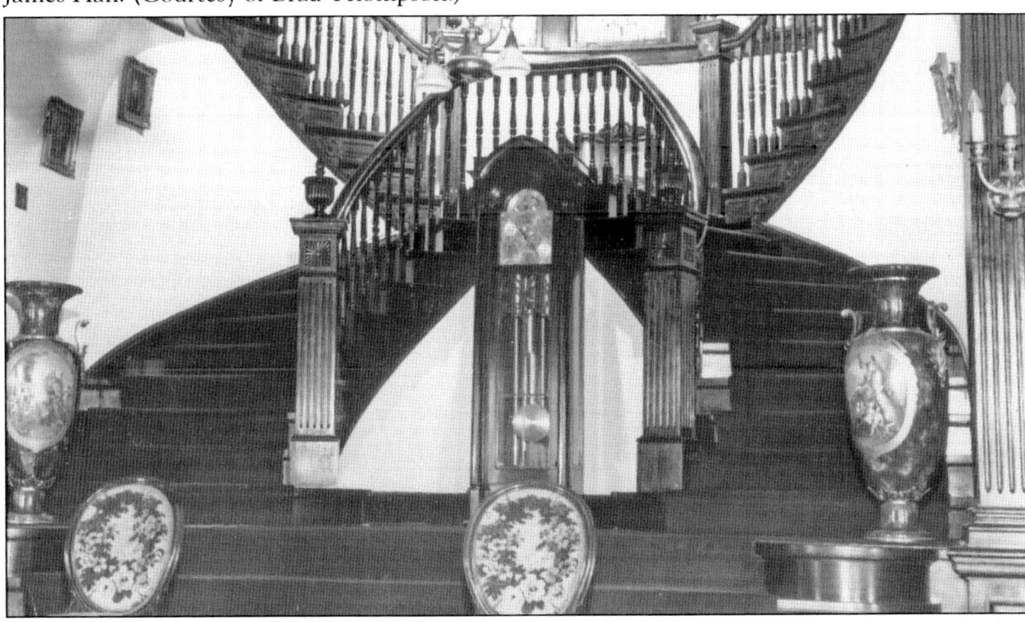

The entry hall of the White home featured a magnificent split staircase with stained-glass windows on the landing. The home had all the modern conveniences of the time, including speaking tubes to connect each room with the staff in the kitchen. The home was purchased by the Chestnut Street United Methodist Church in 1970 and was used as a youth center for several years. It was demolished around 1973, and the land was turned into a parking lot. (Courtesy of Brad Thompson.)

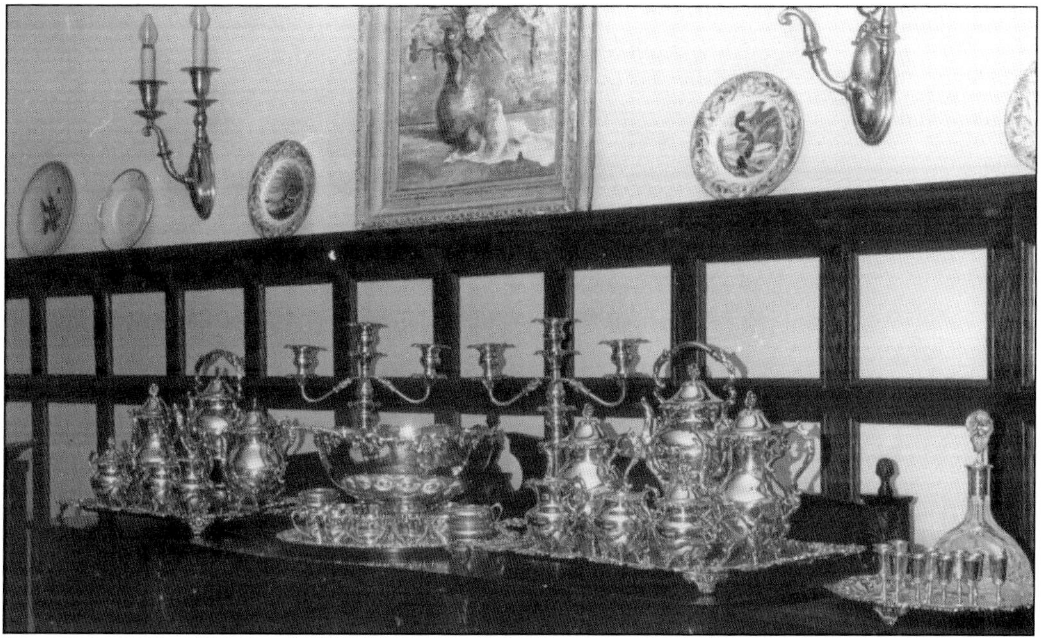

The dining room of the White home featured beautiful mission oak paneling and was the setting of wonderful dinner parties hosted by the Whites. Albert White served as mayor and had extensive business concerns in Lumberton, including a mercantile business and the Bank of Lumberton, and he also served as vice president of the Jennings and Mansfield Cotton Mills. Dr. Beam was president of the Lumberton Theatre Company that operated the Carolina and Pastime Theatres. (Courtesy of Brad Thompson.)

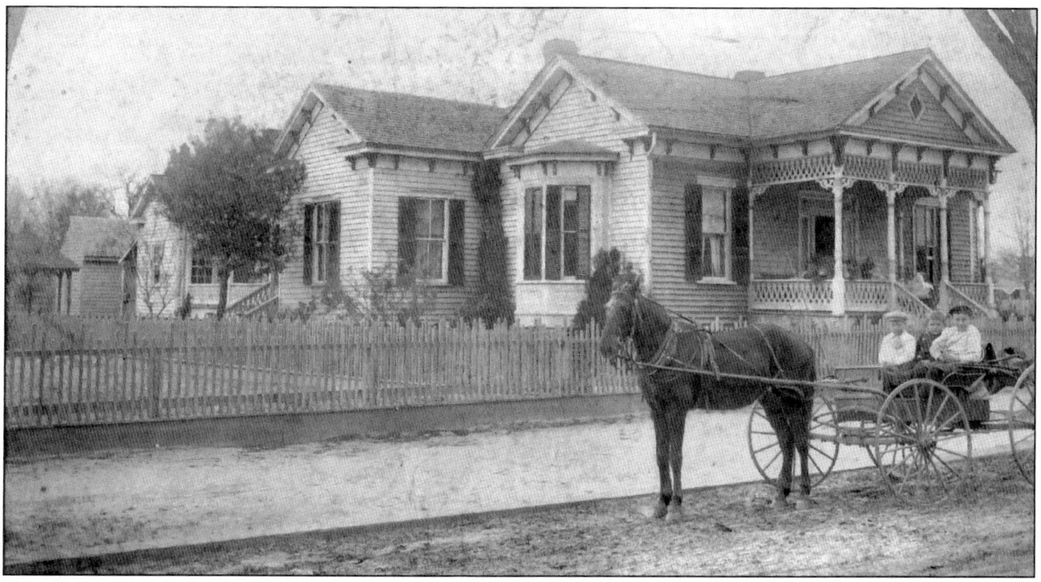

This home built by Robert David Caldwell and wife Dovie Carlyle on Elm Street is where they spent the early years of their marriage. They were parents of Robert David Caldwell Jr., William Edward Caldwell, Simeon Foster Caldwell, Mary Corinne Caldwell, Annie Ruth Caldwell, and Sarah Caroline Caldwell. The home was moved around the corner to face Eighth Street and became the home of their son, Simeon Foster Caldwell. (Courtesy of Ruth Ann Baker McLellan.)

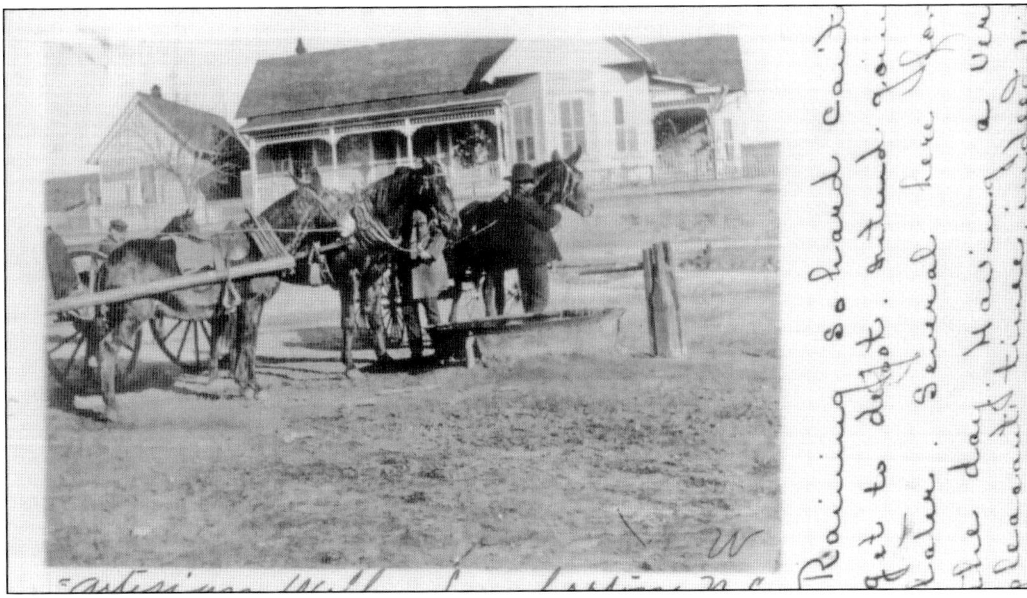

Beside the Caldwell home was an artesian well and gully that ran between Elm and Water Streets. It was this area that Dovie Caldwell used to establish her sunken garden when they built their new home around 1910. It was terraced, grassed, and featured shrubbery and a fountain as a continuation of the grounds of the Caldwell home. It was a place of beauty enjoyed by its owners and everyone passing by. Steps led into it from the Caldwell home. (Courtesy of the Carolina Collection, UNC-Chapel Hill.)

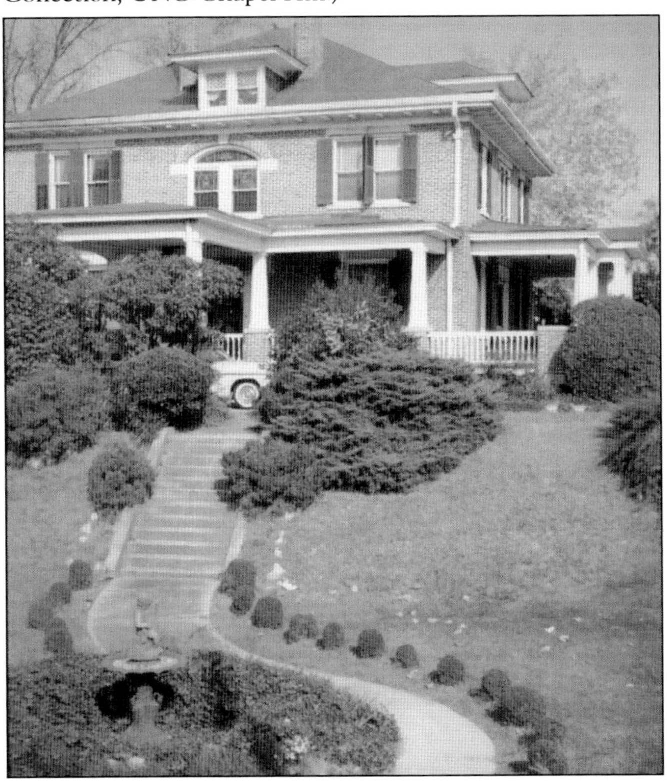

This brick home was built by the Caldwells after they moved their former home around the block. The home's wonderful sunken garden was the talk of the town and the scene of many parties and receptions. This house was later home to their son-in-law and daughter, Dr. Horace and Annie Ruth Baker. The home was razed in 1960 along with the original home to construct the Colonial Store. It is now the site of the of the county's administration offices. (Courtesy of Ruth Ann Baker McLellan.)

Seven

EDUCATION

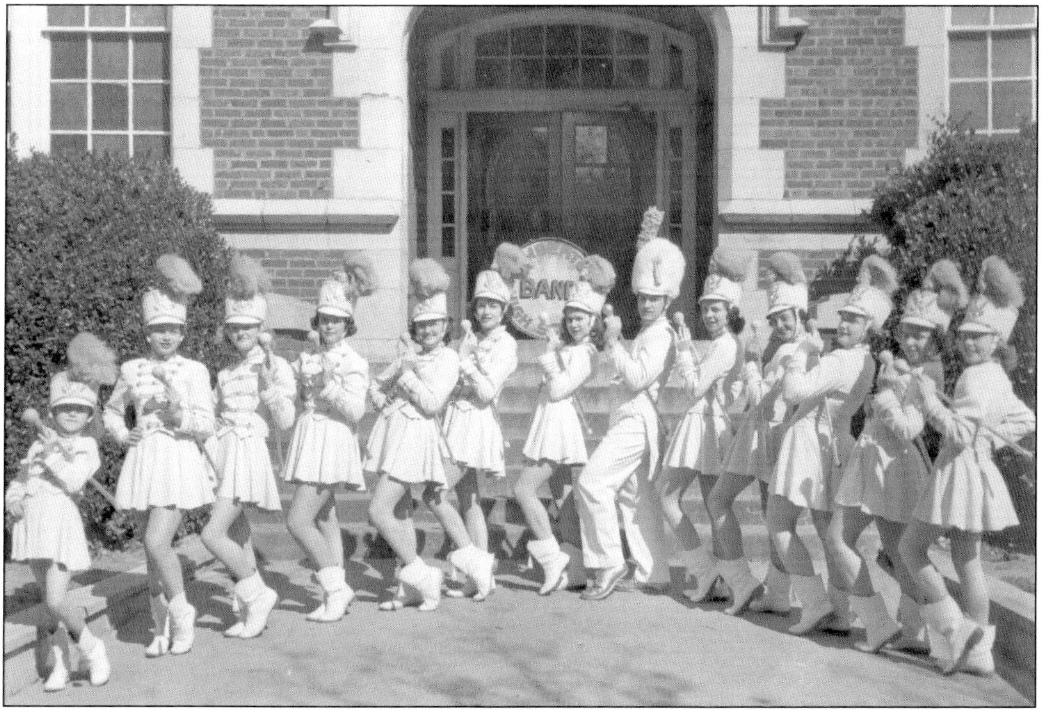

These Lumberton High School Band majorettes are pictured around 1948. They are, from left to right, junior majorette Patsy Bullock Davis, unidentified, Linda Anderson, unidentified, Jackie Kissam, ? Townsend, Shirley Rogers, I.P. Sealey, Nell Boone Crofton Wellington, Nancy Burns, Pat McQueen, Connie Huntley Floyd, and Marilyn Stacy. (Courtesy of Gillespie Studio Collection Robeson County History Museum.)

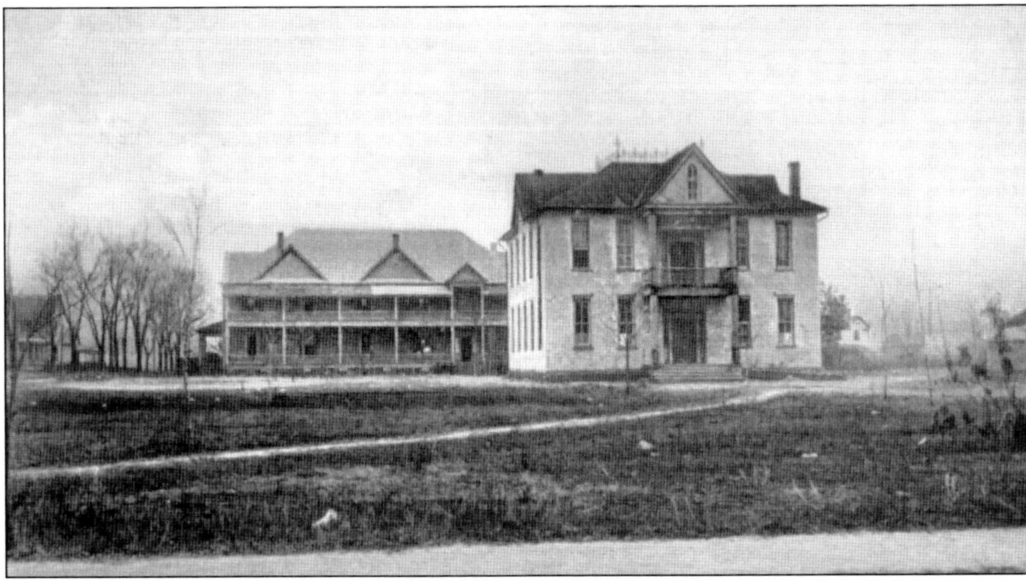

R.D. Caldwell, Berry Godwin, Frank Gough, A.C. Melke, and E.K. Proctor Jr. founded the Robeson Institute in Lumberton in 1891. The school was lead by John Duckett, former superintendent of public instruction in Wake County, and Gen. Thomas F. Toon. The school's motto was "Do Right." Tuition for primary pupils was $1.50 monthly, and for high school pupils, $3. Board ranged from $3 to $4 per month. Special instruction in French, bookkeeping, or commercial law was 50¢ extra per month. (Courtesy of the Hubbard-Tyner Collection.)

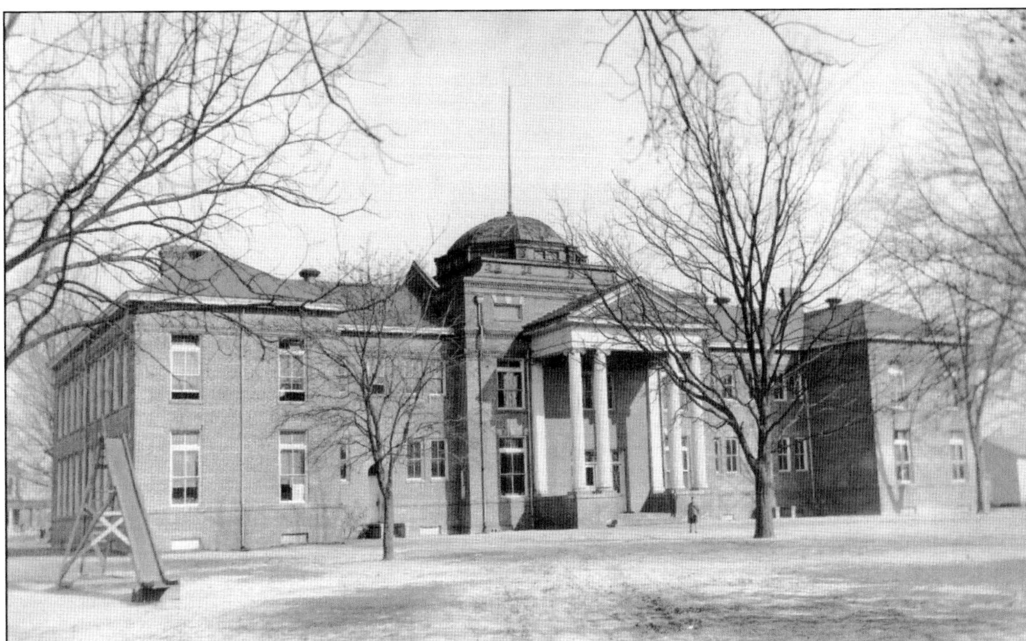

After the Robeson Institute was closed in 1907, the property was sold to the city of Lumberton for use as a grade school. Two wings and a dome were added. In the background is the building used for boarding students, which also functioned as a hotel. The school was demolished in 1941. (Courtesy of Brad Thompson.)

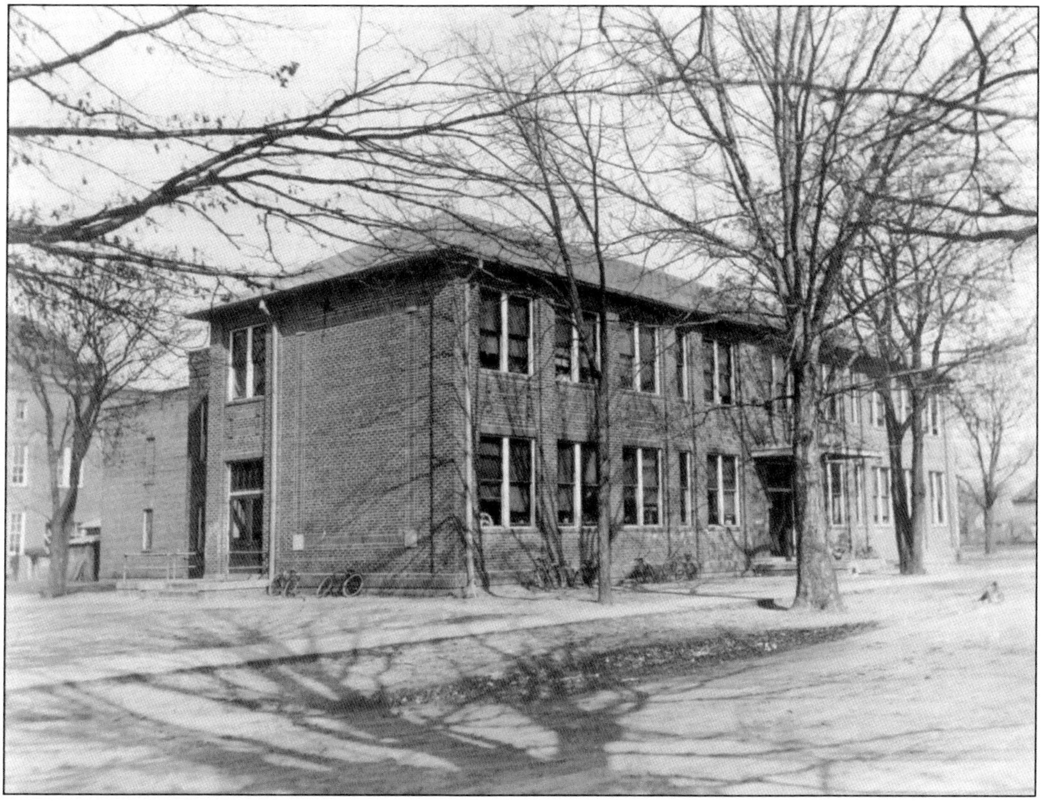

Lumberton's first public high school was built on Walnut Street between 1915 and 1916, but by 1924, it became necessary to build another high school next door. This was later the site of Joe P. Moore School. (Courtesy of Brad Thompson.)

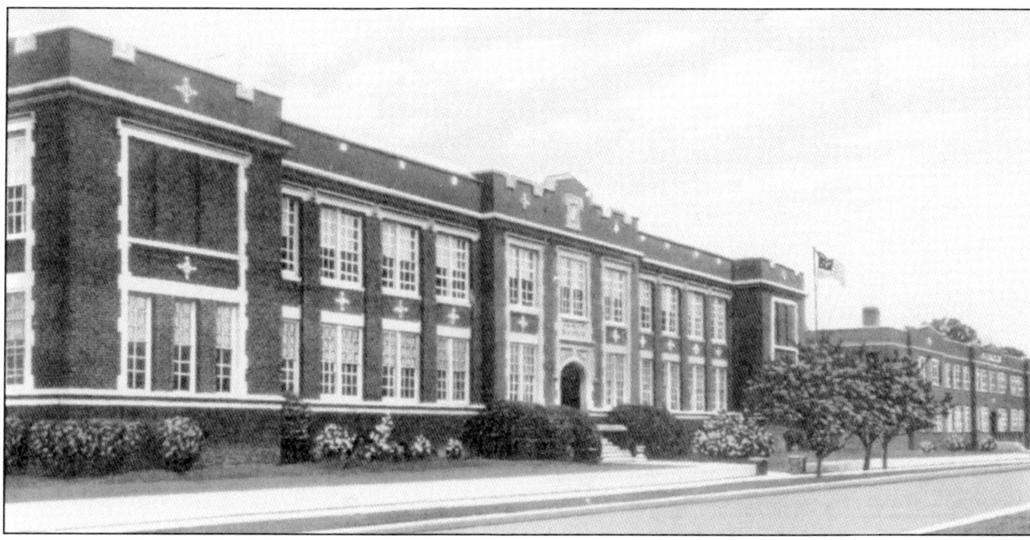

This Lumberton High School was built in 1924, and in 1936, the school term was extended to nine months. The Joe P. Moore School was built next door as a project of the Works Progress Administration. The high school was demolished in 1982. (Courtesy of the Hubbard-Tyner Collection.)

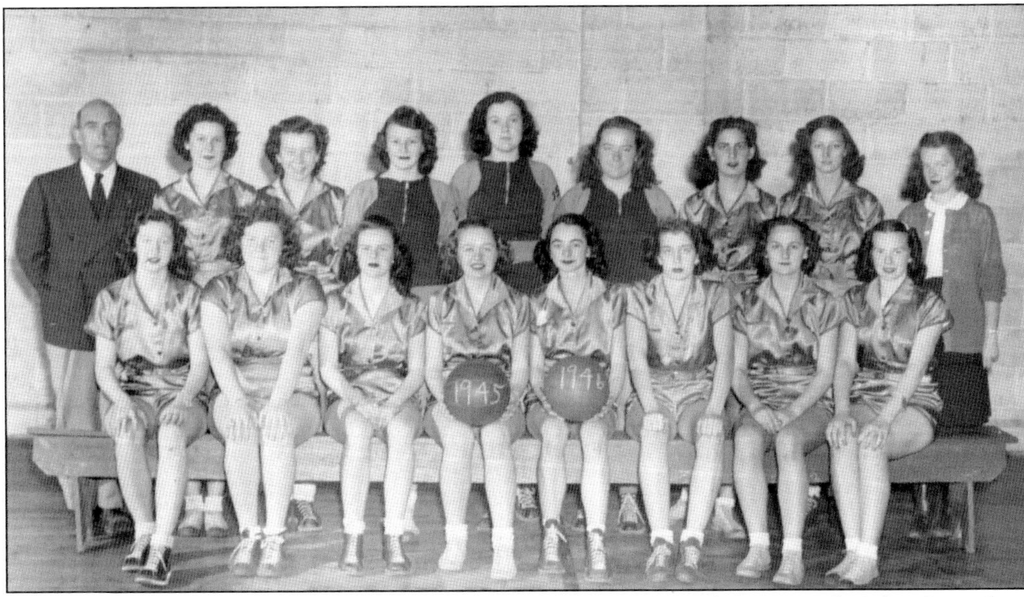

In this photograph of the 1945–1946 girls basketball team of Lumberton High School are, from left to right, (first row) Bonnie Brown (Bunky) Ashe, Rachel Sarbaugh, Oriana McArthur, Jackie Oliver, Kitty Edens, Ann Graham, Peggy Hardee, and Carolyn Lyerly; (second row) coach Jack Richards, Bonnie Ray Wilson, Doris Williams, Marion Skinner, Jeannette Chance, Helen Stone, Doris Everleigh, Margie Brisson, and manager Mary Johnson Stephens. (Courtesy of Jackie Oliver Utz.)

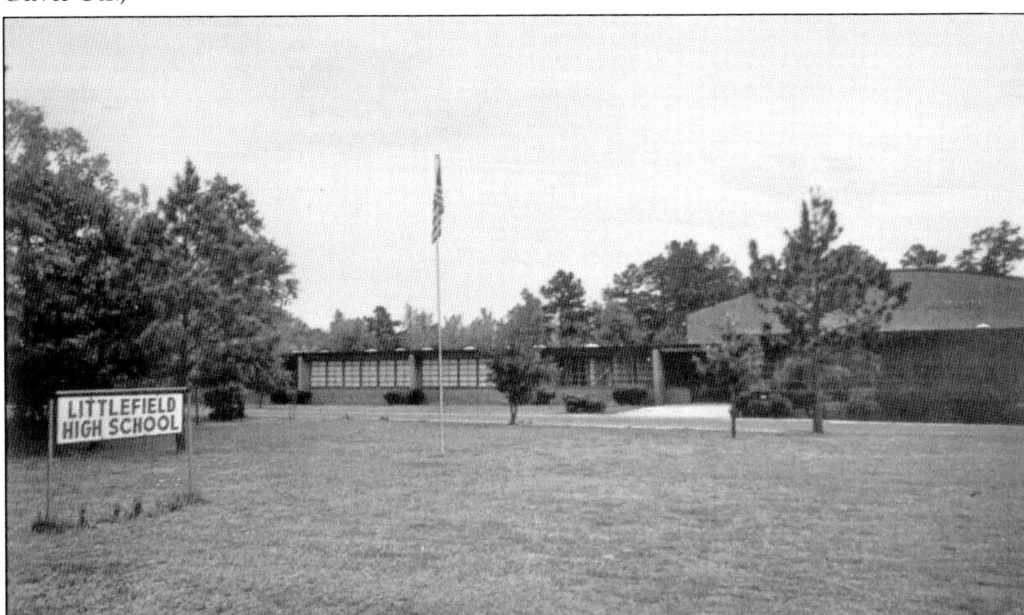

Named for superintendent B.E. Littlefield, this school was opened in the fall of 1955. Barker Ten Mile School, Allenton School, and Smith's Schools had merged to create the new high school, which was located on 17.7 acres six miles east of Lumberton on North Carolina Highway 41. It housed 273 students in its first year. In the fall of 1991, it was made into a middle school. (Courtesy of the Hubbard-Tyner Collection.)

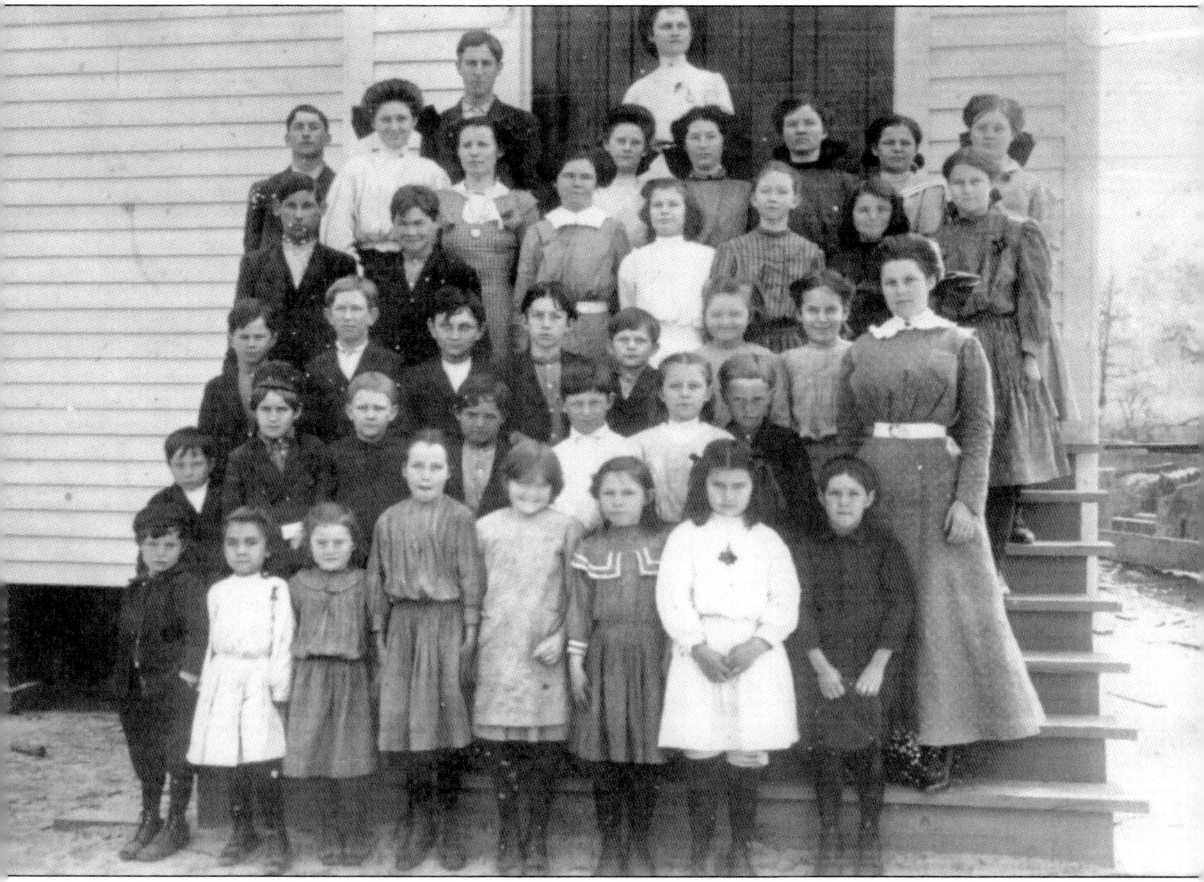

Students of Ten Mile School pose in 1910 on the steps of Ten Mile Baptist Church. The community was so named because of its location 10 miles from Lumberton. Pictured are, from left to right, (first row) Glenn Townsend, Marcy Howell, May Townsend, Janie Martin, Evelyn Regan, Anna Powers, Lizzie Howell, and John Powers; (second row) Edward Musselwhite, Harvey Baxley, Charlie Malone, Murphy Townsend, Sam Britt, Amelia Powers, Leroy Townsend, and teacher Nellie Butler; (third row) Vester Musselwhite, Woody Eubanks, Kindred Howell, Clarence Powers, Frank Malone, Mary Ella Regan, and Libby Baxley; (fourth row) Frank Seals, Pink Barker, Ruth Townsend, Kate Britt, Annie Neal Regan, Tessie Townsend, and Sue Powers; (fifth row) Bertie Seals, Laney Malone, Cora Britt, Polly Malone, Ethel Powers, Nan Willis, Lillie Townsend, and Blache Willis; (sixth row) George Powers, and teacher Florence Butler (Courtesy of Kate Biggs Collection, Robeson Public Library.)

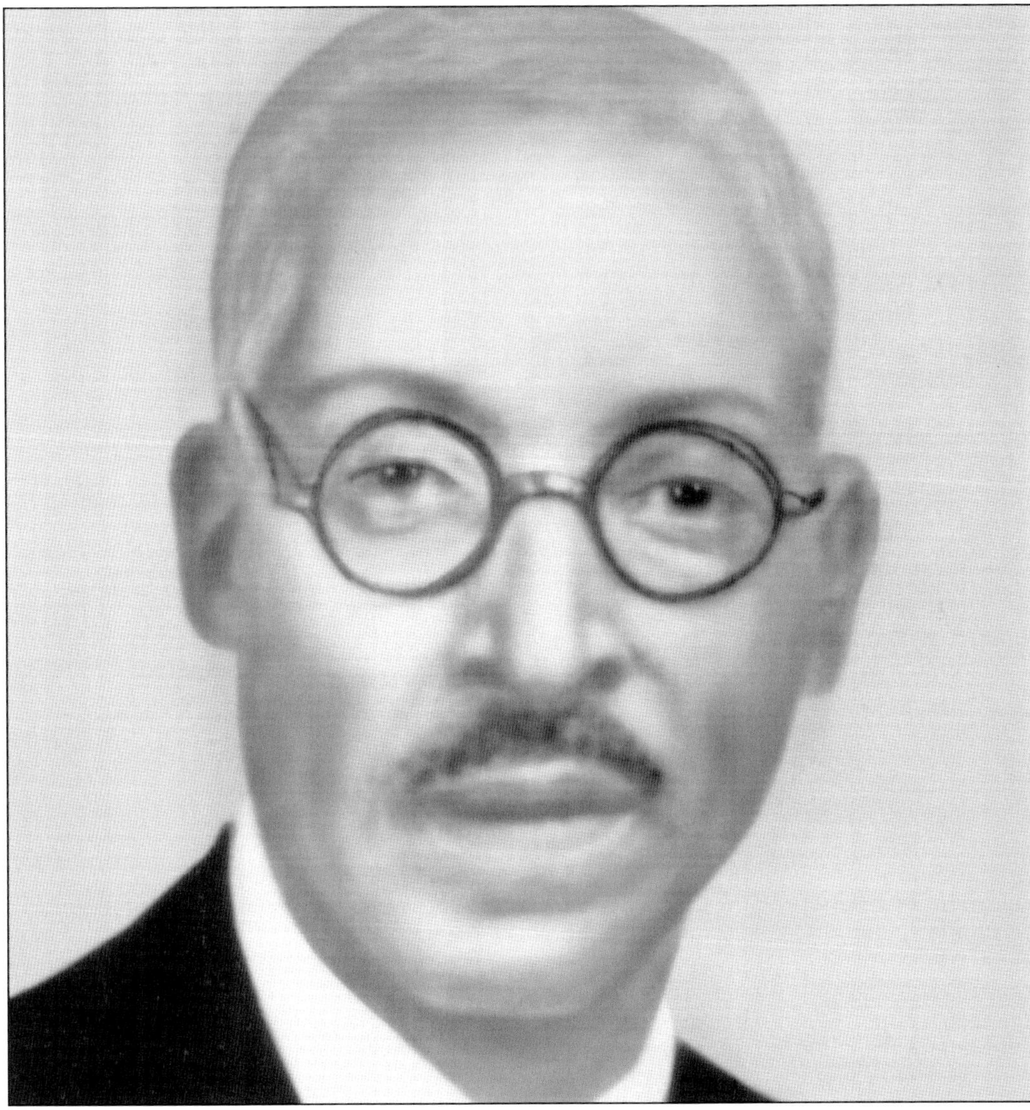

Alexander Hill Thompson was born a slave on June 28, 1828, to the Reverend Alexander A. Thompson and his wife, Margaret. Following the lead of his preacher father, Thompson grew up to be a preacher, educator, community organizer, and also the progenitor of 27 children by two wives. In 1877, he was one of the two founders of the Lumber River Baptist Association, which grew out of the Grey's Creek Association. The Lumber River Missionary Baptist Association was organized in Fair Bluff, North Carolina. The minutes of the Grey's Association show that E.M. Thompson and A.H. Thompson led the way. The association was started to teach the Bible to ministers, who recognized the importance of education for the black population. In 1881, they acquired land and started a school, naming it the Thompson Institute in honor of Alexander H. Thompson and his leadership. The Lake Waccamaw Association donated most of the money, about $1,000. There were three buildings, and Reverend Thompson was the leader while it was a religious school. In 1900, when the institute became specifically an educational institution, the Reverend J. Avery became the first principal, serving two years. Several short-term principals followed until, in 1912, the Rev. W.H. Knuckles became principal and served until 1942. (Courtesy of the Thompson Collection, Robeson Remembers, Robeson County History Museum.)

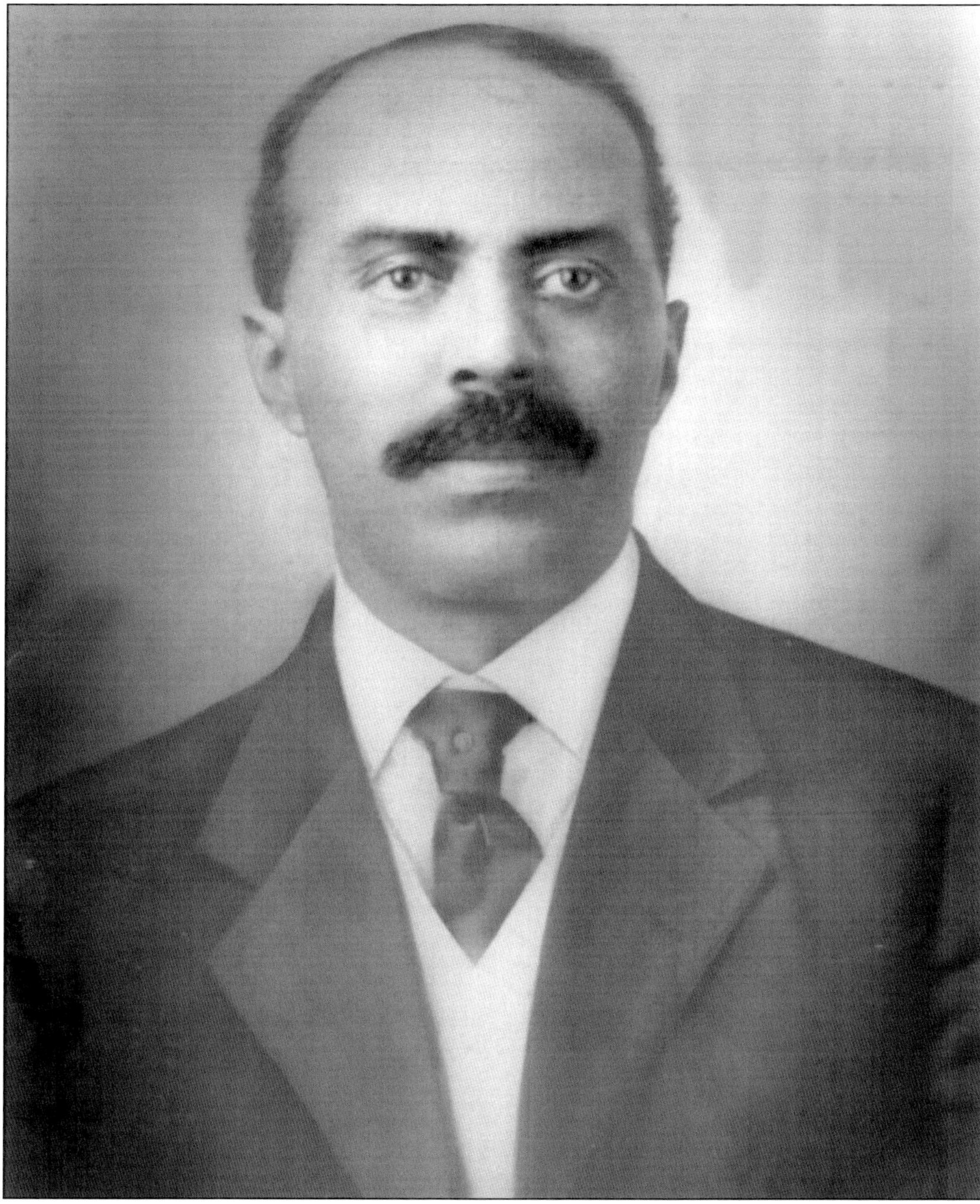

William Henry Knuckles graduated from Shaw University. He came to Lumberton in 1912 to take a position as principal at the Thompson Institute. The original institute was one building, but by 1921, under the administration of Dr. Knuckles, there were five buildings. The main complex—a three-story brick structure with wooden columns—housed dining facilities, classrooms, and living quarters for teachers and students. Under the leadership of Dr. Knuckles, the school attracted students from many of the nearby counties and from several states, some from as far away as New York. Most of the African American teachers employed in the local schools were graduates of the Thompson Institute. Dr. Knuckles passed away in 1942, and W.H. Knuckles Elementary was named in his honor as a lasting memorial. (Courtesy of Knuckles School.)

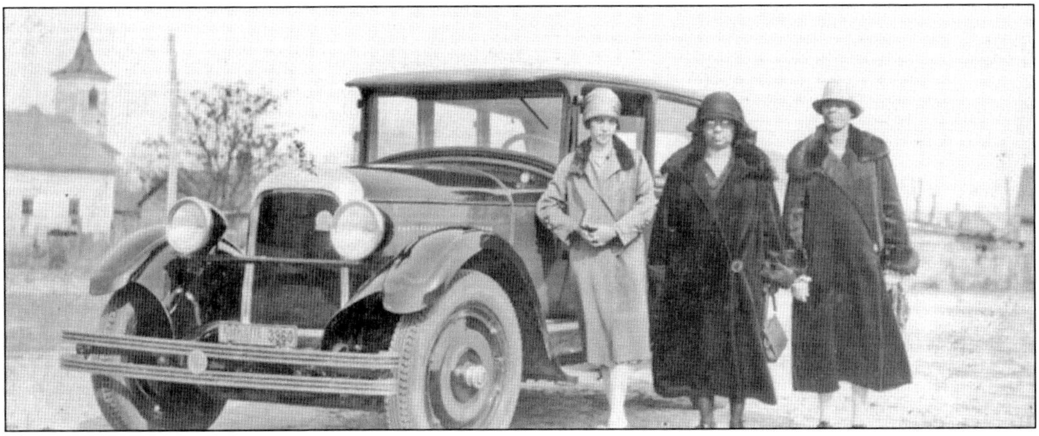

Anne T. Jeanes founded the Jeanes Foundation to train African American educators to teach African American children. Ethel Thompson arrived by train in Lumberton in the 1920s; she had been selected to work as a Jeanes supervisor in Robeson County. Her role was to assist the African American population in their educational objectives, but she found herself a record keeper of black, white, and Indian schools from the 1920s to the 1940s. She developed curricula, recruited and nurtured teachers, and reported on teacher development and student enrollment. Dr. J.H. Hayswood, the pastor of Bethany United Presbyterian Church and an avid educator in his own right, began courting her. The couple married, and though they had no natural offspring, they opened their home to eight children who lived with them at various times. It was understood that all eight would attend college, and they did. Pictured from left to right are Ethel Thompson Hayswood, Annie T. Holland, and Mame Holiday. (Courtesy of the Hayswood Collection, Robeson Remembers, Robeson County History Museum.)

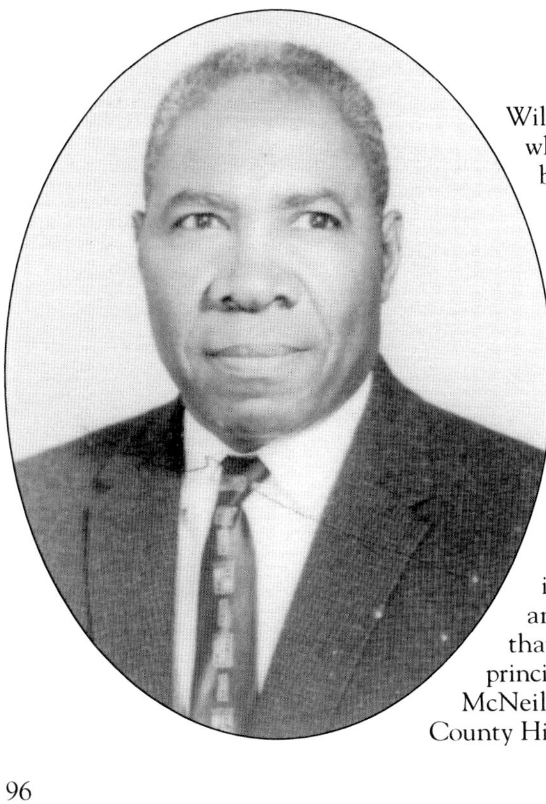

William McKinley McNeill was a local instructor who taught at the Redstone High School. He began teaching there in the mid-1930s. Better known as "Prof" by his students, he wore many hats. McNeill taught math, chemistry, physics and physical education. He coached three sports—football, basketball, and baseball—and served as assistant principal when Dr. John H. Hayswood had to be away from school. McNeill arrived at school at 7:30 a.m. and usually left around 6 in the evening. When his mentor, Dr. Hayswood, retired, the Lumberton School Board named the newly constructed school in his honor and appointed McNeil as principal. At the Hayswood School, his students had the first indoor gym. McNeill was able to hire coaches and other teachers to do many of the activities that he had once done alone. McNeill served as principal from 1949 until his death in 1964. (Courtesy McNeill Collection Robeson Remembers, Robeson County History Museum.)

Eight

CITIZENS

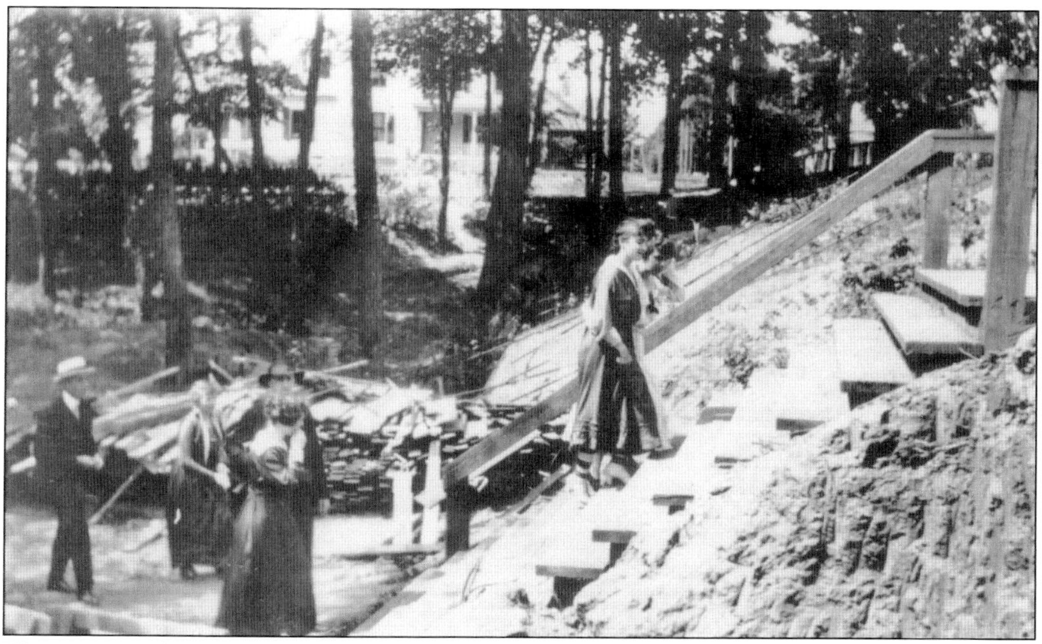

The citizens of Lumberton have always been attracted to the Lumber River that runs through town. Shown here are the wooden steps that lead to the river from Water Street near Sixth Street. Residents used this area to relax and enjoy the water or maybe a picnic. In the background is the Luther Caldwell House. (Courtesy of Historic Robeson, Inc.)

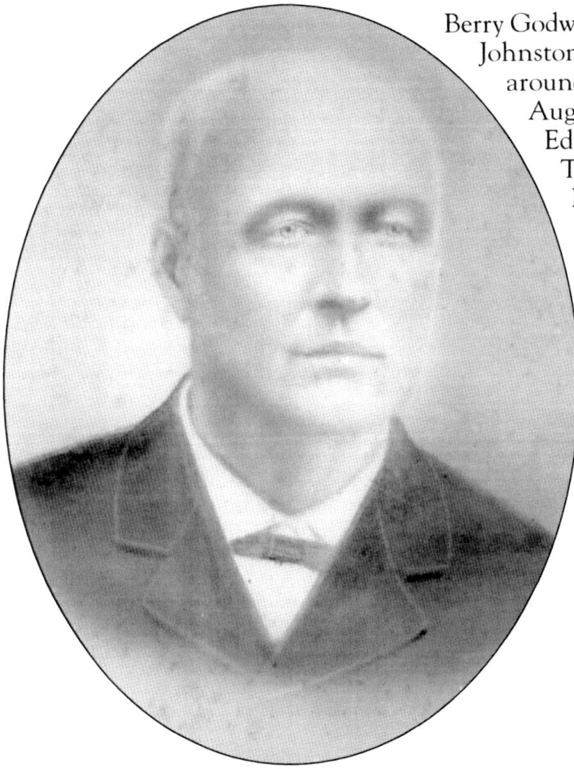

Berry Godwin was born on October 1, 1826, in Selma, Johnston County, and came to Robeson County around 1855 after marrying Martha Faulk on August 27, 1854. They had one daughter, Edna, who married James McDaniel French. The Godwins raised their grandchildren, Margaret Jones French and George Godwin French, after the children's parents divorced. Godwin's interests in Lumberton included large land holdings, a cotton gin, livery stables, and a mercantile business. He also invested very heavily into the Bank of Lumberton and the cotton mills. (Courtesy of the Godwin/French Collection, Robeson Remembers, Robeson County History Museum.)

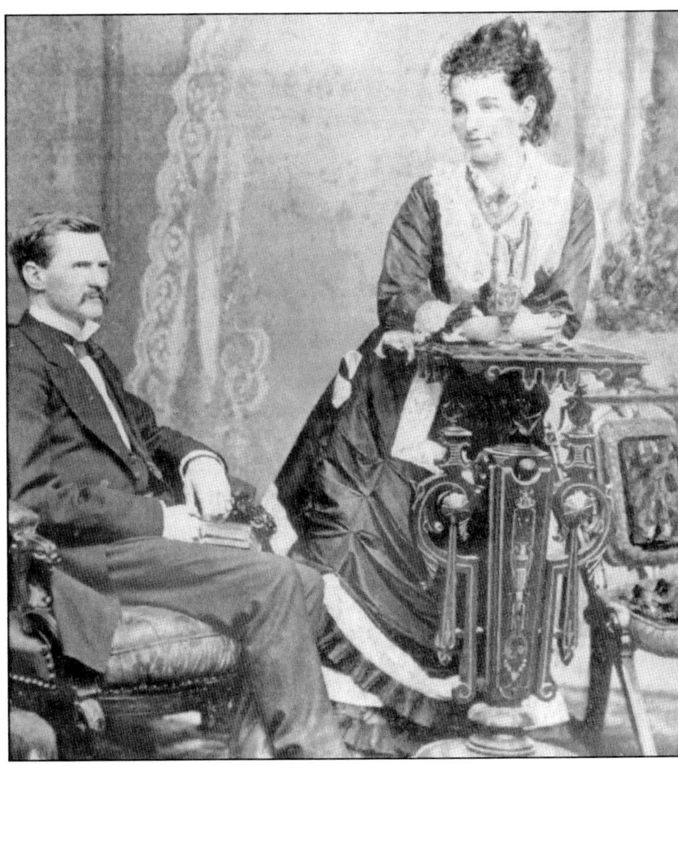

Edna Godwin, daughter of Berry Godwin and Martha Faulk, was born on July 14, 1855, at the family farm, which is in the Bee Gee section of Lumberton. She married James McDaniel French of Wilmington on June 26, 1877. They were the parents of George Godwin French, who married Lee Morrison, and Margaret Jones French, wife of Gov. Angus Wilton McLean. The couple divorced sometime prior to November 1889, and Edna was remarried to a dentist, Dr. John Wesley Griffith. (Courtesy of the Godwin/French Collection, Robeson Remembers, Robeson County History Museum.)

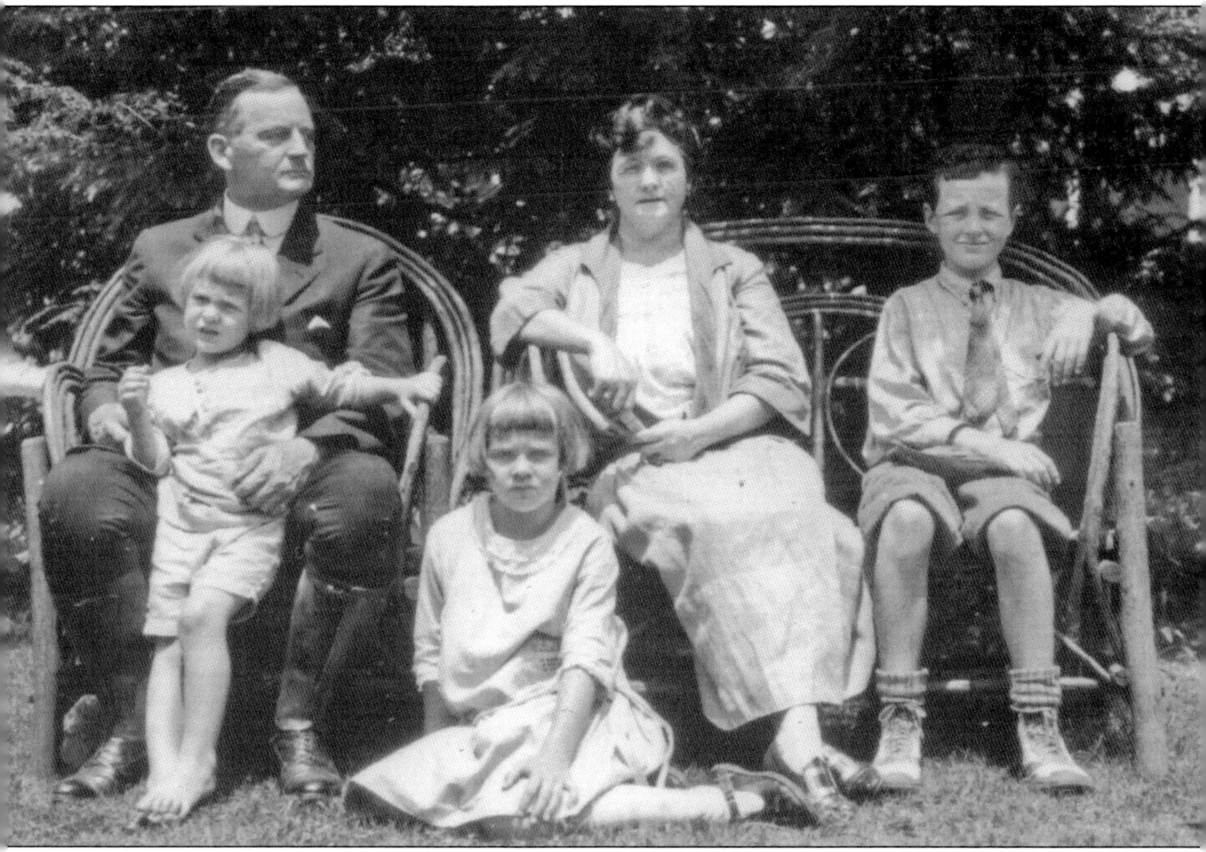

Pictured here are North Carolina governor Angus Wilton McLean, Margaret Jones French McLean, and Angus Wilton McLean Jr., with Hector MacLean, and Margaret French McLean in front. McLean served as director of the US War Finance Corporation and assistant secretary of the US Treasury, and he was governor from 1925 to 1929. McLean organized many Robeson County businesses, such as the National Bank of Lumberton in 1897, which later became Southern National Bank; the Lumberton and Dresden Cotton Mills; and the Virginia & Carolina Southern Railroad. He died on June 20, 1935. Son A.W. McLean Jr. was a real estate developer, and daughter Margaret married Scott Shepherd and was active in charity work throughout the county. Son Hector took the old Scottish spelling of the name, MacLean, and followed his father as a lawyer and politician and as president of Southern National Bank. (Courtesy of Lyl MacLean Clinard.)

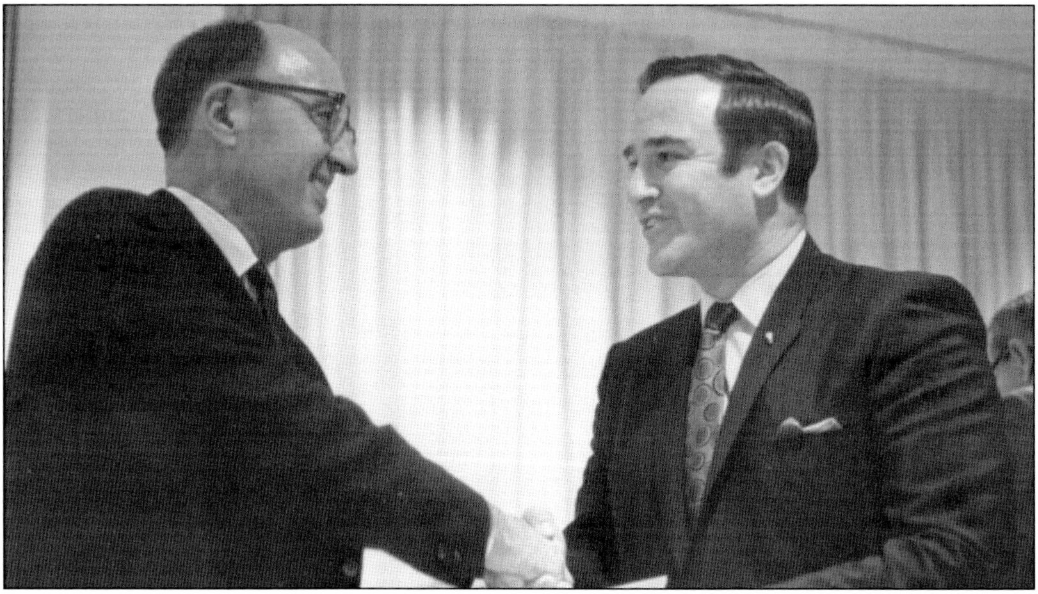

John Allen Sharpe was born on October 20, 1912, and died on May 17, 2009. He attended Duke University, graduating at age 19. He served in the Air Corps during World War II. He assumed the role of editor of the *Robesonian* newspaper after his father's death in 1947, a position he held until the 1980s. He married the former Helen Seawell, a reporter and feature writer at his paper. They have three sons, John Allen Sharpe III, Cliff Sharpe, and Hal Sharpe. Here, Sharpe (left) received the North Carolina Press Association editorial award from Gov. Bob Scott in the 1960s. (Courtesy Sharpe Collection Robeson Remembers, Robeson County History Museum.)

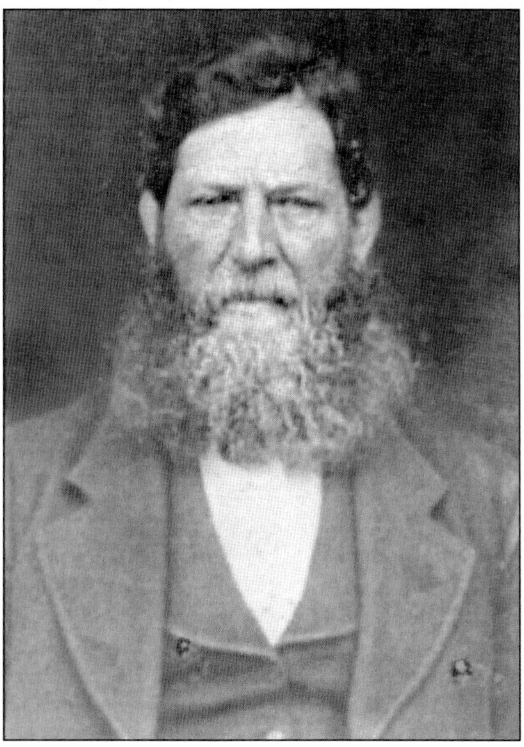

Rev. Elias Davis Johnson was born in Bladen County on August 6, 1828, to Samuel and Sarah Davis Johnson. He married Sarah C. Humphrey in 1849 and was ordained to the gospel ministry in 1855 at Rat Swamp Church by Revs. F. Prevatte and I. Stone. He preached in Robeson, Bladen, Cumberland, Sampson, and Columbus Counties and in a part of South Carolina. He and wife, Sarah, had 11 children. (Courtesy of the Johnson/ Odom Collection, Robeson Remembers, Robeson County History Museum.)

On Thursday, November 1, 1883, at the Raft Swamp Baptist Church, the Robeson Baptist Association met for the first time. The introductory sermon was preached by elder W.T. Jordan. Rev. A.R. Pittman was elected as the first moderator, and D.W. McGugan was elected clerk. Stephen Ward, pictured, served as the first treasurer of the Robeson Baptist Association. (Courtesy of First Baptist Church.)

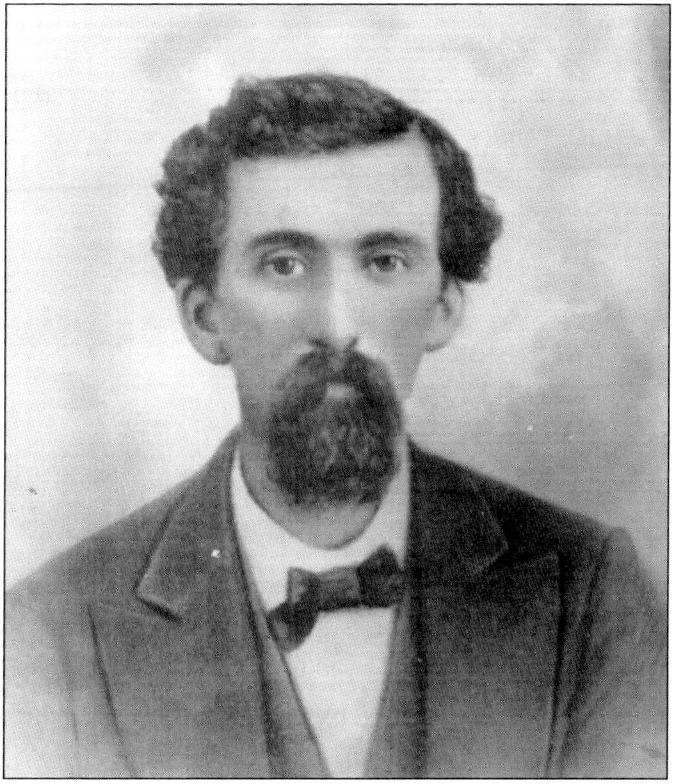

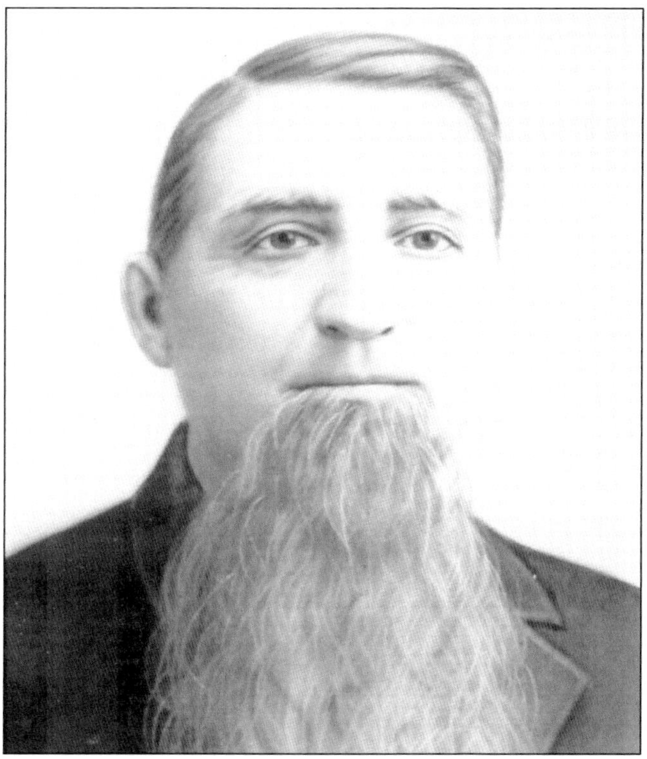

Alexander Hamilton MacLeod was one of the fathers of Lumberton. He was in mercantile business with Maj. John T. Pope in the firm of Pope & McLeod, and he was the founder of the First National Bank as well as many other corporate enterprises. He and his wife, Emily Sarah Blount, were parents of seven children. One son, George B. McLeod, served for years as Robeson County sheriff and as a state senator. (Courtesy of Rev. James Burt MacLeod and Suzie McLeod Dedrick.)

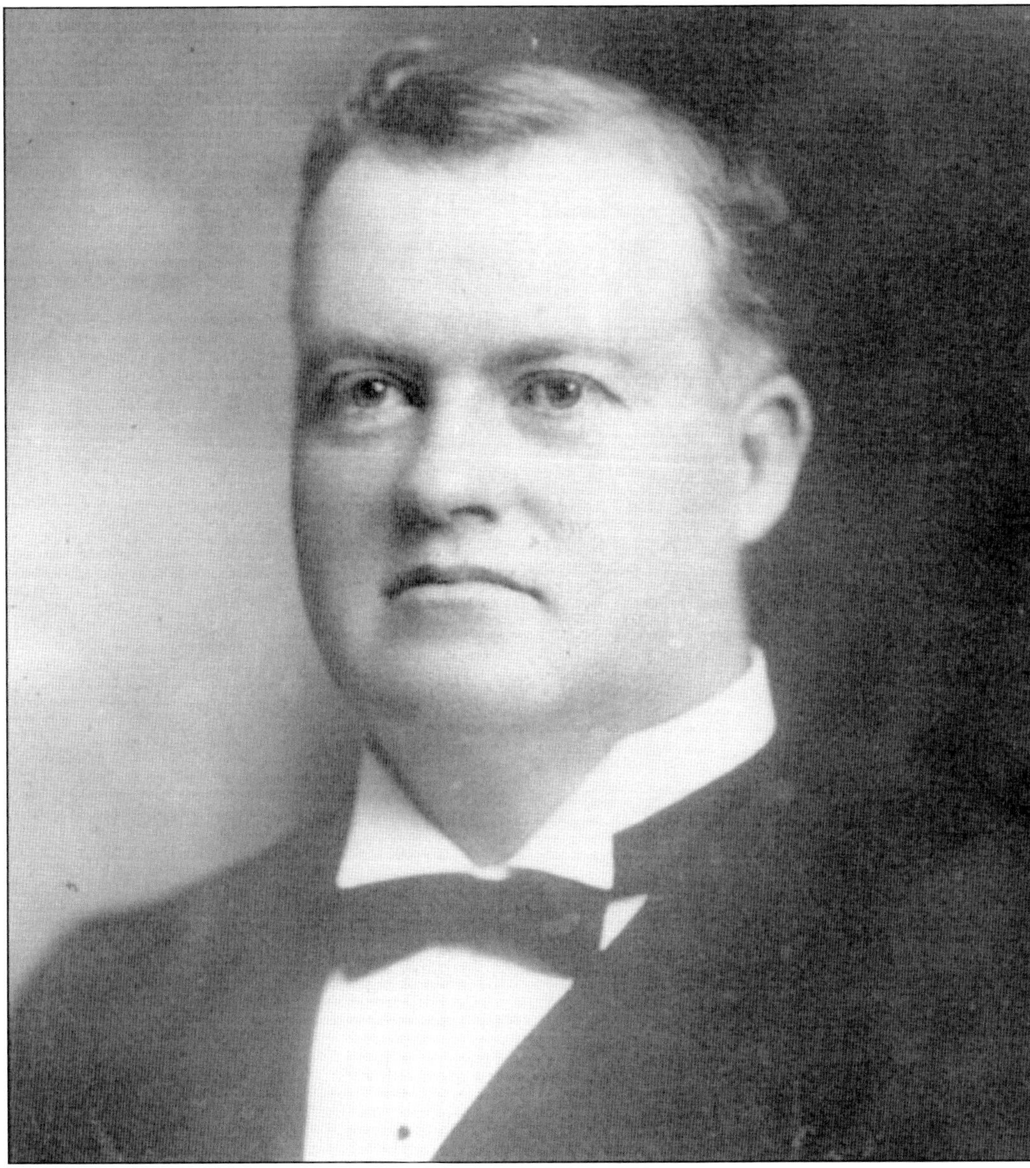

In 1859, Calvin and Caroline Graham purchased 204 acres of what had formerly been the royal land grant to James P. Lewis in 1745. On July 3, 1866, they sold to their newly freed slave Dennis Graham a 50-acre tract of land for $200. It was on part of this land that the town of Proctorville eventually was established. In 1899, Augustus Mellier, president of the Carolina Northern Railroad, purchased a 100-foot-wide tract of land through the property of Dennis and Rose Graham to build his railroad. A month later, he purchased 10 additional acres and immediately laid it out into four blocks and subdivided it into lots with properly laid-out streets. The town was named in honor of Edward Knox Proctor Jr. (pictured), an outstanding Lumberton lawyer, promoter of the Carolina Northern Railroad and other enterprises that were helpful in developing lower Robeson County, and a pioneer Prohibition leader in the area. Shortly after this, Proctor purchased the town with the plans to make it "an ideal town." He died two years later, but his work was carried on by W.R. Surles and J.L. Price, the first postmaster. (Courtesy of First Baptist Church.)

Luther H. Caldwell was the successful owner of L.H Caldwell, "The Home of Good Merchandise," following in the successful footsteps of his father, John Caldwell. He was a man of high integrity, but he shunned the limelight, never accepting public office. In addition to his primary business, he served as director in the bank, cotton mills, the Virginia & Carolina Southern Railroad, the oil mill, and other enterprises. He was very active in First Baptist Church and was primarily responsible for the establishment of North Lumberton Baptist Church and its Sunday school. (Courtesy of the Caldwell Collection, Robeson Remembers, Robeson County History Museum.)

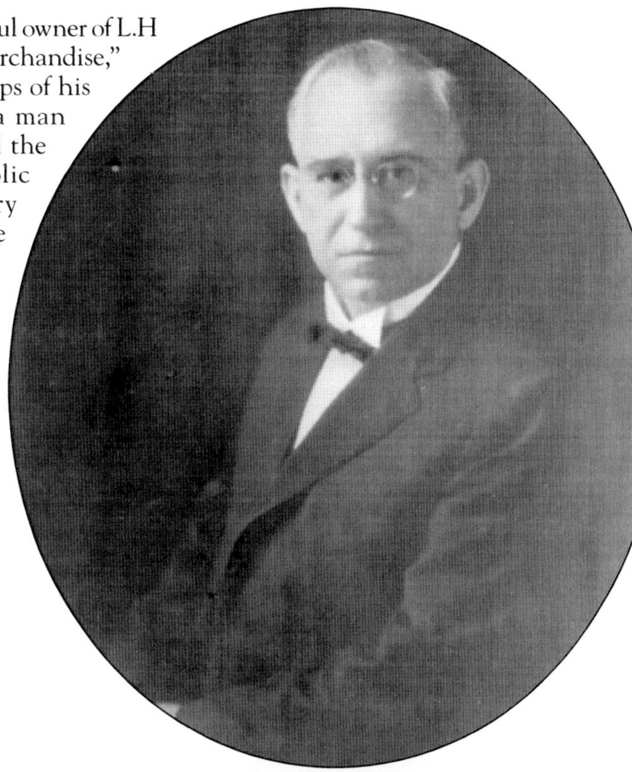

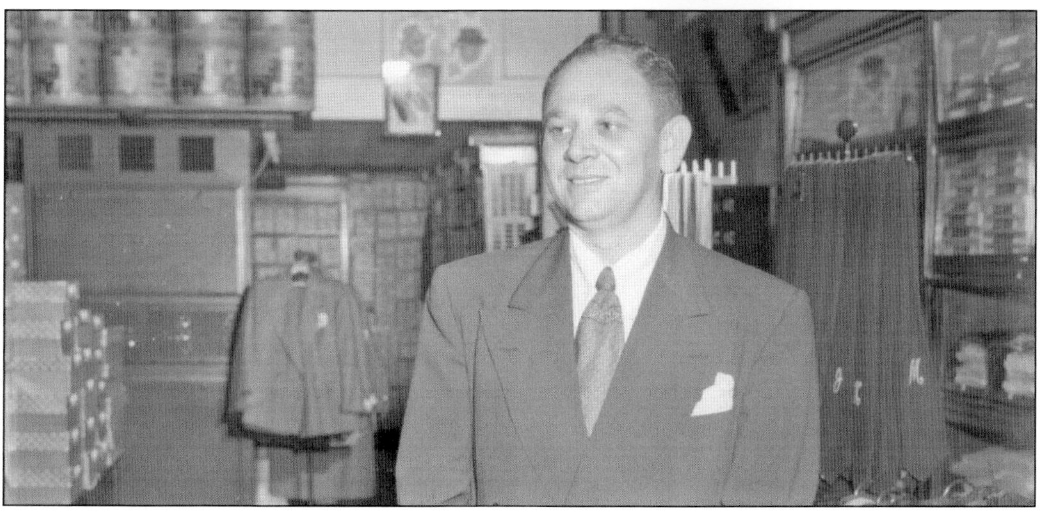

Emanuel Sugar opened Sugar's Men's Store in Lumberton in 1935, but he was not new to the clothing business. He was the son of Joe and Anne Sugar of St. Pauls, who had operated Joe Sugar's Clothing since 1916. He married Evelyn Dilugin, and they had two sons, Alan and Dennis Sugar. His obituary, printed in the *Robesonian* on December 30, 1964, called Sugar Lumberton's "Merchant Prince" and described him as being "in the forefront of such promotional groups as the chamber of commerce and Merchants Association. He was also a Mason, Elk, a member of the Kiwanis Club, and a devoted member of Temple Beth-El." His sons took over the business, operating it for many more years. (Courtesy of the Gillespie Studio Collection, Robeson County History Museum.)

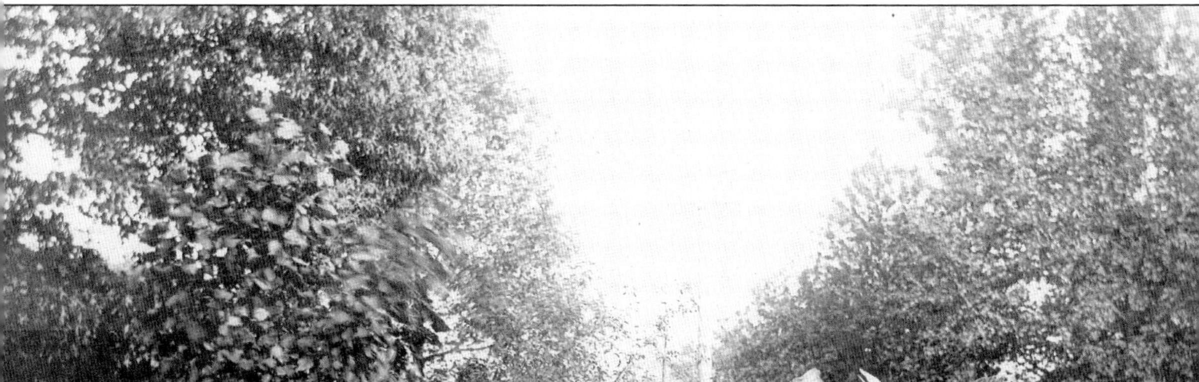

Shown here are in the front of the buggy are Albert E. White and his wife, Ellen Fuller White. The girl behind Albert White is unidentified, and behind Ellen White is their adopted daughter Vashti, who first married Dr. Russell S. Beam Sr. and had one son, Russell S. Beam Jr. After Beam's death, she married James Earl Hall. As a child, Vashti had the honor of turning on the first electric lights in town when her father was mayor. White was one of the town's pioneer businessmen; he was originally a merchant but later served as president of the National Bank of Lumberton and executive of the cotton mills and also established the Lorraine Hotel, just to name a few of his business interests. He served as a North Carolina senator from Robeson County. A favorite story of him concerns the Lumberton Telephone Company, which was organized in 1898 and which White sold to Southern Bell Telephone Company in 1909. He carried the check in surplus of $25,000 to the bank and requested cash. It took all the cash on hand and some silver to make up the amount. He put his arms around the pile of cash and said, "It's all mine, and I wanted to see it" and then deposited it. (Courtesy of Brad Thompson.)

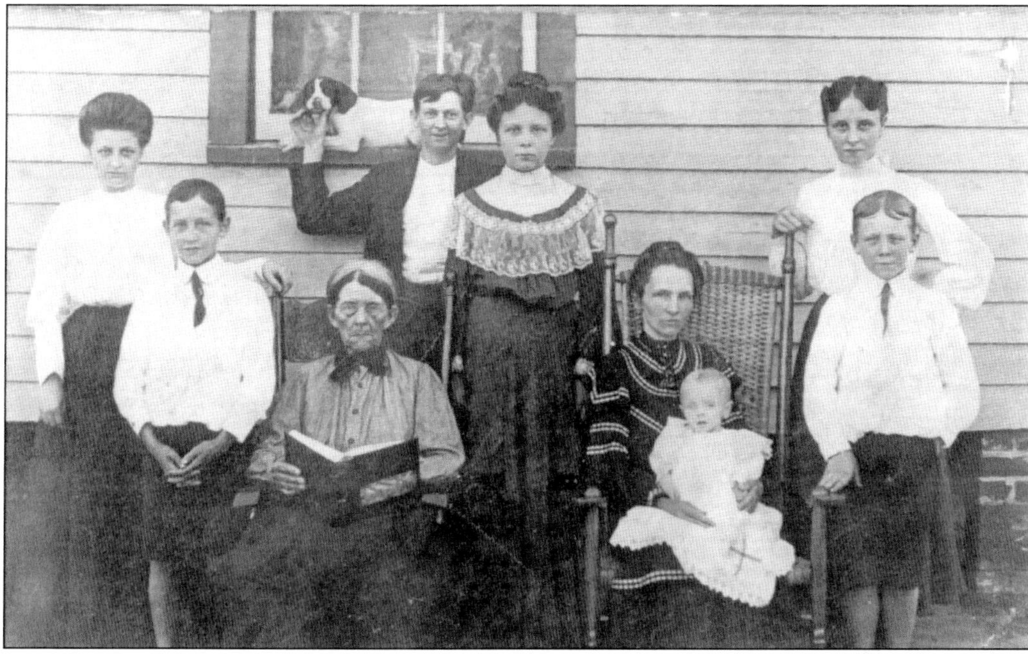

Early photographers traveled through the county, taking pictures of families. They worked similarly to photographers today, collecting their money and mailing the images to the family. This photograph was taken at Charles Upton Spivey's home while he was away on business. Seated are Spivey's mother, Francis Ivey Spivey (left), and his wife, Amerette Prevatte Spivey (right), holding an unidentified child. Behind them stand, from left to right, an unidentified family friend, Raymond Spivey, Warren Wirt Lewis (with his ever-present basset hound), Lillie Spivey Lewis, Lula Spivey, and James Spivey. (Courtesy of the Hubbard-Tyner Collection.)

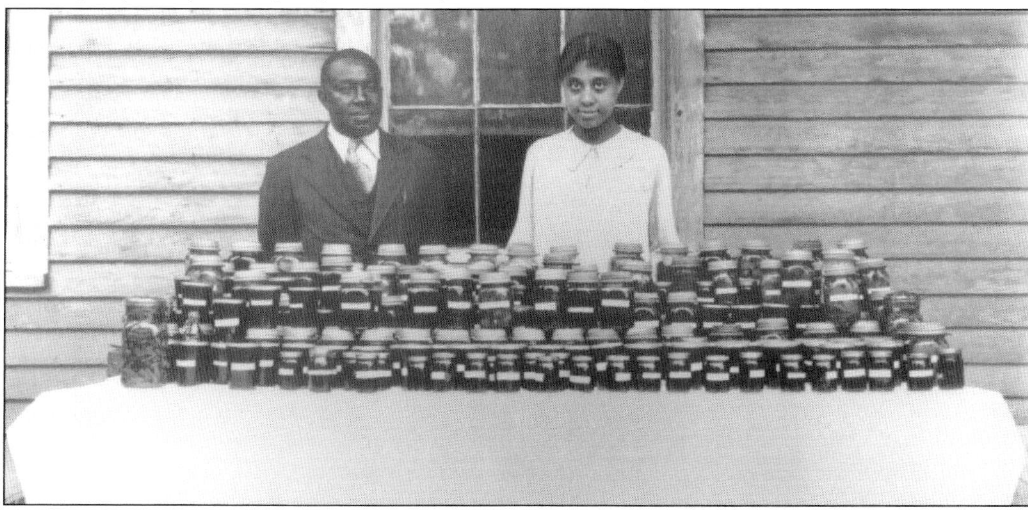

Expert canners Julius E. and Alice Bryan are shown here at their Elizabethtown Road home with their winter supply of canned fruits and vegetables. Canning was a part of everyday life and was essential to feeding a family in the days before refrigeration and supermarkets. This photograph was taken by George W. Ackerman on May 20, 1932. During his almost-40-year career with the US Department of Agriculture, Ackerman took more than 50,000 photographs. (Courtesy of the National Archives and Records Administration.)

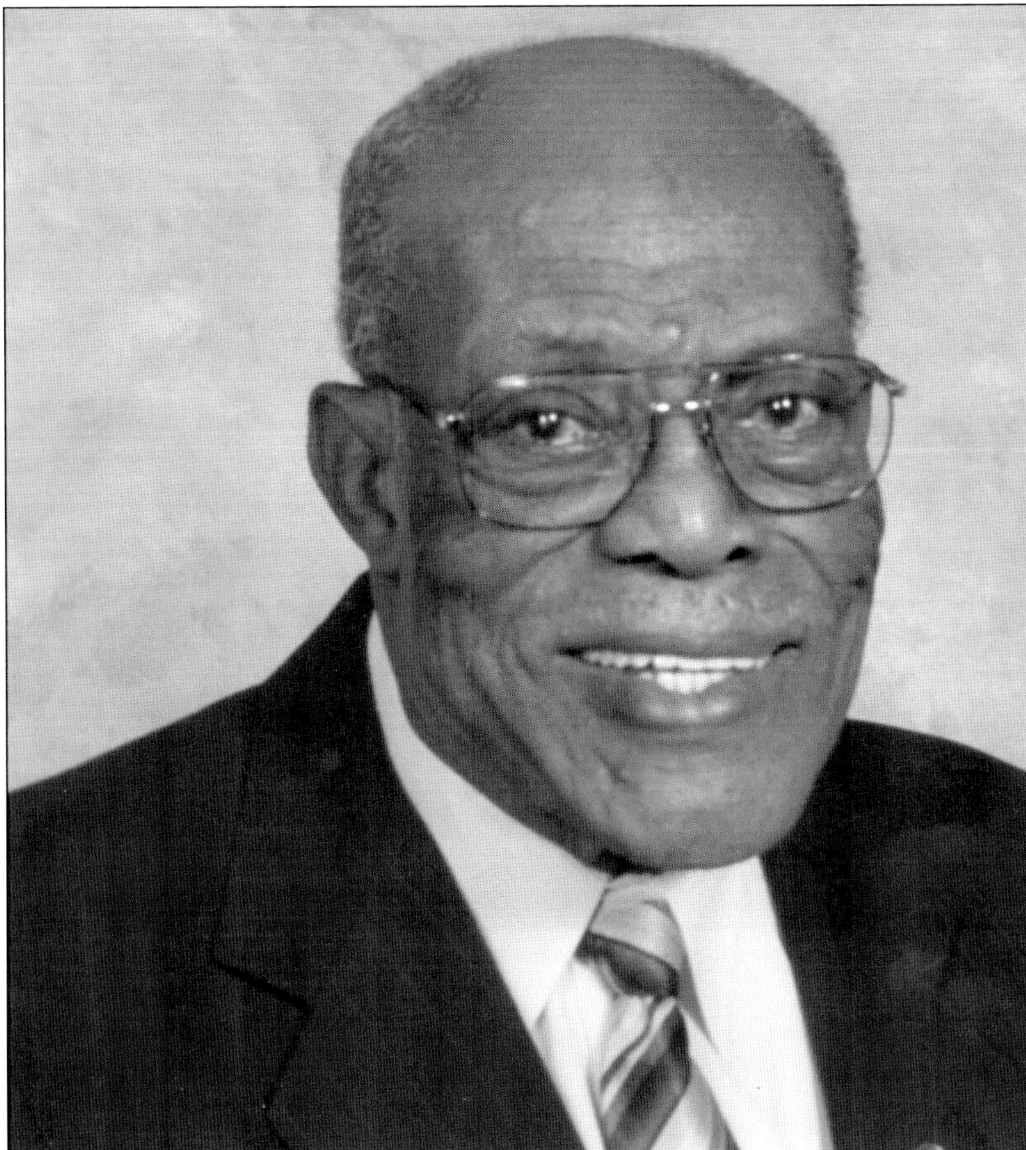

Dr. Eugene Burns "E.B." Turner served as the pastor of First Baptist Church on West Second Street for 57 years with his helpmate and wife, Georgia McNeill. An inspirational leader, he encouraged all citizens, especially African Americans, to find the courage to use their voices to break an oppressive silence. It was upon arriving in Lumberton as a preacher at the age of 22, that he first discovered the harsh living conditions African Americans were force to endure. There were no paved streets in the black sections of town, and most blacks lived in poor housing with little opportunity for upward movement. In the political field, he was chairman of the Robeson County Democratic Party and served 30 years on the Lumberton City Council before being elected to the Robeson County Board of Commissioners in 1992. He was also on the boards of Lumberton Economic Advancement for Downtown, Inc., the Lumberton Housing Authority, Lumberton Community and Economic Development Committee, Lumberton Commission for Youth and the Family, the Lumberton Visitors Bureau, and Historic Robeson, Inc. (Courtesy of Robeson County History Museum.)

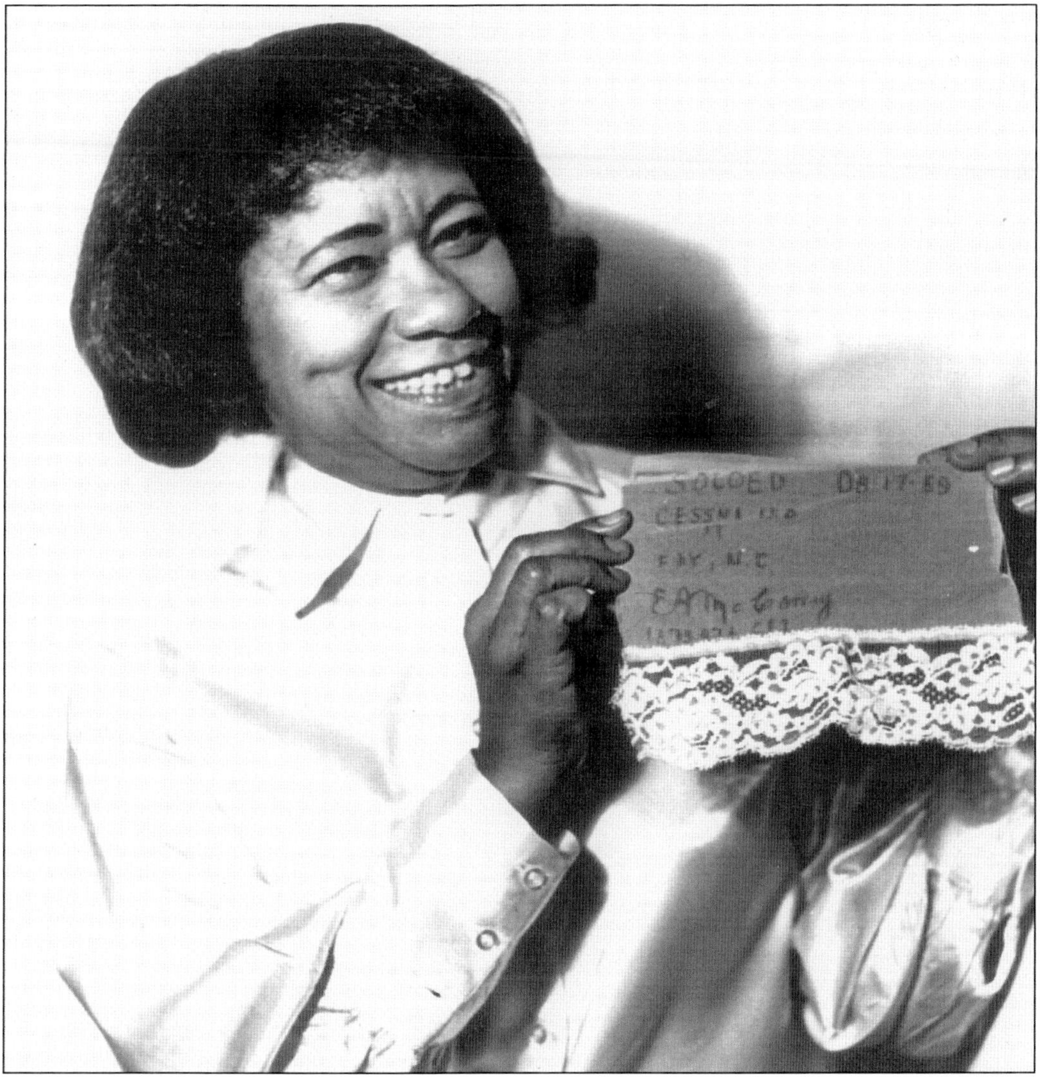

Ida Van Smith knew from her early childhood that she wanted to be a pilot. Her father began taking her to air shows at the old Lumberton airport when she was three years old. She was delighted by barnstorming exhibitions performed by pilots and by the women performing wing-walking stunts on the airplanes. Born in 1917 in Lumberton to Theodore Deland and Martha Jane Larkin, Smith graduated from Red Stone Academy and Shaw University. She earned a master's degree from Queens College and became a teacher in the New York City Public Schools in the fields of history and special education. In 1967, at the age of 50, she finally fulfilled her personal dream of learning to fly. Once she had her private pilot's license and instructor rating, Smith founded the Ida Van Smith Flight Club on Long Island, New York. The flight-training club was for minority children to encourage their involvement in aviation and aerospace sciences. Training for the students was provided in an aircraft simulator funded by the Federal Aviation Administration and an operational Cessna 172. Soon, there were more than 20 clubs throughout the country, with members between the ages of 13 and 19. As a result, thousands of children were exposed to aviation, and many pursued related careers. Smith also produced and hosted a cable television show on aviation and taught an introductory aviation course at York College of the City University of New York. (Courtesy of Robeson County History Museum.)

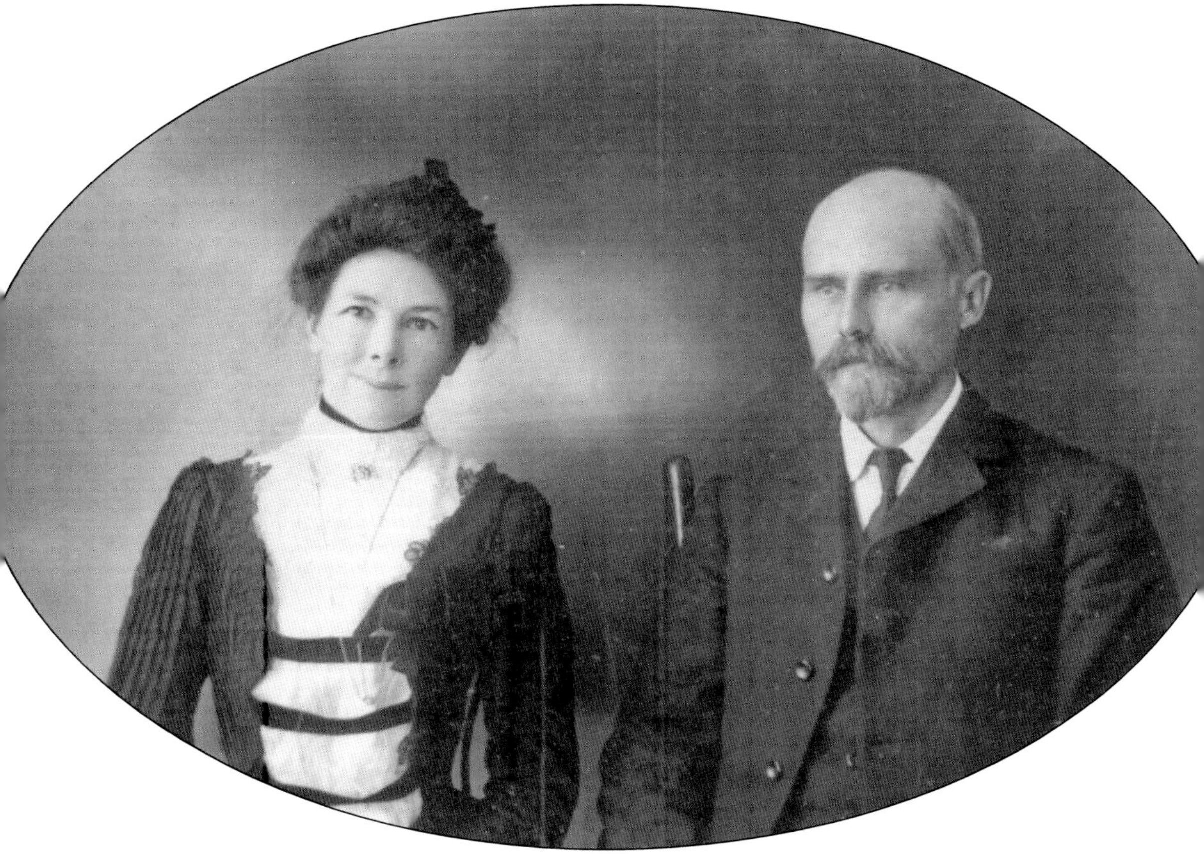

Pictured here are Robert D. Caldwell (son of Mary Ann Caldwell) and his wife, Dovie Carlyle (daughter of Simeon and Sarah Caroline Conoley Carlyle). Caldwell was in business with his brother-in-law William Watts Carlyle in the firm of Caldwell & Carlyle. The firm was located on Elm Street where the plaza is now, and it advertised having everything needed from cradle to grave. After Carlyle retired, the firm was renamed R.D. Caldwell & Sons. Later, Caldwell's son Simeon operated the business as S.F. Caldwell & Co. A list of all the business enterprises in which Caldwell had a hand would look like the Lumberton phone directory. He was instrumental in the formation of the National Bank of Lumberton, the Lumberton, Dresden, and Jennings Cotton Mills, the Lumberton Building & Loan Association, and the Robeson County Loan and Trust Co. He was very public-minded, serving as a member of the town commissioners and as chairman of the board of county commissioners. For a quarter of a century, he was chairman of the board of deacons of the First Baptist Church, and for practically the same period, superintendent of its Sunday school. (Courtesy of Ruth Ann Baker McLellan.)

Nine

LEISURE TIME AND CELEBRATIONS

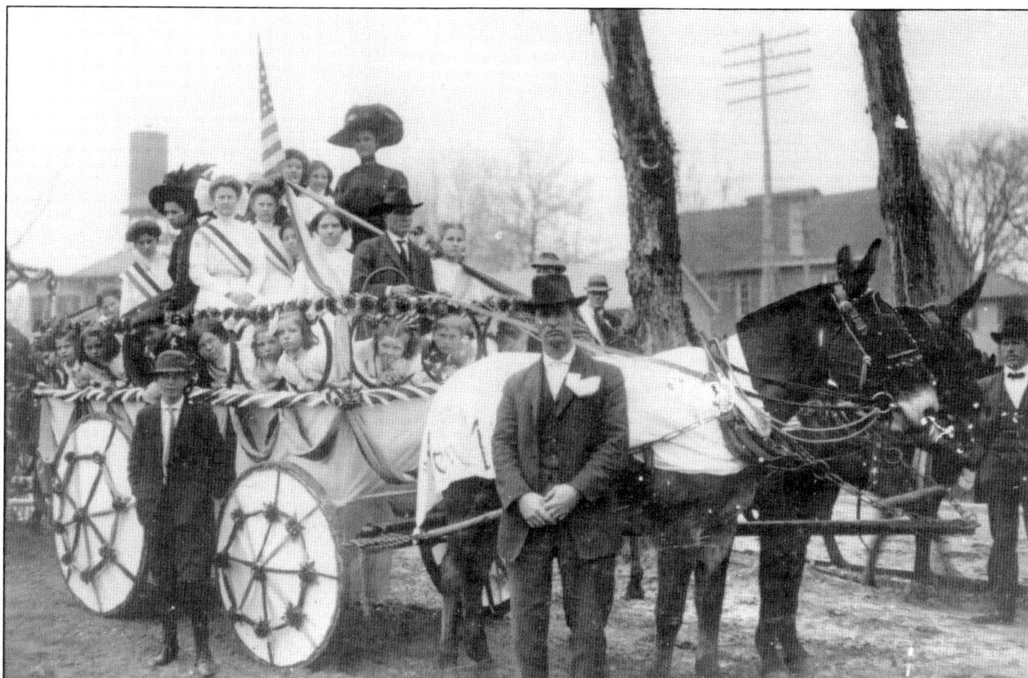

This float from the Ten Mile School won third place in the January 26, 1911, Robeson County School float competition. The women of the Ten Mile community worked long hours decorating this wagon; note that even the wheels are decorated. (Courtesy of the Kate Biggs Collection, Robeson County Public Library.)

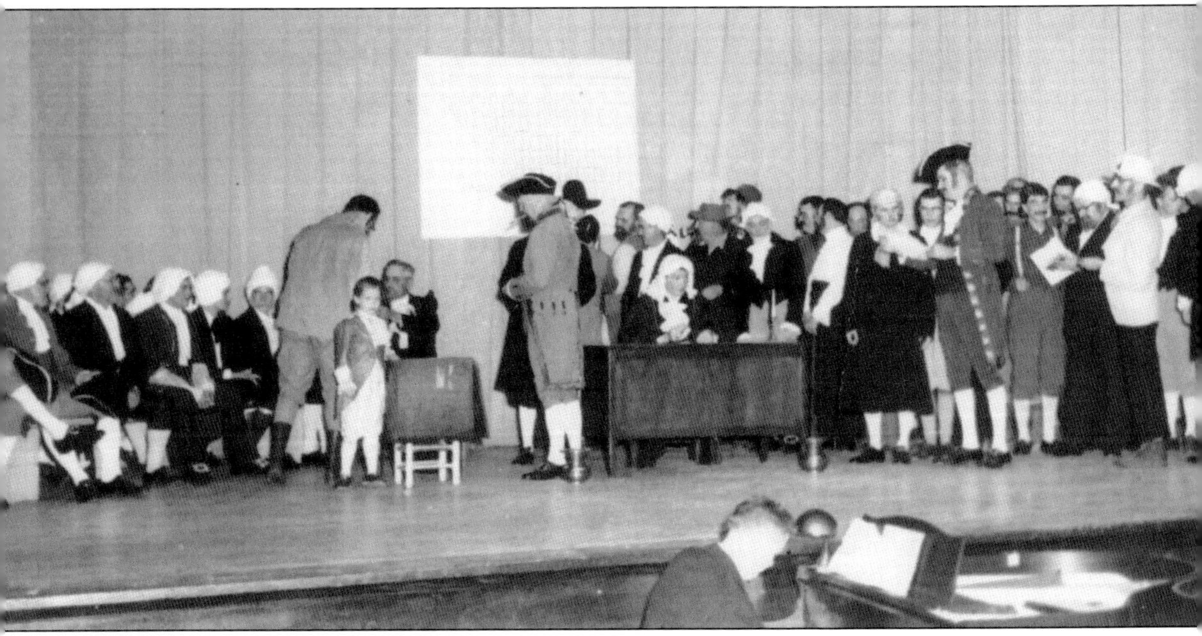

The citizens of Lumberton celebrated the 100th anniversary of the incorporation of the town from November 30 through December 2, 1952. Numerous groups went together to sponsor the events, and hundreds of volunteers spent hours to bring the celebration to fruition. One of the highlights of the festivities was the history pageant called "Progress on the Lumbee Since 1787." The action consisted of a series of scenes narrated by Jim McNeill, manager of radio station WTSB. Local artists Billy Bridger and Lawrence Redmond made music on a pair of Baldwin grand pianos placed end to end just beneath the lip of the stage, and a vocal quartet and members of the high school band performed from the wings. This scene shows the August 16, 1787, lottery drawing that was held for the Lumberton lots. Seated at the desk is I. Murchison Biggs portraying the judge Col. John Blount, and seated behind the box is Wesley C. Watts portraying clerk of court Josiah Barnes; Lubin Prevatte portrayed the young John L. McLean, who actually drew the lottery tickets. (Courtesy of Historic Robeson, Inc.)

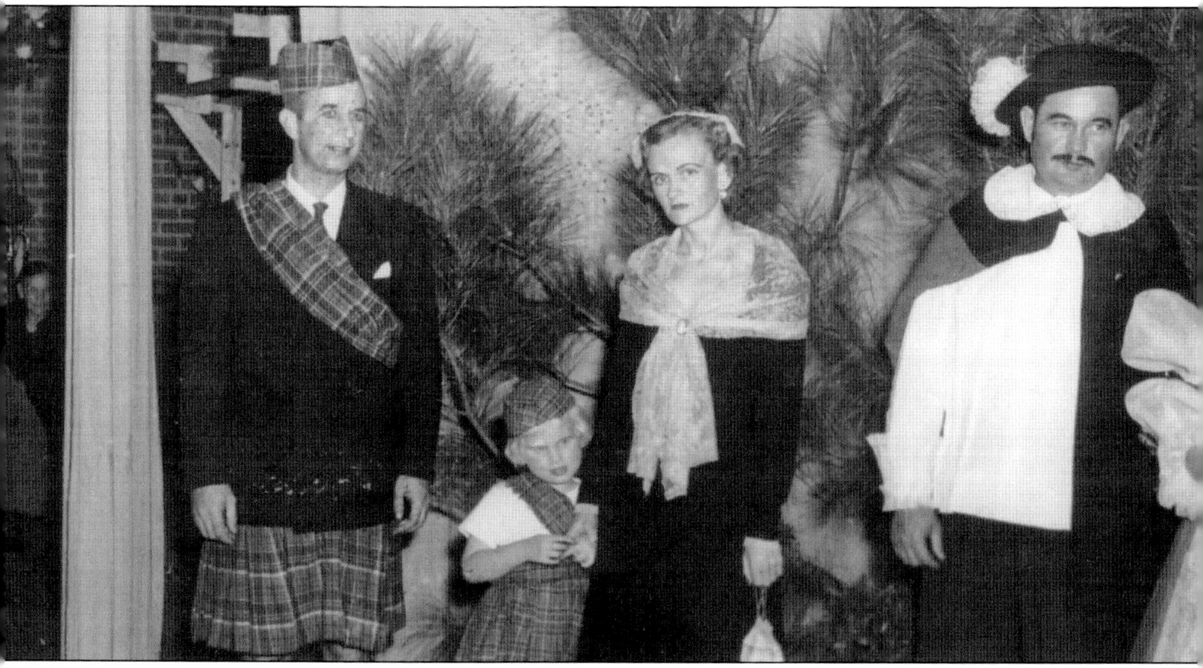

The pageant featured several scenes; the first depicted the white settlers arriving in the county and meeting the Native Americans. The Scottish settlers were portrayed by John Luther McLean, his wife, Isabel McLean, and their son Marshall McLean. W.F. Floyd was chosen to represent the Huguenot settlers. Other scenes included an 1850s wedding with women's costumes by Mrs. J.D. Maude-Stewart, famous at the time for her dress designs, as well as a meeting of the Confederate Ladies Aid Society with founder Susan McQueen, the widow of Lumberton's first mayor. The remainder of the play focused on the history through 1924. The last scene depicted the November 1924 election night when A.W. McLean, Lumberton's best-known public figure, was elected governor of North Carolina. In it, excited men gathered by a telephone in the courthouse awaiting the news from Raleigh. The festivities also included a parade in which Lumberton's 32-year-old mayor ,Hector MacLean, and his wife, Lyl, served as grand marshals. MacLean was the youngest son of Governor McLean. (Courtesy of Historic Robeson, Inc.)

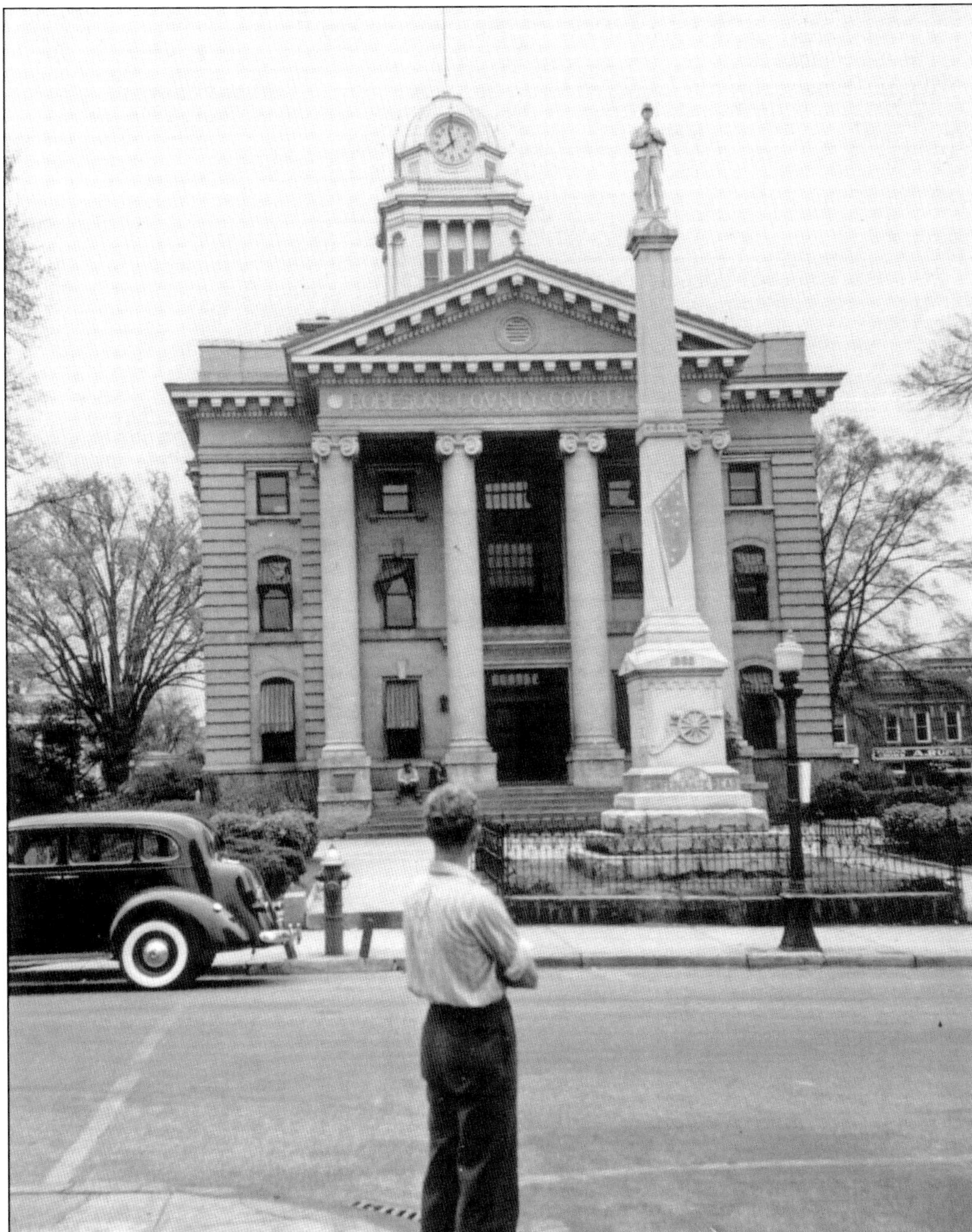

The Robeson County Confederate Monument was unveiled on May 10, 1907, before a crowd of 7,000, including 500 Confederate veterans. The first to donate to the fundraising project was Lumberton attorney and future North Carolina governor Angus Wilton McLean. The monument has survived two courthouses and a major overhaul to the exterior of the current courthouse. Through time and changes, the Confederate soldier has stood high above Elm Street as a silent reminder of the losses the county suffered during the Civil War. (Courtesy of the Hubbard-Tyner Collection.)

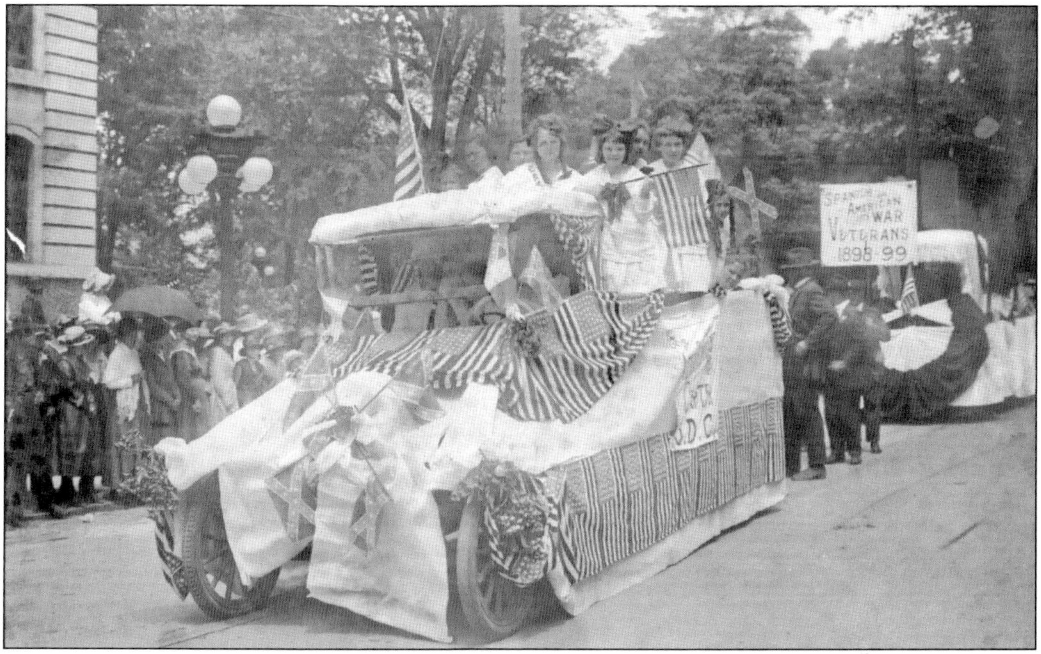

A large parade was held at the unveiling of the Robeson County Confederate Monument on May 10, 1907. Shown here is a fabric-covered truck carrying members of the Robeson County chapter of the United Daughters of the Confederacy. Marching behind them are the few remaining Spanish-American War veterans. (Courtesy of Robeson County History Museum.)

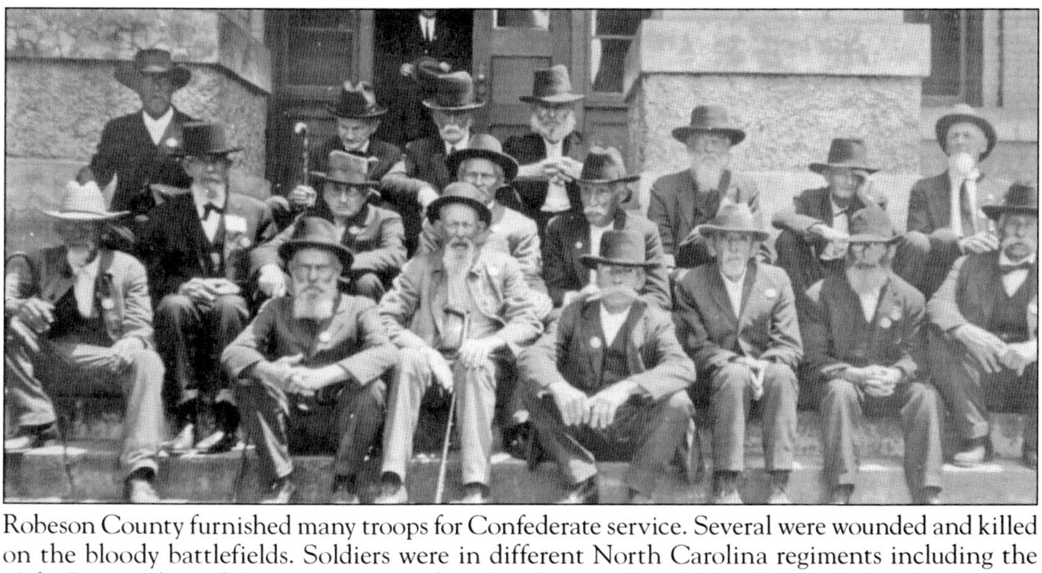

Robeson County furnished many troops for Confederate service. Several were wounded and killed on the bloody battlefields. Soldiers were in different North Carolina regiments including the 18th, 31st, 46th, and 51st. Men of note from Lumberton included William S. Norment; Bunyan Stansel; William Foster French, a distinguished lawyer and legislator; Alfred Rowland, a lawyer and congressman namesake of the town of Rowland; Dr. Edmund McQueen, the first elected mayor of Lumberton; Dr. Richard M. Norment, a veteran of the Mexican war; Francis Marion Wishart, a later head of the local militia that fought against the Henry Berry Lowry Gang, and Rev. Furney A. Prevatt and William H. Barnes, who were the last two Confederate veterans in Robeson County. (Courtesy Historic Robeson, Inc.)

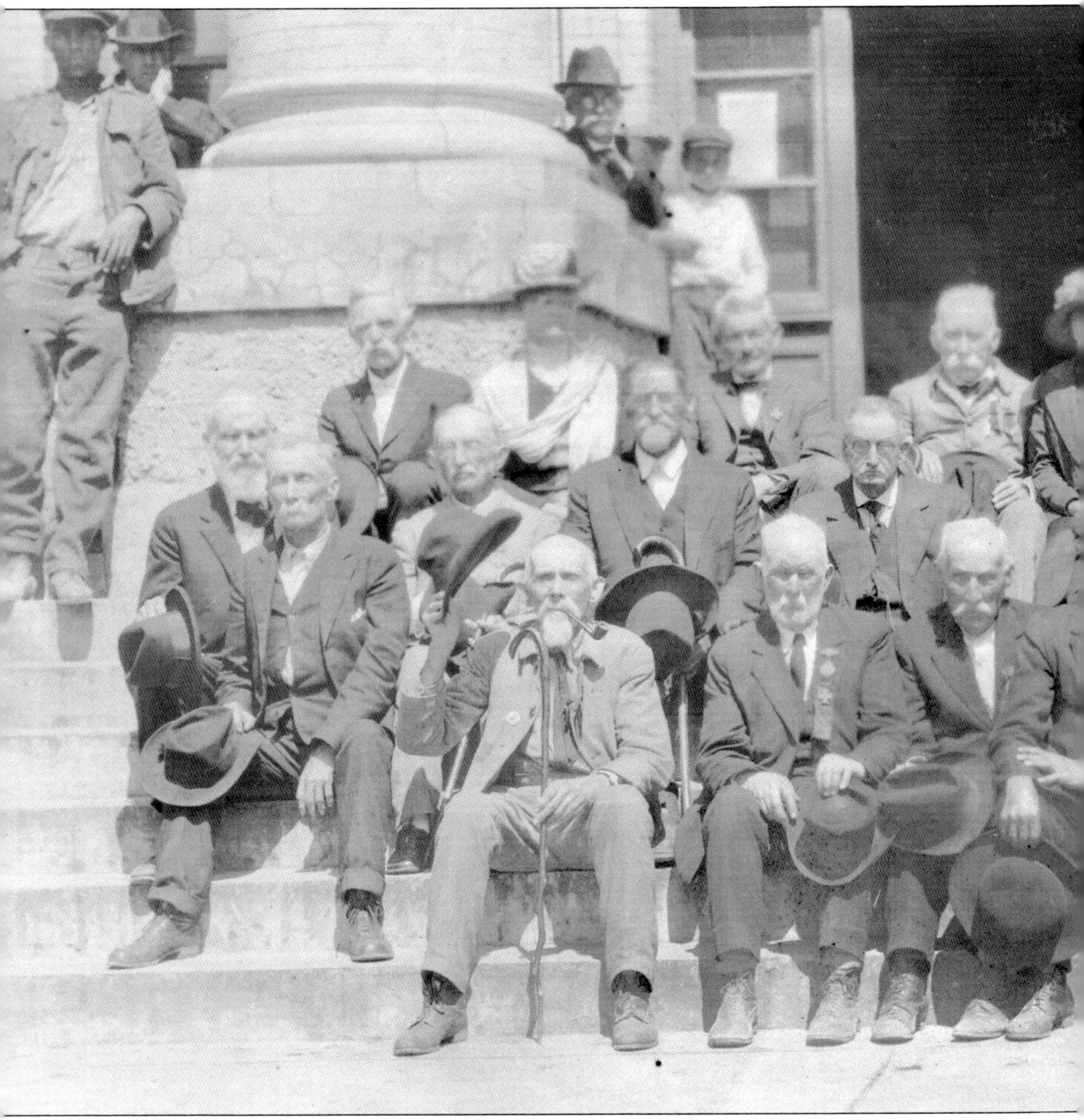

Robeson County's Confederate veterans gathered in 1916 on the steps of the courthouse just a few feet away from the Confederate Memorial that was dedicated in 1907. This photograph was published in the February 24, 1953, issue of the *Robesonian* with no identification. In the days following, the newspaper received letters from citizens offering names of some of the veterans

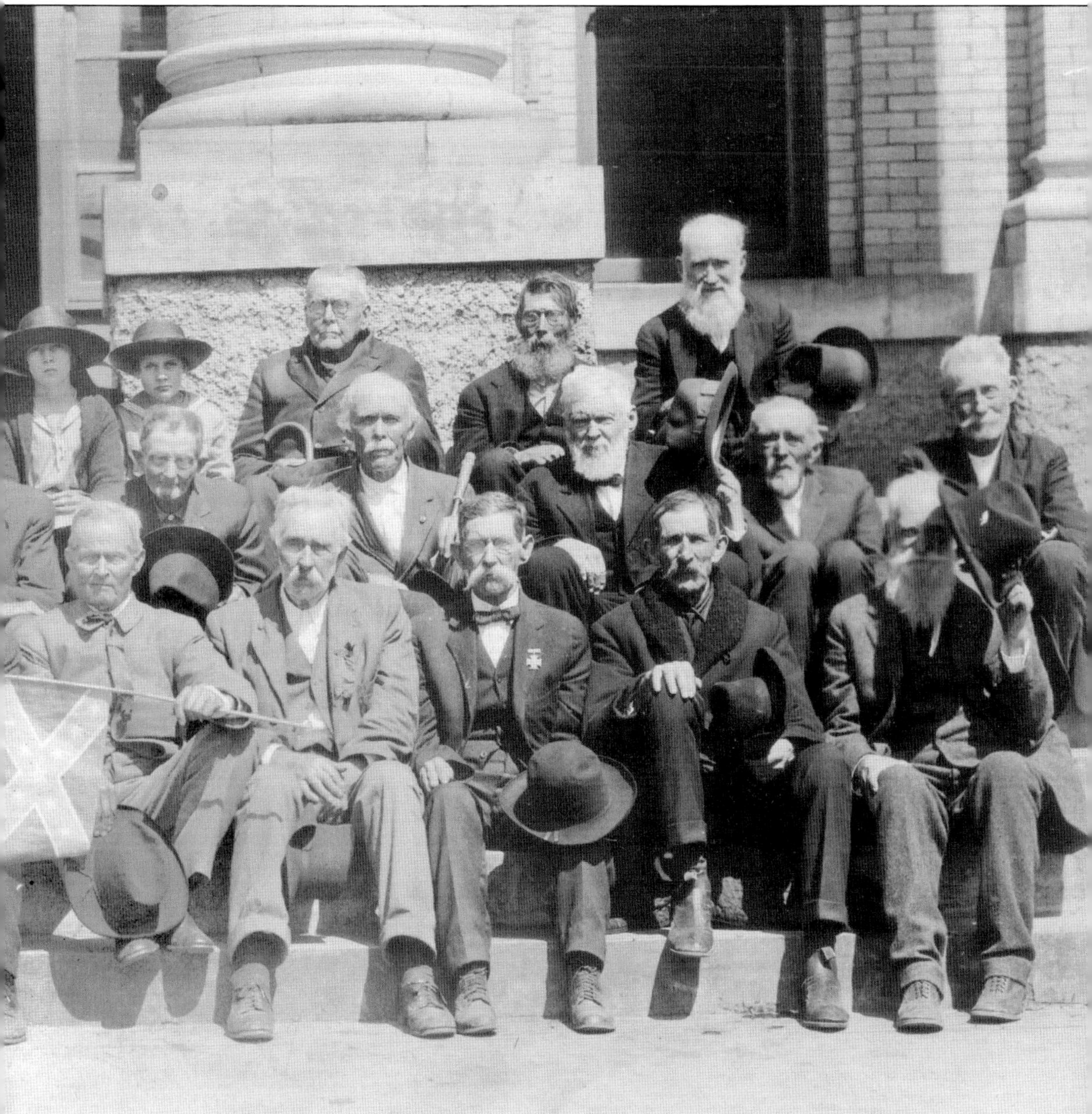

in the photograph, including Joseph Ratley, S.S. Wishart, Isham Lamb, Rev. Furney Prevatte, Calvin Smith, William Haywood Graham, Michael Bullock, A.B. Small, Steven Lawson, Ben Parnell, William Townsend, William P. Norton, W.H. Barnes, and Duckery Allen. (Courtesy Historical Robeson, Inc.)

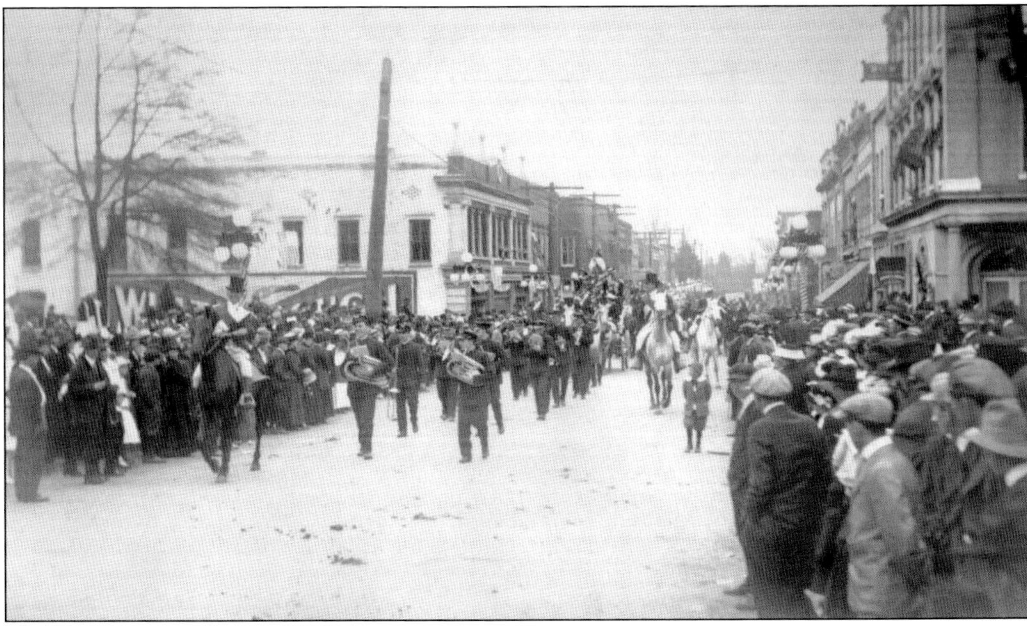

For several years, a main event of the school year was Commencement Day, which included a large parade through downtown Lumberton. The *Robesonian* reported that 3,000 children representing 50 schools took part and were observed by between 8,000 and 10,000 people on April 9, 1915. The parade was led by four grand marshals on horseback. (Courtesy of the Robeson County Public Library.)

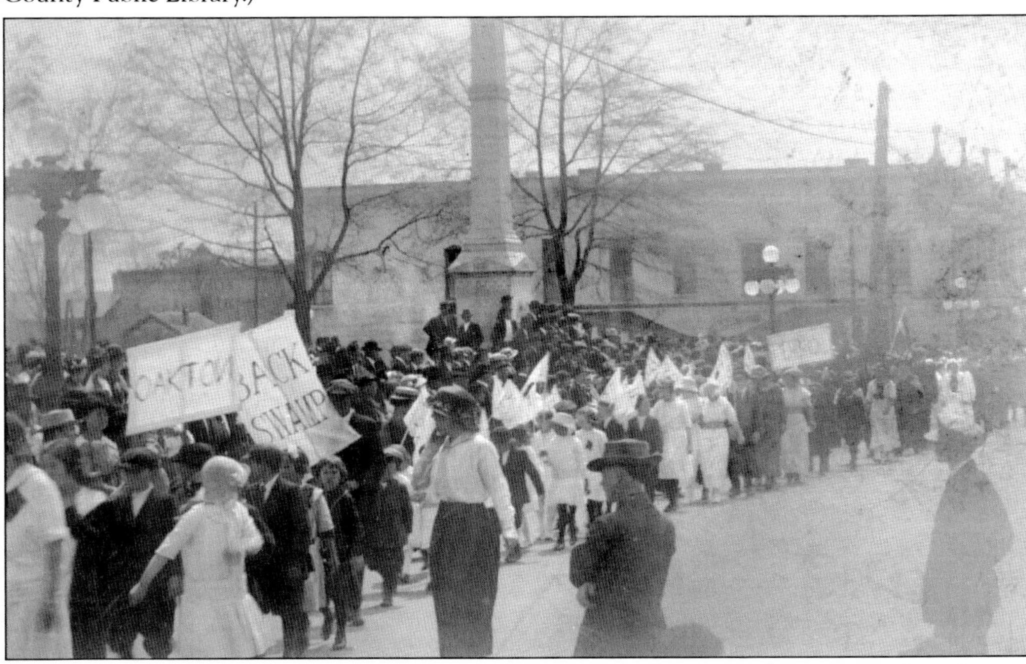

Most schools in the county would decorate a float or wagon, but some chose to march with just a hand-painted banner. The children would march north on Elm Street, past the courthouse. This scene shows class groups from Oakton, Back Swamp, and Pembroke. Note that the *N* in Oakton's banner is painted backwards. (Courtesy of the Hubbard-Tyner Collection.)

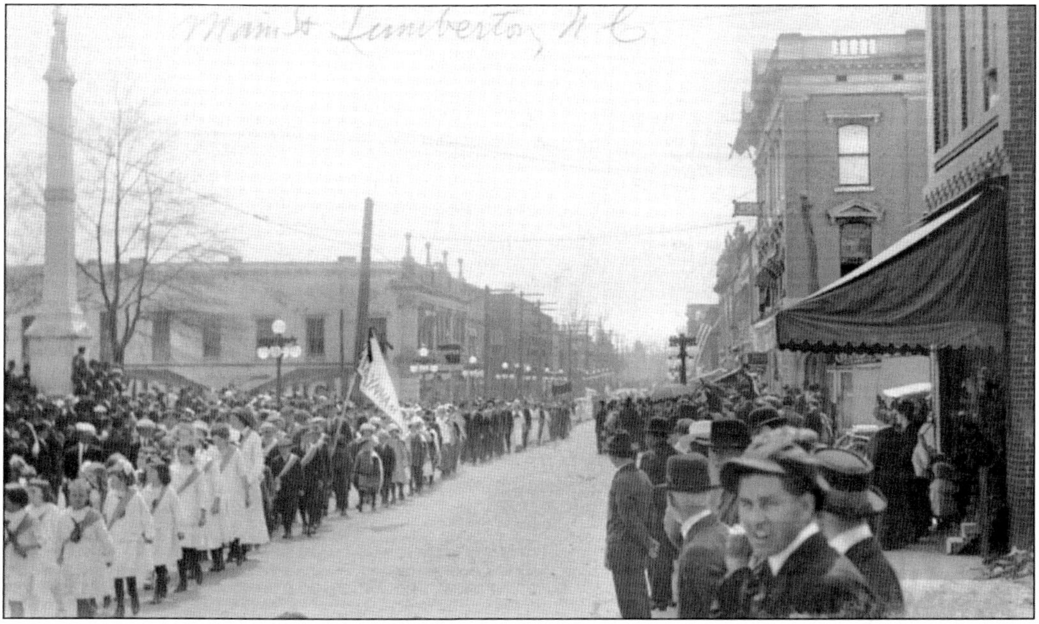

After the Commencement Day parades, there were athletic contests held, including a 100-yard dash, a 450-yard dash, the high jump, and a potato-sack race. In 1915, Wake Forest College president W.L. Poteat delivered the main speech, and 230 diplomas were awarded to those who had completed the first seven years of education, meaning that they were free to enter any high school in the county. (Courtesy of the Carolina Collection, UNC-Chapel Hill.)

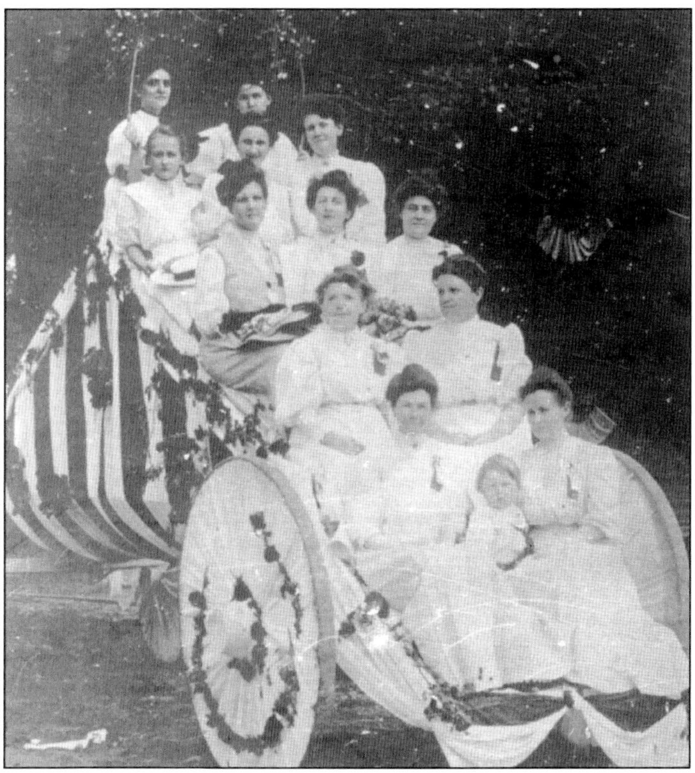

Some of Lumberton's beautiful belles are seen here in their long, white summer dresses as they ride in an early-1900s parade in a flower-bedecked and fabric-covered cart. (Courtesy of Historic Robeson, Inc.)

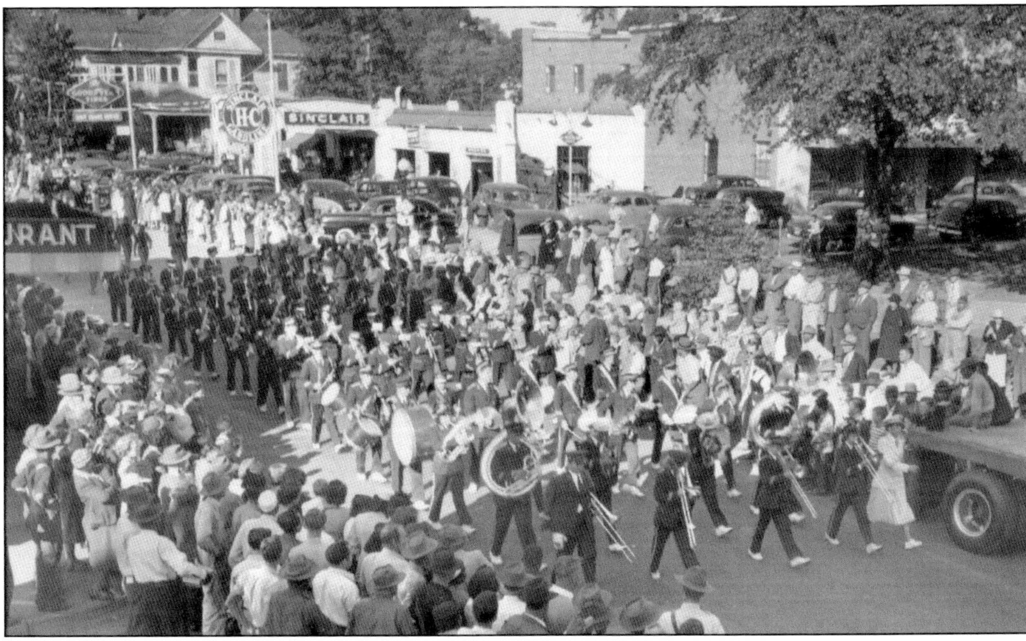

The Lumberton High School marching band was always a big hit during parades. In the background behind the band is the home of Ralph and Ruby Whaley, which was torn down to build the St. Alban's Lodge No. 114 AF&AM Masonic Lodge. The Lodge was chartered on December 8, 1847, with Thomas A. Norment serving as the first Worshipful Master. (Courtesy of Gillespie Studio Collection, Robeson County History Museum.)

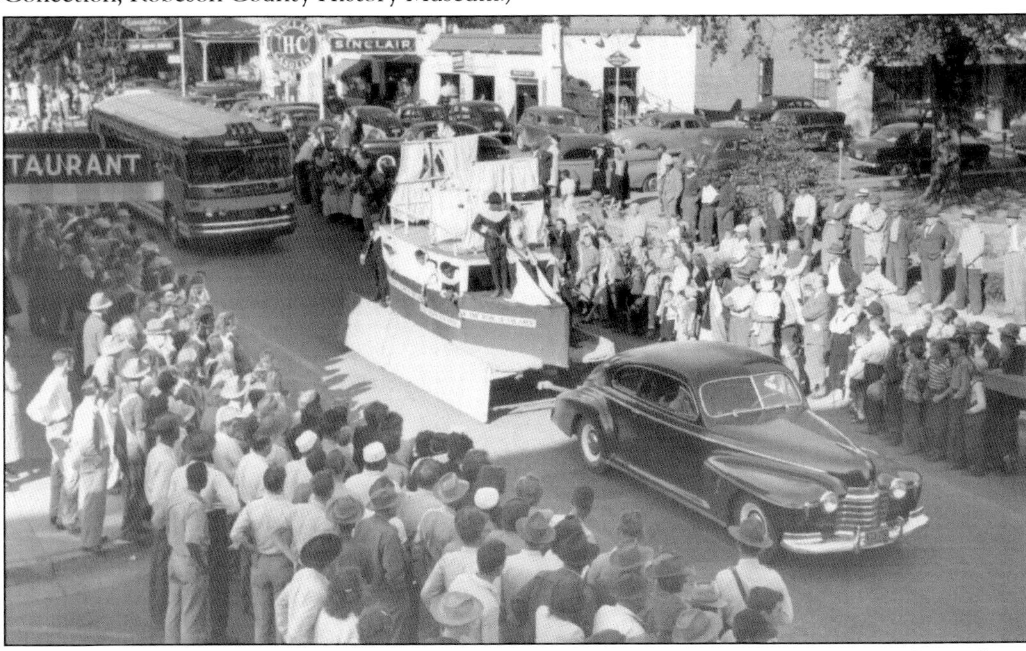

This early-1950s parade down Elm Street featured a recreated Colonial-era ship with a Pilgrim aboard. In the background of the photograph can be seen the Sinclair Station built on the location of the George Badger McLeod home. (Courtesy of Gillespie Studio Collection, Robeson County History Museum.)

The May Day celebrations were the highlight of most schools' spring season. Martha Bowman, daughter of Dr. Earle Ledbetter Bowman and Bernice Smith, is pictured as Queen Persephone at Salem College May Day 1942. Later, she married Judge Sandy McKinnon. Miss Bowman's dress was made by Lumberton seamstress Maude Stewart, who was known for her beautiful gowns. (Courtesy Robeson County History Museum.)

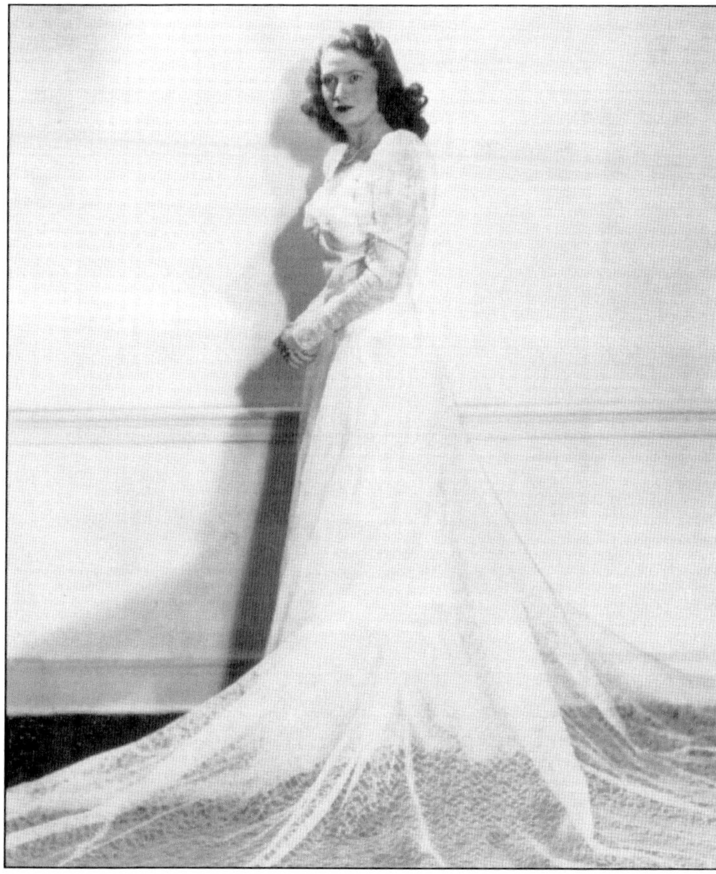

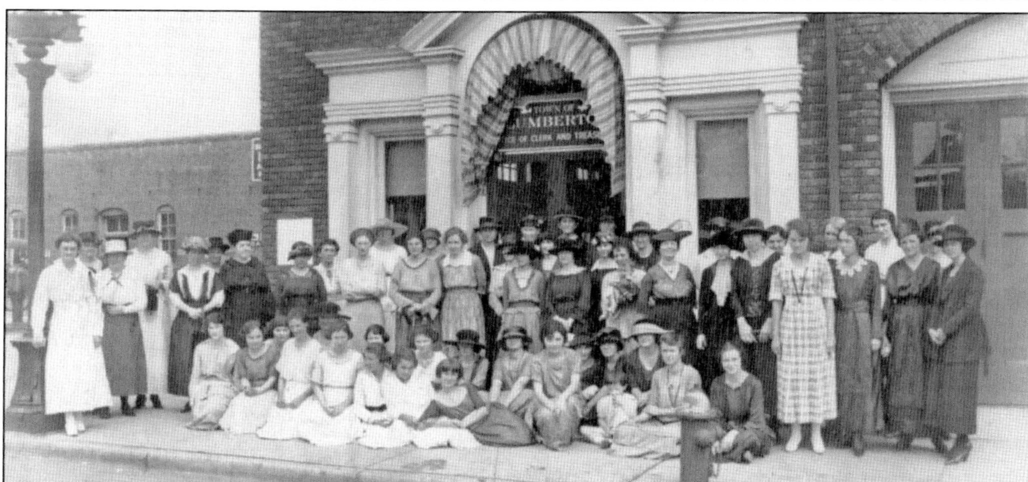

In the early 1900s, farmers attended farmers' institutes, and farm boys would join "corn clubs," through which they would each raise an acre of corn and keep the money after selling it. But there were no educational opportunities for women who wanted to learn the best ways to feed and raise their families. The women of Robeson organized as the first county home extension bureau in North Carolina on September 20, 1920. Here, they pose in front of Lumberton City Hall. (Courtesy of NC State University Library.)

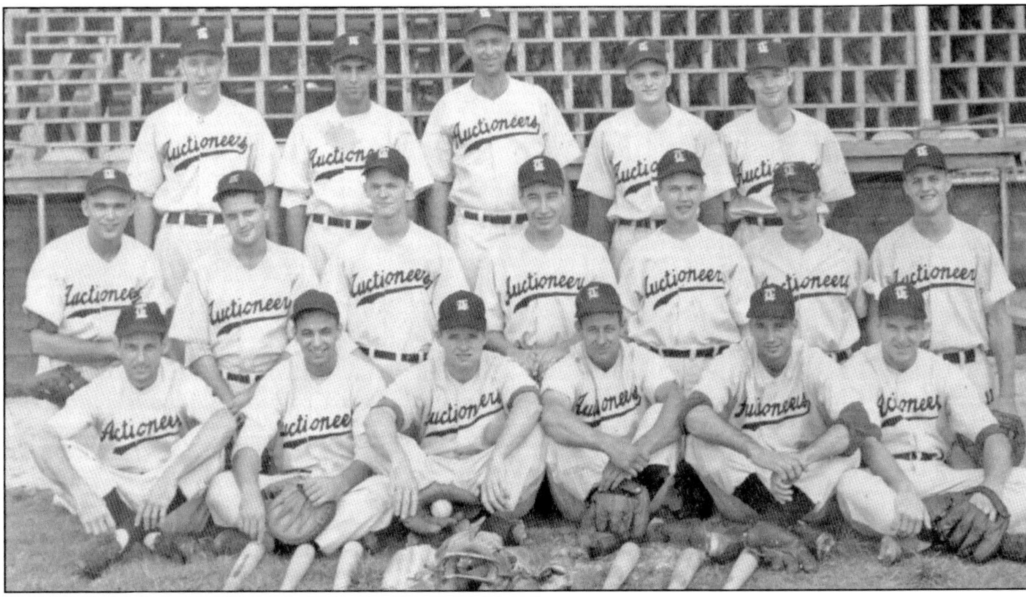

The Lumberton Cubs were founded in 1947 and established a working relationship with the Chicago Cubs. The season opened on April 24, 1947, with 3,000 fans in attendance. That season, the team attracted nearly 51,000 paying customers. In 1949, they were renamed the Lumberton Auctioneers, generally referred to as the "Auks." This is a 1949 photograph of the team; the tallest player on the back row is Cecil "Turkey" Tyson, who married Hester Hayes of Lumberton. (Courtesy of Catherine Currie Ward.)

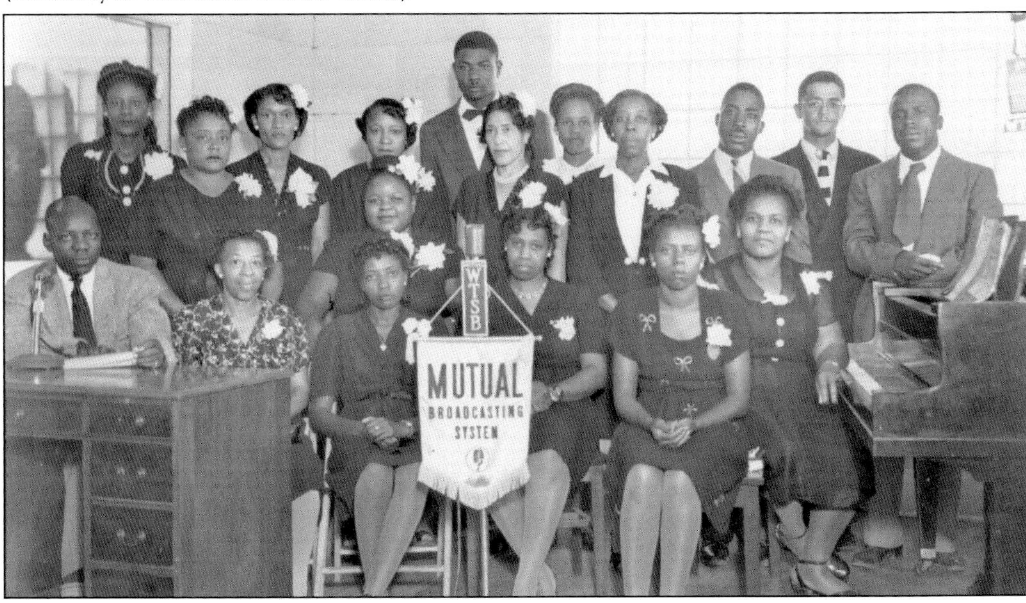

The Nightingale Chorus use to perform Saturdays at 3:00 p.m. on WTSB (the station's call letters stood for "Where Tobacco Sells Best"). Some of the local personalities over the years included Jim Kirkland, Bobby Pait, Greg Barnes, Glenn Kinlaw, Ron Dennis, Bruce Worrell, Don Babson, Tony Prevatte, Dave Britt, Chip Davis, Dave Collins, Al Stanley, Lumberton High School play-by-play announcers Nick McKeithan, "Leather Lungs" Pridgen, and flying weatherman Jim Burkhead. (Courtesy of Gillespie Studio Collection, Robeson County History Museum.)

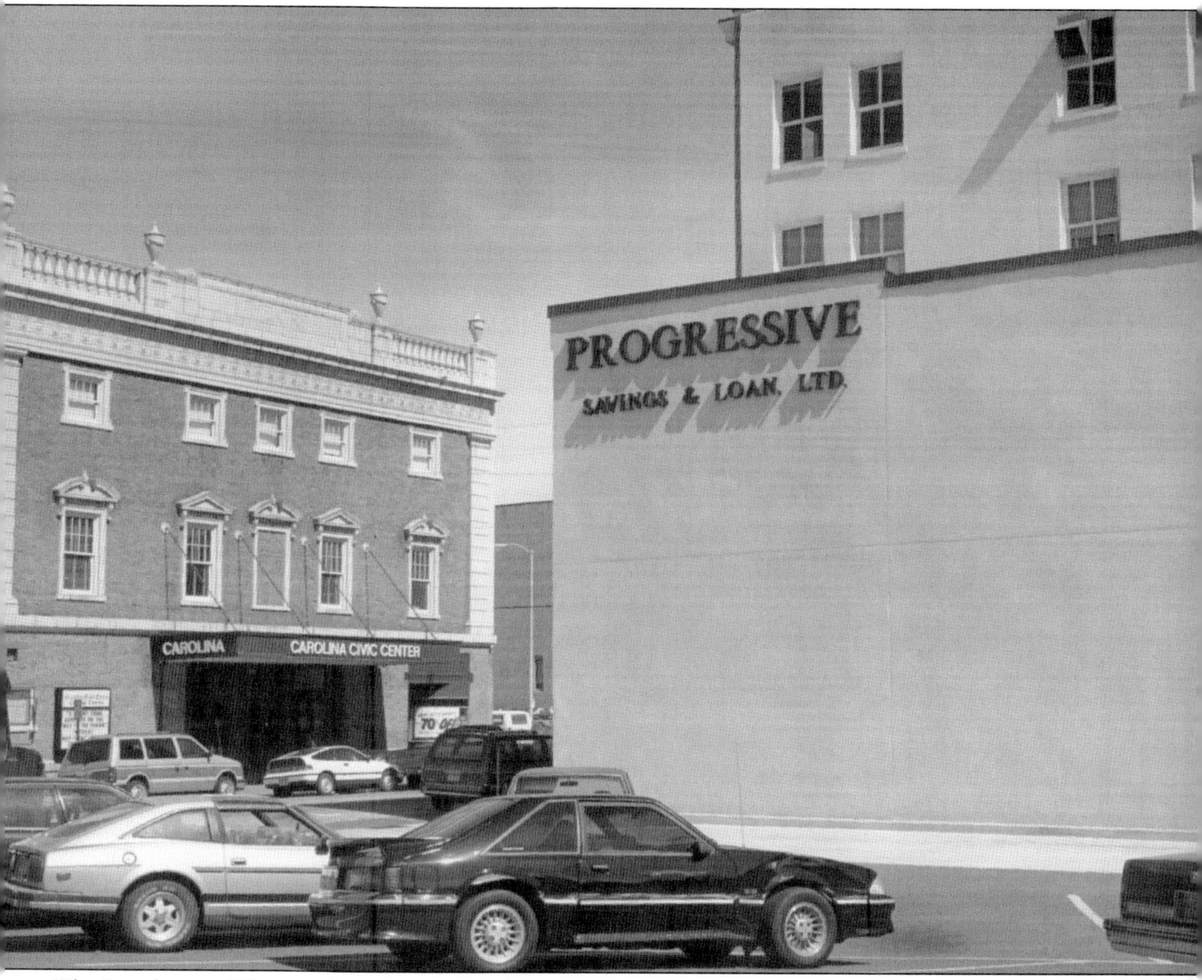

The Lumberton Theatre Company opened the Carolina Theatre on June 18, 1928. The Carolina Theatre closed its doors for business in 1975 and plans were to demolish the theater and replace it with a parking lot. A group of concerned citizens banded together and their efforts saved the historic structure. It reopened on June 18, 1985, as the Carolina Civic Center. The company also opened the Pastime Theatre on August 18, 1934, in the McLeod building on Elm Street. Admission was 20¢ for adults and 10¢ for children. There were about 500 seats downstairs and 100 more in the balcony. It showed second-run films or "B" pictures. (Courtesy Brad Thompson.)

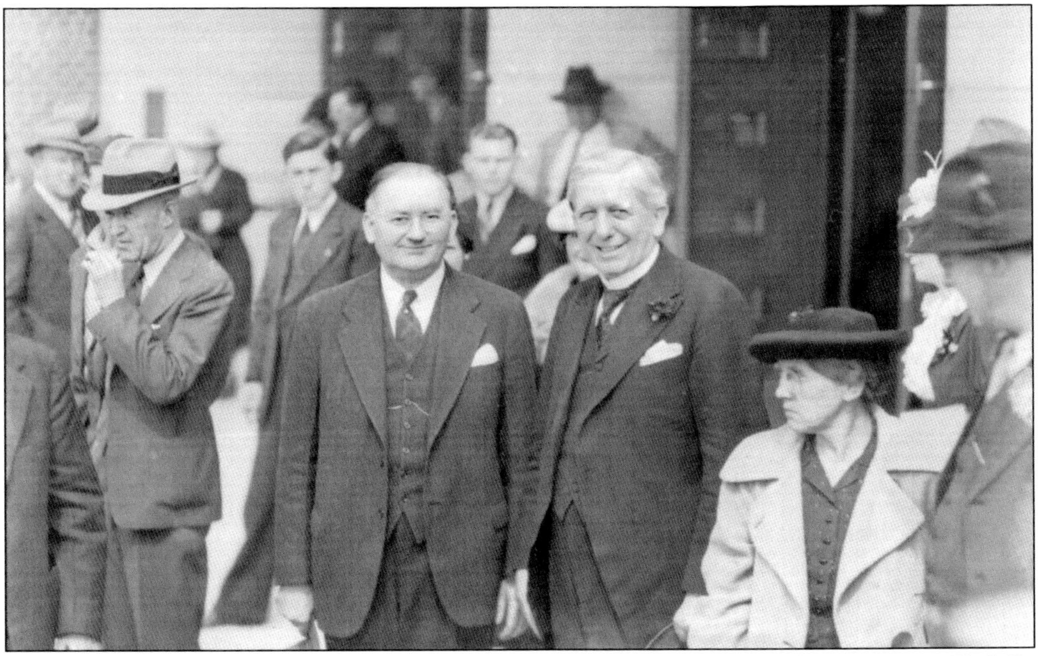

Lumberton mayor Ervin Mosby "EM" Johnson (left) talks with North Carolina governor Clyde R. Hoey during the March 21, 1940, dedication service for the Lumberton Armory, which is now the Bill Sapp Recreation Center. The property was purchased from Penelope and Winnifred Rowland, and the building cost was $100,000. (Courtesy of the Hubbard-Tyner Collection.)

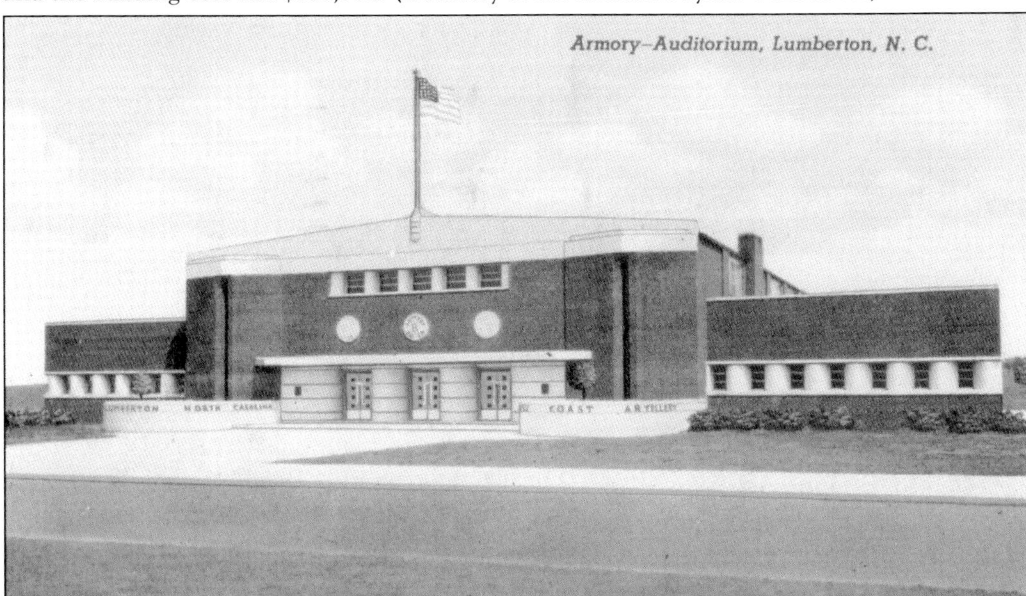

In addition to the armory, Lumberton was the recipient of many Work Projects Administration projects, including the building of a cafeteria at the Lumberton High School, an agricultural building, and a post office. Beautifying projects were done at McMillan's Beach and Meadowbrook Cemetery, and at one time, as many as 1,000 people where employed in the program in Robeson County. (Courtesy of Mitchell Prevatte.)

Helen Allen and Nash Odom were chosen by the *Robesonian* as the June bride and groom in 1960. They posed throughout the city advertising the products needed by every new couple. Here, they take a break for a Pepsi. He went on to become a noted historian and pastor, and she retired as a school guidance counselor. (Courtesy of Brad Thompson.)

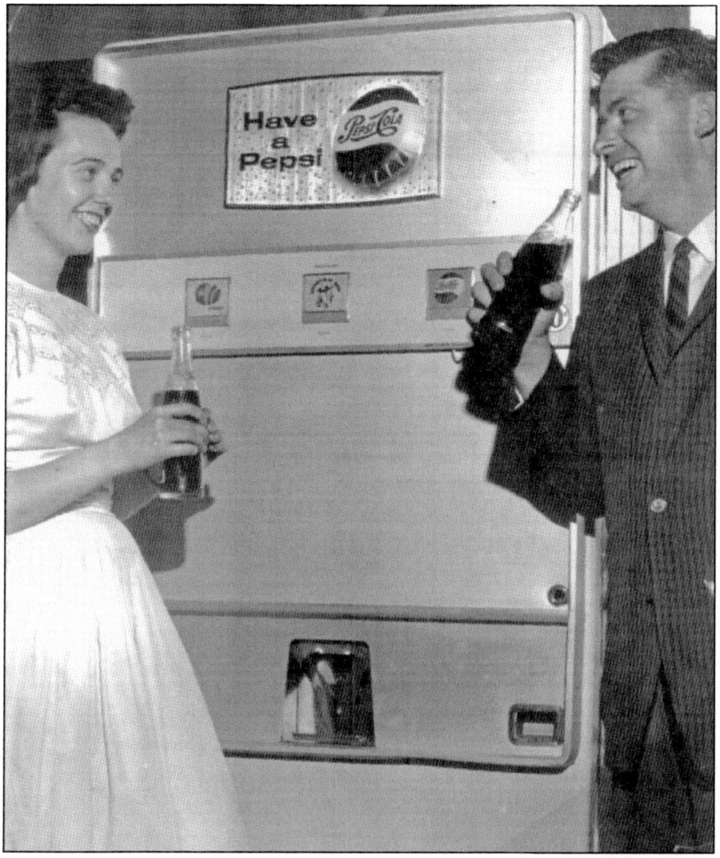

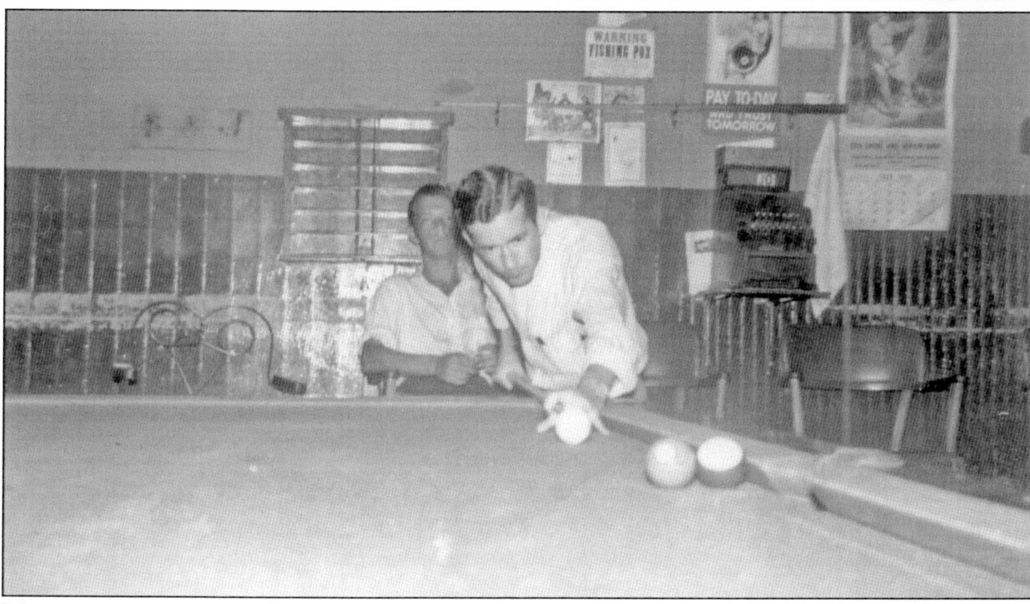

Many young men spent hours hitting the white cue ball into colored balls in Lumberton's pool halls. This pool hall was located in the 200 block of Elm Street where the plaza is now. (Courtesy of Mitchell Prevatte.)

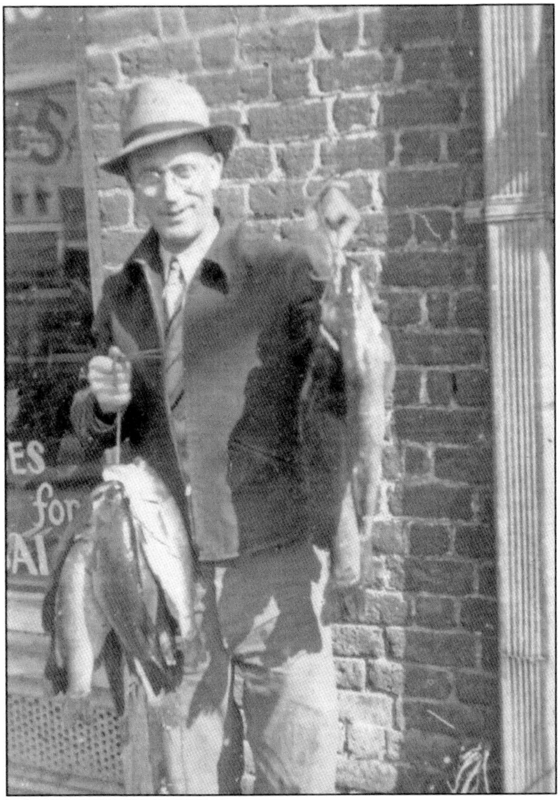

To a true fisherman, there is nothing like spending time in deep thought beside a pond, lake, or river. Roy Miller loved fishing along the Lumber River, and he died doing what he loved. He was on his way down a path to the Lumber River to fish when he had a heart attack. (Courtesy of Alan Prevatte.)

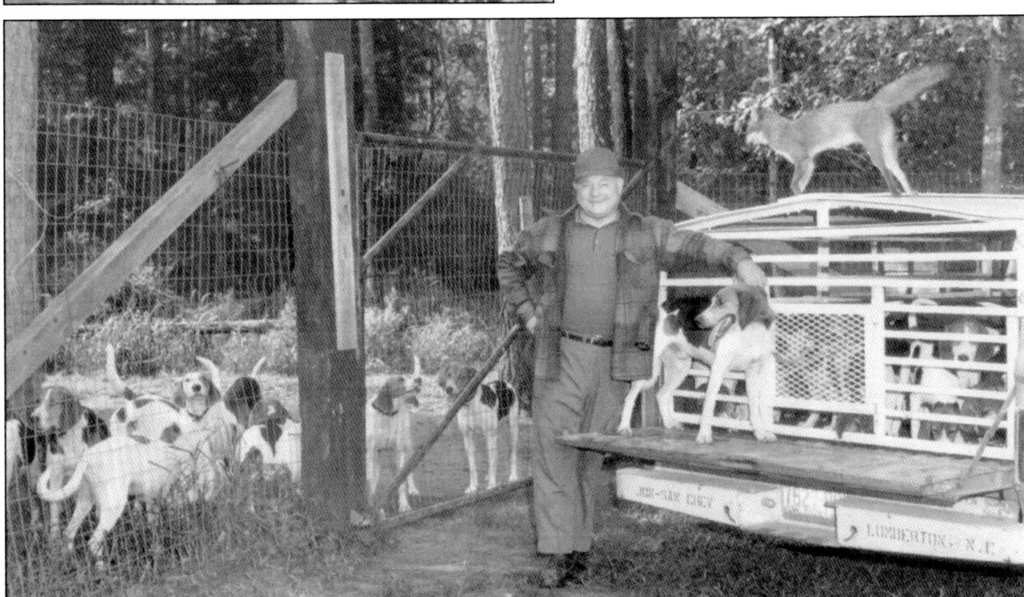

Foxhunting in Lumberton can trace its roots back to the early 1900s, when the horseback sport was wildly popular among men as well as women and children. Special hunts were held on Christmas and New Year's Day. Here, Henry Smith is seen paying a visit to his dogs. (Courtesy of Mitchell Prevatte.)

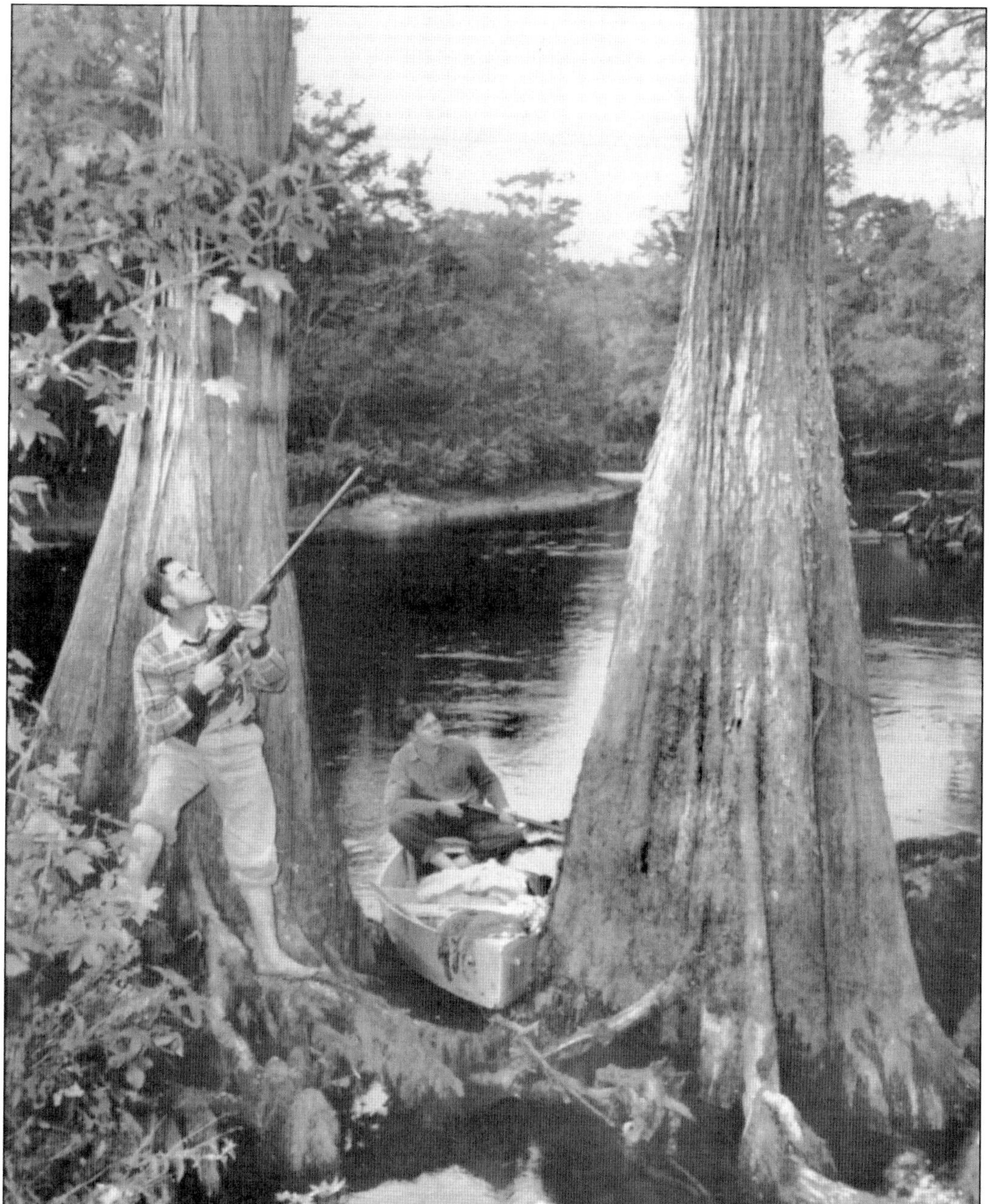

Squirrel hunting is popular in southern North Carolina, and while it is fun hunting the bushy-tailed animals in the backwoods, drifting down a wild river while doing it makes for a real outdoor adventure. Here, Ernest Higley and Clyde Burney (in the boat) beach their skiff at a likely spot for squirrels on the Lumber River. (Courtesy of the Hubbard-Tyner Collection.)

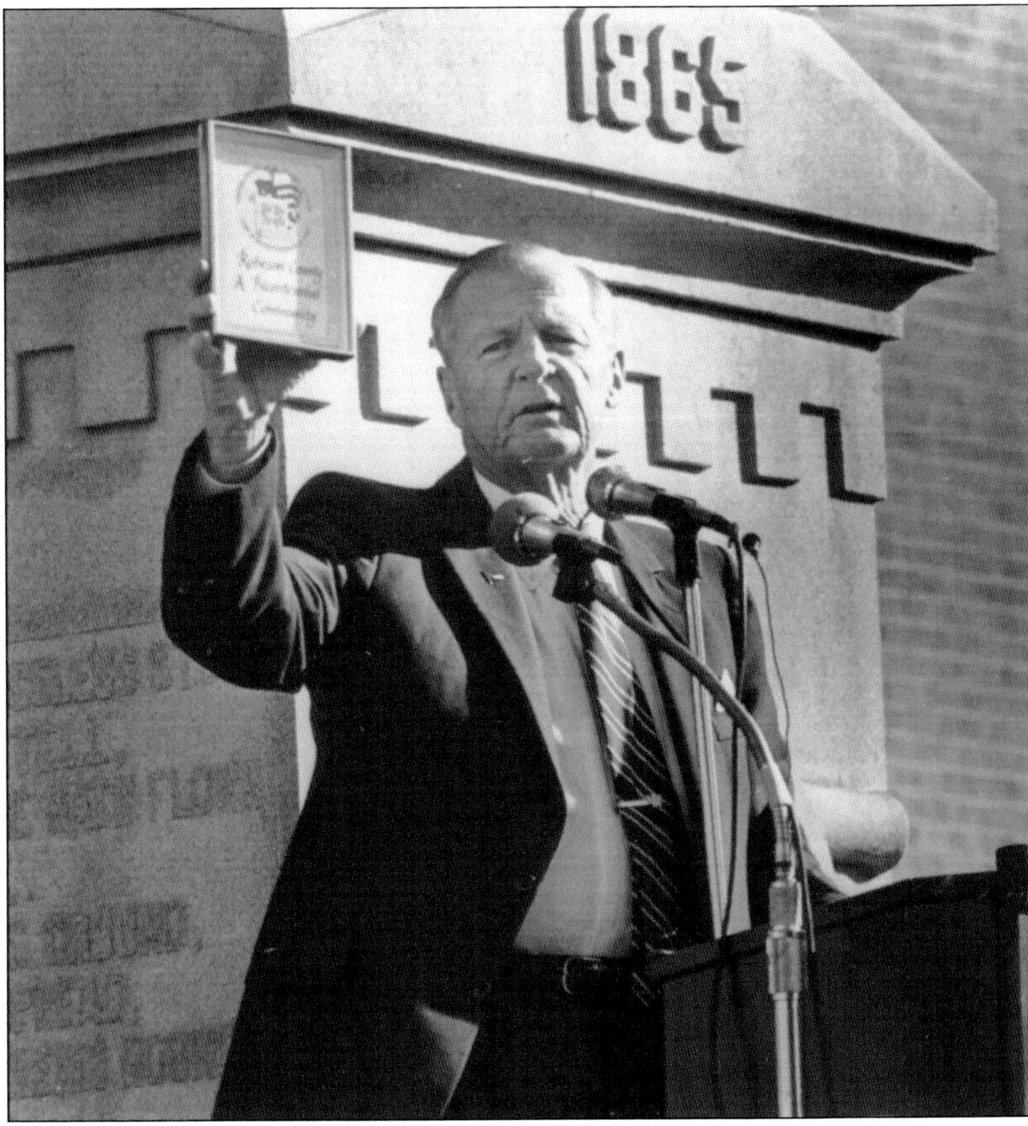

Hector MacLean was chairman of the Robeson County Bicentennial Commission, which organized all of the events for the yearlong celebration in 1987. Here, he opens the year's festivities. MacLean greeted the crowd by saying, "All of you are distinguished guests on this occasion. If you are from Robeson County, you a distinguished guest for that and no other reason." (Courtesy of UNCP University Communications and Marketing.)

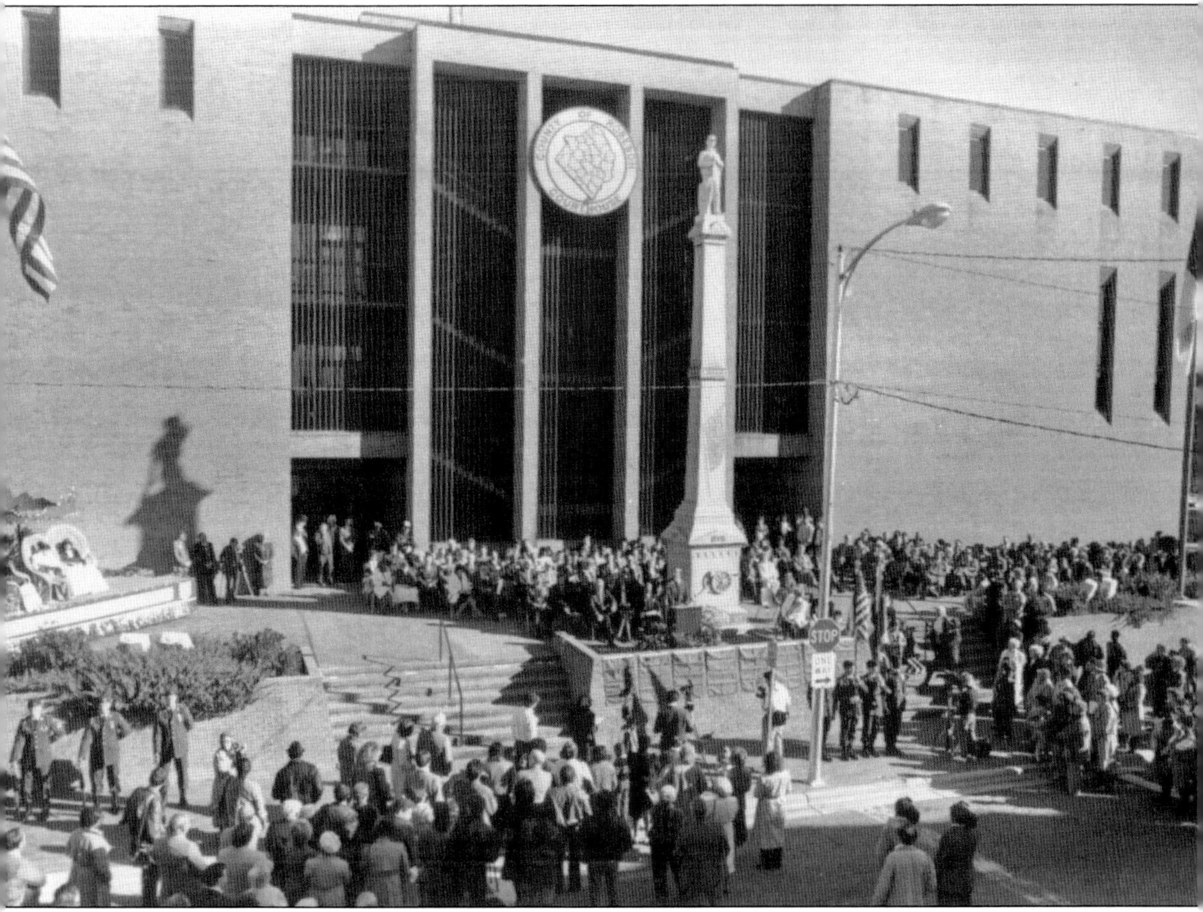

A crowd of nearly 500 gathered in front of the courthouse on January 6, 1987, to hear the Honorable H.A. "Sandy" McKinnon, retired superior court judge, present a brief history of the county. Looking at this bicentennial celebration is a good reminder to look to the future knowing the importance of saving bits and pieces of history. (Courtesy of UNCP University Communications and Marketing.)

Consistent with our mission to preserve history on a local level, this book was printed in South Carolina on American-made paper and manufactured entirely in the United States. Products carrying the accredited Forest Stewardship Council (FSC) label are printed on 100 percent FSC-certified paper.